BEE GEES

BEE GEES

Children of the World

BOB STANLEY

NINE
EIGHT
BOOKS

NINE
EIGHT
BOOKS

NEB 017

First published in the UK in 2023 by Nine Eight Books
An imprint of Bonnier Books UK
4th Floor, Victoria House, Bloomsbury Square, London, WC1B 4DA
Owned by Bonnier Books, Sveavägen 56, Stockholm, Sweden

 @nineeightbooks

@nineeightbooks

Hardback ISBN: 978-1-7887-0541-7
Trade Paperback ISBN: 978-1-7887-0542-4
eBook ISBN: 978-1-7887-0543-1

A CIP catalogue record for this book is available from the British Library.

Publishing director: Pete Selby
Senior editor: Melissa Bond

Typeset by IDSUK (Data Connection) Ltd
Printed and bound in Great Britain by Clays Ltd, Elcograf S.p.A

1 3 5 7 9 10 8 6 4 2

Nine Eight Books is an imprint of Bonnier Books UK
www.bonnierbooks.co.uk

MIX
Paper from
responsible sources
FSC® C018072

For Len

CONTENTS

INTRODUCTION

The Bee Gees didn't fit in. They never really made sense. They have intrigued me greatly since I was a kid, but they weren't like other misfit pop groups that I came to love over the years – the Raspberries, or Felt, or the Zombies – because they were no minor cult group, no one-hit wonders. Instead, they were international superstars, a major presence on the pop scene for four whole decades: rivals to the Beatles in the late '60s; bigger than ABBA in the late '70s; returning like Lazarus with a number one in the late '80s; feted elder statesmen who could still produce top-five hits in the late '90s.

Brothers Barry, Robin and Maurice Gibb had first harmonised together on stage in 1958, as the Rattlesnakes. Rechristened the Bee Gees, they would record their first single in 1963, when Barry was fifteen and the twins just thirteen, and went on to record twenty-two studio albums, producing global hits like 'Massachusetts', 'Stayin' Alive' and 'You Win Again'. They would rack up nine American number-one singles, more than any group save the Beatles and the Supremes. The Bee Gees were still making hit records in 2001, and their run only stopped

1

when one of the twins, Maurice, died in 2003. They have sold an estimated 220 million records worldwide, making them one of the best-selling acts of all time. Occasionally they dipped into the background, sometimes for a few years at a time, but Barry, Robin and Maurice Gibb would always somehow return to the charts, time and again. Still, at no point – save a period in the late '70s – did they seem to fit the pop scene around them; there was no obvious place to file their music. For this reason, in spite of their great success, they seemed somehow easy to mock.

My way into the world of the Bee Gees was through my Uncle Bill. He had shelves of albums in his Habitat-veneered front room in Hastings and in 1975, when I was aged ten, Uncle Bill made me a C90 with the Beach Boys' *Greatest Hits* on one side and a compilation called *Best of Bee Gees* on the other.

After the Beatles, they quickly became my two favourite groups. I equated them in my head, the Beach Boys so full of harmonic positivity and the Bee Gees their polar opposite, so melancholic. On the covers of these albums, the groups were similarly unidentical twins. The Beach Boys were shot in high contrast, bleached out in black and white by their own Californian radiance. The Bee Gees, meanwhile, faced the camera, unsmiling, on a mustard-coloured front cover, while on the back they stood aboard a docked boat on the murkiest January morning imaginable, almost silhouetted by the grey of the day. Even their names fitted together, the Beach Boys signifying seaside, summer, ultimate West Coast high jinks; the Bee Gees were from a strange island in the Irish Sea and ... well, what exactly did Bee Gees mean? It sounded like someone was trying to say Beach Boys, but they'd lost the will halfway through.

By the time I received my magical C90 in 1975, the Bee Gees were scoring hits again after a couple of fallow years; 'Jive Talkin'' had just been a summer hit and 'You Should Be Dancing' would follow it a year later. Down the line they became international pop icons and then, almost overnight, an international punchline. The songs on *Best of Bee Gees* sounded nothing like 'Jive Talkin'', though. The first track was called 'Holiday' and it was the least likely holiday soundtrack you've ever heard, uncommonly sensitive, with Robin Gibb's other-worldly sad voice singing, 'Millions of eyes can see / Yet why am I so blind?' over a bed of mournful strings and church organ. If it hadn't been for Uncle Bill I might easily have sided with pretty much everyone at my school in 1978, falling into line by mocking their falsettos, Robin's teeth, Barry's chest hair, Maurice's lack of hair. But no. Instead, thanks to songs like 'Holiday', 'New York Mining Disaster 1941' and 'I've Gotta Get a Message to You', I was a secret fan. I would look at their other, intriguingly sleeved early albums like *Odessa* and *Trafalgar* in the second-hand shops and wonder what they sounded like, wishing I could afford them.

To my mind, the Bee Gees were up there with the Beach Boys, and knocking on the Beatles' back door. They were inventive, shape-shifting, writers of death-haunted melodies, with voices that sounded like no one else. They were deeply odd, and quite wonderful.

Other people did not see the Bee Gees this way. Many still don't. I've written this book as an attempt to give them their rightful place at the very top of pop's table. They always seemed to be out of step with almost everything, yet had an indirect impact on so much. I also want to explain why and how the Gibb brothers have been othered, and − unlike the Beach Boys − rarely treated with the respect they should have earned as a right.

Even now, twenty years after the group ceased to exist, and in spite of earning enough trophies, gold discs and accolades to fill a museum, they don't really receive their dues.

Why is this?

As an inventive musical family, the Gibbs were on a par with the Wilson brothers of Hawthorne, California, and the Davies brothers of Muswell Hill, north London. Their lack of a geographical grounding, thanks to their peripatetic upbringing, has led the Isle of Man, Manchester and Australia to all claim them as their own, though the Gibbs would be residents of Miami for more than half of their career. From an early age, Barry and Robin had both demonstrated a remarkable versatility and malleability as both writers and performers. They always seemed able to step out of the pop picture, see it all, clear-eyed, then rewrite the whole thing in their own unique, Gibb-like way. At a glance, Barry and Robin looked like very different people and, sure enough, they developed significantly different writing and recording styles quite quickly. Barry preferred to have his songs written and his arrangements crafted before making a record. Robin liked to work in the studio, spontaneously, intuitively, often alone. In the middle was Maurice, the bassist and the peacemaker, who pretty much abandoned his songwriting ambitions when the family left Australia in January 1967; peeping through the studio window would be kid brother Andy, a full eight years younger than the twins, who was always waiting for his invitation to the party. The brothers' story would become a little slippery in the telling, a little complicated, largely because they were such unreliable narrators. But like Frank Sinatra and Elvis Presley, they had almighty rises and falls, and their career would become a three- or even four-part saga. Their lows would never be as low as Sinatra's 'Mama Will Bark' or Presley's 'Do the Clam', thankfully, and their records were never less than intriguing.

The Gibbs' unusual upbringing partly explained their responses to pop, which were always vivid and effective without ever really being canny or knowing. Throughout their story, they often seemed unaware of how things worked, musically or on a more intuitive level; they seemed almost consciously anti-hip – Barry, in particular, would automatically shut down any conversation that didn't suggest they were simply entertainers purveying the most regular pop music currently available. When pop's zeitgeist touched them, they often shied away. They could be praised by the Beatles or Oasis but, like children, they never seemed sure how to take compliments.

Barry, Robin and Maurice Gibb were outsiders, even though – with stacks of hits and their adopted Miami Beach lifestyle – they could come across as the ultimate insiders. They had grown up in poverty. They had studied and developed their craft from scratch. They learned how to disguise their social awkwardness. With help from friends and family, they then made some of the most commercial and most successful records of the '60s, '70s and '80s.

In the art world, 'outsider' is a term that is usually used to explain and define self-taught, obsessive art by loners and odd-balls. I would like to repurpose it here. Vast commercial success does not preclude an outsider tag, and some of pop's most sin-gular outsider musicians are right there in plain sight: the Bee Gees, Dexys Midnight Runners, Terence Trent D'Arby. (It's also notable that, often, their most 'outside' work spectacularly fails to sell.)

Maybe the Gibb brothers' singularity came from childhoods spent in a state of flux. Moving house every six months, finding it hard to make friendships with peers, they had to lean on each other for support and inspiration. They would also turn to the radio. The young Gibbs learned music in a completely untutored way, listening closely – though not informedly, let alone analytically – to pop music and filtering what they discovered through their unique Gibb family worldview. They were fans, and they were magpies, borrowing indiscriminately from things they heard on the radio or in their dad's record collection. They performed their songs in the most natural way, with fraternal harmonies, yet their music always seemed quite unnatural – how could three teenagers have come up with something as expressive and bereft as 'New York Mining Disaster 1941'? No cold-eyed songwriter aiming squarely for commercial success would have come up with music and lyrics in the way the Bee Gees did, or sung them like Barry or Robin Gibb.

From the start, though, they were drawn uncritically towards potential mass success – this desire never left them. For years, they had nothing to back up their self-belief beyond the enthusiasm of their parents, a speedway track owner, and a couple of Australian DJs; they felt it was their destiny. When it arrived out of the blue in 1967, real fame did not seem to come to them as any kind of shock. All families are unique, of course, but few are as tight, self-absorbed and self-protective as the Gibbs were. And simultaneously, they called out to the whole world with their songs of love and fear and death, reaching out beyond the walls of their compound for the biggest public hug imaginable.

INTRODUCTION

If the three brothers' personalities weren't as familiar to the public as the Beatles, the Beach Boys, or even ABBA, then that was a triumph of their wilful anti-fashion. No one was keener to paint the Bee Gees as regular guys, shying away from the rock 'n' roll lifestyle, than the Bee Gees themselves. In reality, naturally, they were highly unusual and all the better for it. In an ill-conceived 1980 biography called *Legend*, they were quite happy to be portrayed as cartoon animals – Barry the lion, the leader of the pack; Robin the red setter, his King Charles locks reflecting his fascination with history; and Maurice a beaver, presumably because of his ever-ready, toothy smile. This was not a children's book (it really doesn't work as a children's book, believe me). Was this an intentional anti-cool move? It was certainly a rather strange one. Regular pop stars would never have signed off on *Legend*; regular pop stars could never have come up with anything as far outside conventional pop music as Robin's 'Farmer Ferdinand Hudson' suite, or Maurice's Moog-folk drone 'Sweet Song of Summer', or a title as wilfully uncommercial as 'Fanny (Be Tender with My Love)'.

In their lyrics, they used English as if it was a second language. The results could sound gently psychedelic ('Ev'ry day's Saturday, feeling in steadily / Laughing at people with stars in their eyes' – 'Sir Geoffrey Saved the World', 1967) or lightly cosmic and new age ('Life is a moment in space / When the dream is gone, it's a lonelier place' – 'Woman in Love', 1980), depending on the direction in which the pop world was spinning, but their lyrics were rarely literal. This can prove a barrier to acceptance among pop fans who liked their lyrics either literal (like ABBA, Westlife or Kylie Minogue) or mystical (Bob Dylan, Van Morrison). But the Bee Gees' approach was closer to abstraction, the work of people who used words intentionally incorrectly, who could paint a scene more vivid than one that used direct language. The Bee Gees' outsider status and worldview is something that will crop up throughout this story.

You would think this approach would have set the Bee Gees up to have a sizeable cult following, like the Beach Boys and the Kinks, groups with an everyday radio presence but whose catalogues and back stories scratch an itch for pop historians and obsessives. This is not the case. I have set out to write this book to show just how unique and fascinating the Bee Gees are as a group, as well as how varied and endlessly rewarding their back catalogue can be. Unlike the Beach Boys and the Kinks, both of whom have been very cool and deeply unfashionable at different phases of their career, the Bee Gees have never really been seen as hip. Even today, people can talk about the brothers as if they wrote great songs by accident – 'It's the Bee Gees . . . but it's really good' – and partly this is because they are so hard to place in a straightforward pop context. The influence of their 1960s strings-and-Mellotron-soaked material on early progressive rock (Genesis, Yes and especially the Moody Blues) is ignored. A cover version of a Bee Gees song with no side – like Feist's 'Love You Inside Out' – is unusual. More recently, Manchester band Whyte Horses did a faithful cover of 'Mr Natural' and it was received as if they had unearthed a previously unknown Mississippi blues obscurity; how on earth had they found this diamond in the dirt? Most frequently, Al Green's version of 'How Can You Mend a Broken Heart' is spoken about as if the Reverend had made gold from the basest material, as if he had somehow shaped a deep soul classic from the *Scooby Doo* theme.

At the tail end of the 1970s, the Bee Gees were the most successful and recognisable pop group in the world; they had become one of the biggest acts of all time. But their child-star upbringing resulted in a lack of worldliness, and they struggled to deal with their brutal fall from favour at the turn of the '80s. They had never wanted to come across as outsiders, not at all. Their greatest achievements – the slew of classics used on the soundtrack of *Saturday Night Fever* – somehow became a curse. It's hard to imagine what that could do to your mind: you have created hugely successful and popular music and then, as a reward, you are ostracised from polite society. They were ridiculed and shut down, having perfected their craft. In spite of everything they achieved over four decades as singers, writers and producers, they felt they were required to keep proving themselves, over and over, right to the end.

For reasons that are now hard to gauge, the abreaction to disco affected the Bee Gees far more than other acts like Donna Summer, Chic or Michael Jackson, all of whom survived the backlash, adapted and prospered. Yet it's clear with hindsight that the resultant American kickback against disco – slick rock acts like Journey and REO Speedwagon, and especially Toto – owed far more to silky late '70s Bee Gees recordings than it did to the guitar ethos of Bruce Springsteen or Led Zeppelin. And, beyond this brief adult-oriented rock boom, it is now hard to listen to the biggest names of the mid- to late '80s – Michael Jackson, Madonna, Whitney Houston – without understanding their unspoken debt to the R&B/pop-blurring influence of the Gibbs. Does all of this mean that the brothers invented large swathes of pop, from string-driven prog, to international disco, to big-haired AOR and MTV-era pop R&B? Not exactly – but this gives you some idea of their underdiscussed impact.

A lot of their work is now in the ether, as standards that seem to have always been there: 'Islands in the Stream', 'Heartbreaker',

'Massachusetts', 'If I Can't Have You', 'Words'. Other songs, though, are as associated with the brothers and their image – 'Stayin' Alive', 'You Should Be Dancing' – as 'I Get Around' and 'Good Vibrations' are with the Beach Boys. The Bee Gees can be both everywhere and nowhere in their own music. While the late '70s floor-fillers and ballads were golden, it was their work in the '80s that I'd argue places them among the greats: between them, the brothers cut twelve full-length albums in the first seven years of the decade, and only one of them bore the Bee Gees name. Under duress, seemingly unwanted and out of the spotlight, they worked their magic for Barbra Streisand, Dionne Warwick, Diana Ross, Kenny Rogers and Dolly Parton.

They would continue to write and record worldwide top-twenty hits until the end, just after the turn of the twenty-first century. Not even Paul McCartney could do this.

The writer Dave Marsh once recalled being in a limousine with Roger Daltrey in 1978. 'Stayin' Alive' came on the radio, which – in 1978 – it did roughly every hour, on the hour. Though he'd been complaining to Marsh about punk groups stealing all the Who's moves and proclaiming themselves as year-zero origi-nals, Daltrey went quiet as the song came on. Listen to the lyrics, he told Marsh. 'That's a great song. Bruce Springsteen could sing that lyric.' Marsh listened. He thought Daltrey was right. And that voice was pretty great too, come to think of it – Marsh was a long-time fan of falsetto kings like Del Shannon and Frankie Valli, after all. For the first time, he heard 'Stayin' Alive' without preconceptions.

When Marsh wrote this story up in 1989, in his book *The Heart of Rock and Soul*, his praise was still freighted with concern for his cool. 'Beyond the numbing banalities of the beat', he said, 'is a first-rate piece of pop falsetto. Not at the Stylistics level, mind you, but real good. And a good, class-based lyric. Not at Springsteen's level, mind you, but real good.'

It is so strange. No other group of the Bee Gees' standing has had to face such consistently distanced good reviews, as if the writer feels like he's putting his hand in a fire by even discussing them. No other group has had to consistently defend themselves, their approach and their music. And what music it is.

1

THE ISLE OF MAN

It's a warm summer night in 1941. This is the summer of exotic big-band records like Jimmy Dorsey's 'Amapola', Xavier Cugat's 'Perfidia', and Glenn Miller's reimagining of 'The Song of the Volga Boatmen'. There's always news on the radio about parts of the world you were never previously aware of; the music of the moment seems to amplify the international intrigue.

Closer to home, the radio waves sing to Noël Coward's 'London Pride' and Flanagan and Allen's 'Down Forget-Me-Not Lane'. In a corner of Lancashire this evening, a dance band are providing the entertainment – Hugh Gibb and his Orchestra travel wherever work takes them, and tonight it's the Stretford Trades and Labour Club. Hughie Gibb is both bandleader and drummer, and he has got his eye on a slim, kind-faced girl he just spotted dancing to the saxophone and clarinet hum of 'Sweet Georgia Brown'. Hughie is the boss. He's the one who has to work out the travel costs, the one who does the accounts, the one who keeps the boys' uniforms tidy and clean, and the one who keeps the boys' boozing in check. Sometimes it feels like he's managing a football team. Hugh Gibb and his Orchestra may not be in the first division of dance bands, but in 1941 he's not fussed – there's plenty of work to go round.

In London, the dance bands play in wood-panelled restaurants and chandeliered hotels, all within a couple of square miles around Piccadilly and Mayfair. Brylcreemed and debonair, Bert Ambrose, Geraldo, Harry Roy and Jack Hylton are as famous as movie stars, with their performances broadcast live on the BBC Light Programme. Though playing at clubs in the West End is not without its risks in 1941; that March two bombs had landed on the Café de Paris, shot straight down a ventilation shaft, and destroyed the basement ballroom, killing thirty-four people, including handsome young bandleader Ken 'Snakehips' Johnson.

Manchester is also in the sights of the Luftwaffe, but the BBC are not doing a remote broadcast from the Stretford Trades and Labour Club tonight or any night. Hugh isn't bothered. He is more than keeping his head above water; he can even afford an apprentice drummer, for a start. 'Fancy stepping in? It's your lucky day,' he tells the lad. 'Play "Moonglow" for us.' Hugh approaches the kind-faced girl with melancholy eyebrows. Her name is Barbara, and she's originally from Bolton. She can claim to be a direct descendant of the inventor of the spinning mule, Samuel Crompton, who transformed both the cotton industry and the landscape of the region. Quite possibly, she doesn't mention this to Hugh as they dance. It's her night off, after all.

Barbara is a 'canary', as the girl singer with a dance band is known – she solos on the occasional chorus, tucked in between the silver saxes. Her one night off is also her one chance to go out dancing. Barbara and Hughie dance to 'Moonglow', then 'I'm in the Mood for Love', before the bandleader steps back onto the stage to resume his drumming duties. But at the end of the night he gets to walk Barbara back home to her mum's house in Stretford. She tells her mum about Hughie over breakfast the next morning. She talks about his immaculate swept-back hair, *de rigueur* for bandleaders, and his big winning smile. 'We liked each other very much,' she says.

Hughie Gibb's own parents did not approve of his chosen profession. They considered musicians to be 'vagabonds'. He told them it was all he wanted to do, and that was that. By 1940 the Hugh Gibb Orchestra had steady work on the Mecca ballroom circuit across the north of England and Scotland, hinterlands the BBC patronised with daily broadcasts of *Music While You Work*, light music to get your head nodding gently. BBC bandleader Henry Hall and the director general John Reith are both Calvinist Scots who mistrust jazz, frown over anything too hot, and also scorn crooners like Al Bowlly and Hutch as if soft, soothing, microphone-aided vocals might somehow weaken the resolve of the nation's armed forces. But the Calvinists are safely down south at Broadcasting House, and the rest of Scotland carries on dancing. Hugh Gibb goes on to earn himself a residency at the Palais in Edinburgh in January 1945 and stays there until the war is over. Among the regulars at the Palais are George and May Gray – twenty-five years later these families will be related, and living in neighbouring houses on the other side of the Atlantic, but of course no one was to know this in 1945.

By this time Hugh and Barbara are married with a daughter, Lesley, and living in a rented house on the outskirts of the city. Barbara isn't singing anymore, as Hugh has told her that there can only be one musician in the family; she acquiesces, and history will not preserve her voice on record.

In spite of his wishes, however, Hugh will not be the only musician in the family.

Ellan Vannin sits in the Irish Sea, with Scottish Galloway to the north, Welsh Anglesey to the south, Irish Dundalk to the west, and England's Lancashire coast – the tinselly, bleary-eyed resorts of Blackpool and Morecambe – to the east. Known on the mainland as the Isle of Man, it is an island with a strange mystique, living in self-appointed exile, quietly discomforting to outsiders: its cats have no tails; its roads have no official speed limits; it has the oldest functioning parliament in the world, which goes by the part-gothic, part-hobbit name of Tynwald. Ellan Vannin has never been part of the United Kingdom, and it seems unlikely it ever will be: these days, Manx Gaelic is taught in its schools; the Union Jack has been replaced by a flag with three legs joined at the thigh, each armoured and wearing golden spurs; and full independence from fading motherland Britannia seems an encroaching inevitability.

It didn't seem quite as independent from the British mainland in the late 1940s, but the island still did things very much its own way – it used the birch for capital punishment, and it only deigned to help out the UK when the mainland was in a bind. During the Second World War, when Britain was in a lot of trouble, the island allowed itself to effectively become a huge internment camp, with Jewish refugees and potential German spies hurriedly bundled together, sleeping on adjacent beds. At Rushen, in the south of the island, there was a camp entirely populated by women and children, 3,500 of them. There were sculptors and painters working in the camp, and there were language schools for the interned. The camp was run by local landladies and female civil servants, rather than the military.

In Douglas, the island's largest town, one of the buildings requisitioned as a site for wartime refugees was the Alexandra Hotel. Engineer and inventor Barnes Wallis was also resident there during the war while the navy tested his 'bouncing bomb' off the Dorset coast – maids would recalled his generous £5 tips, which more than doubled their weekly wage. Just a few weeks after the war ended, the Alexandra would be packed every night with dancers listening to the sound of Hugh Gibb's band. In the rationed, straitened Britain of the late '40s, a visit to the Isle of Man would be as close to a foreign holiday as most people were going to get, and so Douglas became the next home of the peripatetic Gibbs. Hugh had to go where the work was, even if that work was just for a six-month season. And Douglas provided plenty of work. In fact, it was positively booming – there were star names like Joe Loss at the Villa Marina, and the Squadronaires at the Palace Ballroom, while Hugh Gibb packed out the Alexandra. Locally, at least, he was now on a par with the biggest dance band names.

In Manx mythology, the island was ruled by the sea god Manannán, who kept it safe from its larger neighbouring islands with a protective cloak of mist. The maniacal, dangerous TT motorbike races, the self-preserving tax rules, that three-legged freak flag – all of these Manx totems intentionally emphasised its otherness to the outside world. Barry, Robin and Maurice Gibb would all be born on the Isle of Man. They would make it their playground, a sandpit they could return to when times were rough, a place entirely other to the pop world. Robin, in particular, went on to write loving laments to the mountainous island, naming his last solo record after one of the houses the infant brothers lived in.

Barry was born on 1 September 1946, when the Gibbs lived in a flat above a chemist's on Strand Street, Douglas, right in

16

the centre of the town. When he was eighteen months old, with afternoon tea on the table, he tugged at the tea cosy, and the close-to-boiling water went all over his chest and down his front. He was badly scalded; taken to the hospital, he went into a coma. There were no skin grafts back then. At one point doctors told Barbara he might not survive. Barry did survive, but he didn't speak a word until he was three. He was a serious baby. According to Barbara, he never even made a sound when he cried.

By the late '40s, the big band scene was mutating as its costs spiralled. Now smaller groups were becoming popular, such as the Nat Cole Trio and the George Shearing Quintet, led by a Battersea-born pianist. Inspired by this, Hugh too scaled down; he began to play with a trio at the Glen Helen hotel, a popular spot on the TT circuit. When Barbara became pregnant again the family moved to an anonymous, pebble-dashed, interwar semi-detached house at 50 St Catherine's Drive. On 22 December 1949, twins Robin and Maurice were born. Barry told sister Lesley he was unimpressed: their cat Tatty had produced six kittens. 50 St Catherine's Drive was not a quiet house, as baby Robin and baby Maurice cried all the time. Baby Robin had his mum's melancholy eyebrows – one time Barry was caught shaking him. He asked his mum to take the babies back.

Ten days after the twins were born, the world had moved into the second half of the twentieth century, and modern times. The family were now at Smedley Cottage in Spring Valley, on the outskirts of Douglas. Virtually next door to the now demolished cottage was Ward's ice cream factory; along with Manx Ices in Peel on the west coast it was one of the twin engines of the island's daytime holiday profit. By now, Barry wasn't a silent, traumatised toddler. He had two kid brothers to boss about and Gene Autry movies to draw inspiration from. He would stand on the loading dock of the ice cream factory and pretend it was a stage; first-year primary school girls watched him singing 'Home on the Range'. Barry Gibb had his first ever audience.

The twins were too young to pronounce each other's names properly and called each other Woggie (Maurice) and Bodding (Robin). And they were too young to be left outside playing without adult supervision, too, but this was the early '50s, and one day they toddled off with Lesley. Running by the side of the factory, with a nunnery on the other side, was a thin strip of water called the River Doey, known locally as the Café River. Baby Maurice, eighteen months old, fell into it – he was weighed down by what Barbara called his new 'eskimo coat', a thick downy thing with a massive hood, and he couldn't turn himself over to get out of the water. Lesley later told the *Daily Mirror*: 'I remember him floating along. I went in up to my waist and grabbed him under the arms until people came to help us both out of the water.'

The other kids ran back to get Hugh, who carried Mo home; it was 1951 and the brothers had already chalked up two near-death experiences. Hugh and Barbara shook their heads, bawled them out, but they didn't coddle their kids. Far from it. Hugh had a green Norton motorbike, and he loved to sit Maurice on the front and ride around the island's TT course. 'It was bright green,' remembered Mo, 'and I used to hang onto the tank, and my dad would fly around the track.'

The Gibbs were on the move again in 1952, first to Chapel House on the Strand Road, then to 43 Snaefell Road on the newly built Willaston council estate. Every house move involved a change of school for Barry and Lesley. The house on Snaefell

Road was bigger and cheaper – but the cost of the rent was not insignificant. By now, band work was more seasonal and in the winter Hugh was delivering bread for Quirk's bakery. Barry sat in the bread van with him and, when his dad's back was turned, ate the middles out of the loaves.

Feeding the people of Ellan Vannin hollowed-out bread wasn't a way to keep four kids alive and pay the rent. When his band began to splinter, things got worse; Hugh lost his contract. The Gibbs moved back to Manchester in January 1955.

2

MANCHESTER

New Musical Express UK top ten, 28 January 1955

1. Dickie Valentine – 'Finger of Suspicion'
2. Rosemary Clooney – 'Mambo Italiano'
3. Ruby Murray – 'Heartbeat'
4. Ronnie Hilton – 'I Still Believe'
5. Billy Eckstine – 'No One but You'
6. Dickie Valentine – 'Mr Sandman'
7. Bill Haley & His Comets – 'Shake, Rattle and Roll'
8. Alma Cogan – 'I Can't Tell a Waltz from a Tango'
9. Ruby Murray – 'Softly Softly'
10. Tennessee Ernie Ford – 'Give Me Your Word'

The number-one record in the UK when the Gibb family arrived back in Manchester was 'Finger of Suspicion' by Dickie Valentine. It was on the blue Decca label which, just two months earlier, had begun pressing 7-inch singles that played at forty-five revolutions per minute. In 1955, most people would have bought a shellac, 10-inch, 78-rpm copy of 'Finger of Suspicion', as the vast majority of houses in the UK still had a wind-up gramophone. Dickie V. had been a singer with the Ted Heath band, the most popular in the country, but he got out as the scene began to fade. Solo for eighteen months, by 1955 he had become Britain's number-one heartthrob, and the winking, extended chat-up line 'Finger of Suspicion' would remain his calling card. 'Someone broke into my heart and stole a beat or two / The finger of suspicion points at you.'

Hugh Gibb on the other hand had no singer, no band, no job. The family was dirt poor. Barry, Robin and Maurice's life was more like a folk song than 'Finger of Suspicion' – the Childe Ballad of the Brothers Gibb. Barry was now eight years old, and when they first arrived in Lancashire he had to move in with his dad's family; Maurice, Robin and Lesley lived with their mum's sister. Barry didn't understand why he had been separated from his siblings and sent to a new school called Manley Park where he had no friends. He was lonely. Because they couldn't afford to buy him another pair of trousers, Barry was sent to school in shorts, even though it was so cold that the water in the taps was frozen in the morning. After school, he played in the streets with a knackered bike that had no tyres.

The family had no income, no home. The decline of the dance band scene had left them high and dry, rootless, holding out for help from relatives in the UK. None of the Gibb children had seen Manchester before, so unlike Douglas with its grand hotels, ice cream factories and seaside entertainments. They were unfamiliar with the industrial north of England. According to the BBC, the north was a uniform conurbation of mills and factories, with everyone getting along like they were in a Gracie Fields movie.

In reality, Newcastle and Liverpool had their handsome Georgian centres, their rivers and ships; Sheffield had sooty, millstone grit architecture and dramatic topography; the similarly hilly Bradford was built from a rich, golden sandstone. But Manchester? Manchester was not like this, or much like Douglas either. Its flat, wide streets linked relentless red-brick houses, red-brick factories, red-brick churches, and red-brick schools. Everything was red brick and everything was dirty. Everywhere, 1950s Manchester felt wet and cold and in decline.

After more than six months apart, the family would be reunited in September 1955 and living together in a boarding house in Whalley Range. Barry was moved to Oswald Road Junior school with Lesley, Robin and Maurice, not that he showed up very often. He bunked off all the time, and the truant officer gave Barbara a stern word. Worse yet, while skiving one day Barry fell through the corrugated roof of a hut in the local park and landed on his back. He would suffer from back pain for the rest of his life. Just for good measure, he was shortly afterwards knocked down by a car and ended up in hospital over Christmas 1955. Lesley promised she would bring him a guitar, his Christmas present, and then he felt more like Gene Autry than ever, the only difference being he was a nine-year-old Gene Autry with a bad back and car-twisted legs lying in a hospital bed.

The number-one record that Christmas was again by Dickie Valentine, this time with 'Christmas Alphabet'. But just behind, and about to dislodge it from the top spot in the first week of 1956, was 'Rock Around the Clock' by Bill Haley & His Comets. Valentine's career was heading for Butlin's; 1956 would see the British hit parade conquered by Haley, Elvis Presley, the Platters, Gene Vincent, Frankie Lymon and Little Richard. In the tatty boarding house that passed for home, Hugh looked at the situations vacant in *Melody Maker*. Then he looked at his fast-thinning hair in the mirror. He remembered his parents saying that a musician's life was the life of a vagabond. He finally decided to find other work – just as Barry, in his hospital bed, learned the three guitar chords necessary to have a go at playing 'Rock Around the Clock'.

By the summer of 1956, the summer of 'Hound Dog' and 'Heartbreak Hotel', Hugh was managing a TV shop and, on the side, had a gig as a refrigerator salesman. This enabled the Gibbs to move out of forbidding Whalley Range and into a ground-floor flat at 51 Keppel Road, in the slightly leafier Manchester suburb of Chorlton. Home life became a little less chaotic. Still, neighbours would give biscuits and sandwiches to the Gibb kids because they looked half-starved. One night, when they were home alone, Lesley brushed up against the fireplace and an ember landed on her nightie – it caught fire, and so did she. Barry was smart enough to quickly wrap her in a rug, but she still received third-degree burns. Looking back, it seems miraculous that all the kids made it through to adulthood.

A neighbour on Keppel Road had heard about Barry and his new guitar. Most kids in 1956 were showing no such interest, and this former serviceman, who had been stationed in Hawaii, took Barry in: 'He started showing me chords that he'd learnt in Hawaii, playing Hawaiian guitar. So basically, I play the guitar completely wrong. I play totally unconventionally. If you watch Dolly Parton play the guitar it's the same as me. We bar all our chords. There's very little fingering going on, it's just barring, which is basically steel guitar.'

Hugh had his drumkit set up in the bedroom at Keppel Road, his back to the window. When he wasn't in there, the boys (Barry now nine, the twins aged six) would sit on the bed with make-believe microphones – empty tin cans placed on top of their mum's hairbrushes. The furniture in the room was so spartan that the emptiness gave their voices a natural echo. The brothers, being brothers, started to harmonise instinctively. What's more, they liked the sound of their voices together. Hugh played them his Mills Brothers 78s, but was not at all pushy about their singing. He also played them Glenn Miller and Bing Crosby records. The gramophone was an essential luxury. Robin and Maurice even had a crack at harmonising 'God Save the Queen' in school assembly, and got a thick ear for their troubles. At Oswald Street, they used to lean against a wall in the playground, tell jokes and sing. Most choirs in school would kick them out for improvising.

Maurice would later claim he was a 'goody two-shoes at school. I was Mr Perfect. And Robin and Barry always burned down shops and billboards and things. I couldn't do that.' Maybe not, but he stole toys from Woolworths. He would sneak bikes and prams across the road, or a couple of streets away, just to see if he could get away with it. With his mate Paul Frost, he stole a whole crate of orange juice from a neighbour's doorstep, and that was enough for the police to knock on the door at 51 Keppel Road. According to Barry, all three brothers would be out until eleven or twelve most nights, playing on the streets.

The twins once overheard Barbara complaining that Hugh never brought her flowers. Robin and Maurice pinched a wreath and gave it to her – it still had the lettering on it that read 'Rest in Peace'. Another time, Barbara had left twelve pounds in notes on the mantelpiece to pay an electricity bill. Robin took it and gave it away to kids at school. It's 'disagone', he told his mum.

Robin remembered the brothers were usually in 'a spot of bother. It was kind of light-hearted stuff . . . well, it wasn't really light-hearted stuff, we were firebugs. We used to run around setting fire to allotments.' Robin had begun by putting leaves and sticks under his bed and then setting fire to them. Satisfied with this, he moved on. His next project was an abandoned car, which was left gutted. A TV and radio shop in Chorlton – not his father's – burned down. After he destroyed a shed at the back of a butcher's shop, the police came around again. First Maurice, now Robin.

Two ways for kids to break out of a dead-end life are sport and music. Manchester offered plenty of opportunities for young footballers; Manchester United were league champions in 1955/56 and 1956/57 with the legendary Busby Babes team – but all the brothers ever cared about was singing. That was their only option. No wonder Hugh fed them the Mills Brothers for breakfast. 'It was a shock to us when we heard them singing in harmony,' Barbara Gibb would say years later. 'Robin always laughingly says his father got dollar signs in his eyes when he heard them sing. But he didn't. I mean, he just thought it was great, he just thought they could sing at parties.'

'We were experiencing all sorts of music,' Barry recalled, 'and then suddenly our sister brings home the Everly Brothers' "Bye Bye Love" and "Devoted to You", and all these beautiful harmony records. That was it. So from then on, it was listening to the Everly Brothers, being influenced – we want to do this, this is what we want – and finding the first juke boxes, and listening to those, and sitting in front of those juke boxes and listening to these new pop records.'

'Bear in mind', said Hugh, years later, 'that they were still school kids, and you know how some kids want to be train drivers at one time or another. But singing was the only thing the boys ever wanted to do. We just couldn't stop them. Even in those early years, their whole lives revolved around waiting to be discovered. They'd stand on street corners singing songs like "Wake Up Little Susie". They had to have an audience.'

'We knew we wouldn't want to be doing anything else when we grew up,' said Barry. 'We knew that's where we were going.' Far from being pushed by Hugh, the brothers would pester him to listen to their harmonies. They needed a stage, and in November 1957 they found one. The plan was for them to mime to a record, a 78, at the Saturday matinee at Chorlton's Gaumont Picture House; this was at a time when UK cinemas were generally one large screen with several hundred seats and a stage at the front. Saturday mornings meant Laurel and Hardy, the Three Stooges, Hopalong Cassidy, Flash Gordon, and Gene Autry in *Goldtown Ghost Riders*. In between, with the blessing of the cinema manager, kids would get up and mime to a hit of the day. Years later, Maurice thought the 78 they took was by Tommy Steele, Barry remembered it being Paul Anka, or − on other occasions − the Everly Brothers. What they did agree on was that on the day they were called the Rattlesnakes, and that the Rattlesnakes were a five-piece. Schoolmates Kenny Horrocks (tea-chest bass) and Paul Frost (drums) made up the numbers, and they would rehearse in the cellar at Paul's house, playing in a pre-teen skiffle style.

The Gaumont wouldn't allow them to take their instruments on stage, but Barry took his guitar along just to look a little more pro. Entering the cinema, the over-excited Barry managed to drop the 78, its brittle shellac cracking at once, their plan foiled. They couldn't back down now. So instead of miming to the 78, they took the stage and sang the Everly Brothers' 'Wake Up Little Susie' in three-part harmony.

The Mills Brothers were Hugh's. But the Everlys belonged to his kids. Don and Phil, one-time child stars on KFNF in Shenandoah, Iowa, were the harmonic model for any aspiring kids in England – the Quarrymen in Liverpool, the Hollies in Manchester. But neither the nascent Beatles nor Graham Nash and his mates ever had what the Rattlesnakes had: that sibling sound. The Gibbs could even add a third harmony and go one better than the Everlys. No wonder they didn't lack for confidence. The Gaumont was their debut show. Barry was eleven, Robin and Maurice were nearly eight years old.

Paul Frost and Kenny Horrocks didn't know it, but they were the first of what would become a very select group – outside musicians who were invited in by the Gibb brothers. Barry, Robin and Maurice were already way more insular and independent than most of their contemporaries – and they weren't even teenagers yet. Moving schools so often meant that it was tricky to ever form strong relationships with other kids, so instead they leaned on each other. 'We were like the Brontë sisters,' said Robin. 'We created our own world and fed off our fantasies and ideas. Once we created this inner world we immersed ourselves in that.' Like contemporaneous groups of boys in Brooklyn and the Bronx, the brothers would find street corners and empty churches where they could get some echo to flesh out their harmonies, replicating the acoustics of a theatre. Their favourite location was Lewis's department store in Manchester, specifically the toilets. Years later, writing in Miami, Barry said how the brothers would still fill the room with echo to get ideas going – 'like a big toilet, if you would'.

Money remained thin on the ground. Hugh struggled to pay the electricity bills. One night they ran out of candles, and Paul Frost kindly brought some over. In the darkness he sat down on an armchair, without realising that he was also sitting down on Barry's guitar. It was eventually repaired, but maybe something was telling the Gibbs that they weren't about to make the grade in Manchester. Broken guitars were only part of the problem. 'We were sort of delinquents. We were always on the streets,' Barry told Melvyn Bragg in 1997. 'We built a fire behind a set of billboards and it took the whole lot down, to the main road. I remember us going to the baths to go swimming after we'd started the fire and watching the police and the fire brigade, and the crowds filling out on the road.' The brothers had the brass neck to stand in the crowd, watching the results of their handiwork. 'We were standing next to a policeman and we said, "What's happened?" The policeman said, "Don't worry. We'll get 'em." We were very defiant. Not good kids.'

To Hugh and Barbara's surprise, they discovered there was going to be a fifth Gibb baby; Andy was born in March and Keppel Road was suddenly a squash and a squeeze. The family moved on in May 1958, to Northen Grove in West Didsbury. Frost and Horrocks left, leading to a name change for the group – the Gibb trio were now Wee Johnny Hayes and the Blue Cats, with Barry as 'Johnny'. They played more Saturday morning shows at the local Palatine cinema, with the Chordettes' 'Lollipop' a new harmony favourite, and began to get tongues wagging. Hugh's band were now regulars at the Russell Club, a converted cinema in Hulme – it would go on to become Tony Wilson's legendary club the Factory in the late 1970s and host names like Joy Division, Iggy Pop, Public Image Ltd. and Wire. Twenty years earlier, Hughie Gibb decided to smuggle his well-underage lads into the club to sing a couple of songs in front of a real audience. It's hard to imagine how the three kids wouldn't have gone down well, but the enthusiastic response buoyed them – this was a real step up from the Gaumont and the Palatine. A proper venue, with a proper adult crowd. Heck, it was even dark outside! Their set extended beyond teenage pop to include crowd pleasers for grown-ups. They learned 'Alexander's Ragtime Band'. Hugh became their de facto manager. It was starting to look a little more like a budding career.

The boys remained budding criminals, too. Barry stole a kid's pedal car with a mate who already had a criminal record – to help him out, Barry took the rap on his own. He 'ended up in court and got two years' probation. It was not good.' When the police came to the door for a third time, they gently suggested to Barbara that the boys were running out of chances, and the next step might be reform school. One policeman suggested there was another country that could handle the rambunctious Gibbs, maybe one on the other side of the world. Barbara's sister Peggy had been thinking about emigrating to Australia, taking advantage of the 'New Life' scheme which meant you could cross the world for just £10. Leaving cold, damp, red-brick Manchester wasn't a hard sell to the boys. Fancy swapping this place for the sea and the sun? What kid wouldn't? If they were going to create their own world, be the male Brontës, they may as well do it in the sunshine rather than a damp back yard. And so the Gibbs decided to leave England behind and start again.

3

BRISBANE

Brisbane rainfall: 12 mm per annum
Manchester rainfall: 1,047 mm per annum

'We left nothing behind, except Manchester, and I wouldn't want to die there. I suppose I've got to look back fondly on my childhood. I've got no other life.'

– Robin

'Between 1960 and 1965 was the era of rock 'n' roll in Australia, with its own environment, its own TV stars, its own pop stars, rock stars, totally unknown to the rest of the world.'

– Barry

Billboard US top ten, 8 September 1958

1. Domenico Modugno – 'Volare'
2. The Elegants – 'Little Star'
3. Everly Brothers – 'Bird Dog' / 'Devoted to You'

4. Jimmy Clanton – 'Just a Dream'
5. Pérez Prado – 'Patricia'
6. Ricky Nelson – 'Poor Little Fool'
7. Jack Scott – 'My True Love' / 'Leroy'
8. Bobby Day – 'Rockin' Robin'
9. Frankie Avalon – 'Ginger Bread'
10. The Olympics – 'Western Movies'

The ocean liner *Fairsea* left Southampton with the Gibb family on board. Five-month-old Andy would be christened at sea; he'd have no memories of frozen taps and raw, bruised knees from red-brick playgrounds. He also wouldn't remember his older brothers taking full advantage of this strange new opportunity to show off their harmonies. The *Fairsea* became a floating version of the Russell Club, with the boys effectively living in the dressing room. They were supposed to be off the decks by nine, after which the grown-ups had the ship to themselves, but the boys would sneak out of bed at night and sing in their pyjamas. Hugh would walk around a corner, see a crowd had gathered, and know his lads would be in the middle singing Everly Brothers songs: 'It happened every night. We couldn't do a thing about it.' They had found themselves another short-lived, rather functional name – Barry and the Twins. Their parents were probably just relieved they weren't hawking stolen toys or turning the purser's quarters into a tinderbox.

The *Fairsea* travelled down the Suez Canal and had a stopover near Cairo. Barry, now eleven, was old enough to appreciate the magic of the journey: 'We saw the pyramids and all these exotic countries at such an early age. We've always had a feeling that had something to do with our songwriting, you know?' They navigated the Red Sea, crossed the Gulf of Aden, passed India, and headed to Perth across the Indian Ocean. The *Fairsea* docked on 1 September 1958, Barry's twelfth birthday. The weather seemed to have followed them from Manchester. Robin and Maurice tried to hide their disappointment, but as they peered through the drizzle they saw no kangaroos or koalas on the streets of Perth.

They travelled on to Queensland and found a house at 394 Oxley Avenue in Redcliffe (main districts: Scarborough and Margate), overlooking Moreton Bay, just north of Brisbane. There were still no kangaroos, but there were fat, almost spherical mango trees in the Brisbane suburbs. And fig trees. This wasn't West Didsbury.

Barry would recall 'being in bare feet all the time, going to school in your bare feet, and that kind of life. That's why I say you have to go: to understand the Tom Sawyer, the Huckleberry Finn type of life. The tyre over the creek, you know? So simple and so uncomplicated.'

The city of Brisbane was an odd place, though – unreconstructed, five years behind the rest of Australia, let alone Britain or America. Hugh quickly found work as a 'bush photographer', taking family photos for people who either couldn't afford a camera or lived in places so isolated that they had nowhere to develop film; Hugh would take his own caravan of equipment.

What did they make of their new home? Browns, bottle greens and battleship greys had been replaced by iridescent yellows, brilliant blues, sparkles of light catching on the warm water. They had left behind peeling paint, black mould growing around soft, damp window frames, bitter cold that got into your bones. The brothers felt instantly at home. And, encouraged by their appearances on the *Fairsea*, they also quickly sensed an opportunity.

'We were never bad kids, we were just mischievous,' Barry would later tell writer Alexis Petridis. 'We always thought we could get away with things. But the Australian police, that's not like England. You don't want to mess with these people. We found that out real quick. We'd shoplift from Woolworths and things like that, in Redcliffe. And finally, on Redcliffe Pier, which has now gone, which is where we would dive and swim amongst sharks – God knows why we ever did it, but we did – on that pier, on a certain day, we all decided never to break the law again. We had to make a choice. Doing what we were doing, we could actually become famous.'

The British pop scene was fairly primitive in late 1958, but it had real stars, boys with real presence – Cliff Richard, Marty Wilde, Lonnie Donegan, with Billy Fury and Adam Faith breaking through the following year. It would even have its own competing variations on the Everly Brothers' blueprint before too long, in the shape of the Allisons and the Brook Brothers. Australia's scene, by comparison, was very much in its infancy. The only local act with name recognition was the hot-headed Johnny O'Keefe, who could cause riots in his home town of Sydney but hadn't yet scored a top-ten hit. Australia's number-one hits in 1958 would have been familiar to anyone passing through from Britain or America: Perry Como's 'Catch a Falling Star'; the Everly Brothers' 'Bird Dog'; Tommy Edwards' 'It's All in the Game'; David Seville's nursery-friendly 'Witch Doctor'. The country's best-selling record of the year was the Kingston Trio's 'Tom Dooley', a folk song, a murder ballad even, though hardly recognizable as such thanks to the trio's collegiate, coffee house delivery. The only homegrown release to have reached number one in Australia in 1958 was another folk song, another horror story if you like – Slim Dusty's 'A Pub with No Beer'. It would take a bunch of families travelling on a £10 ticket from Britain to give Australian pop any sense of direction. It was amateur hour – a vast country, and wide open.

Brisbane wasn't so backward, though, that it didn't have its own radio station. Barry and the Twins entered *Talent Quest*, a search-for-the-stars show on local station 4KQ. They didn't win. Singing wasn't especially encouraged at Scarborough State School, where Barry's red-necked sports teacher made the kids play football barefoot to build up the calluses on their feet. In the face of such good old-fashioned Aussie masculinity, the brothers would slink off and give private concerts for their classmates.

Apart from their screwed-down, crew-cut schooling, life had improved immeasurably. They still had no money, but they went swimming every morning before school off the dock on Deception Bay; after school they would go fishing off Woody Point jetty, or there was Redcliffe Pier with its pinball arcade, fish and chips, and pie and peas imported by homesick Yorkshiremen. In 1999, Barry would write a letter for the Redcliffe Museum. 'It was a wonderful tropical existence that I re-live over and over in my heart and mind.' In search of a new life, they found themselves in a place that Barry called 'paradise'.

The biggest thrill came when they discovered Redcliffe's Speedway. By the beginning of 1959 Barry and his schoolmate Ken Griggs were selling Coke and Fanta there on Sundays. The roar of the bikes and the cars, and the smell of the dust flying off the red, sandy track, was irresistible. The Speedway's mix of oil and hot sun was a scent different from anything the Gibbs had known before. Gaps between races were long and uneventful, so Barry got the brothers to do what they loved to do, singing 'Lollipop', 'Wake Up Little Susie' and the odd Barry Gibb original for good measure. A crowd formed, and the crowd bought more Coke and Fanta.

This got them noticed by the track's owner, a man called Bill Goode, a natural-born car nut whose hands were always covered in oil and grease. The day the Gibbs started their impromptu show, he was doubling up as a mechanic because his marshal hadn't arrived, and he came out of the pits to see what was going on. 'One of my drivers, Bob McMahon, came to me and said there were three young boys outside and they wanted to come and sing for a coin toss at half-time. So I said, "Well, get them in."' Goode thought the boys could sing on the back of a fruit truck: 'Another of our drivers, Barry Watt, got an oil drum so they could hop up . . . I was chasing the stock bike riders out through the gate when I heard these beautiful, melodious voices coming through the speaker. It stopped me in my tracks. I thought, *Geez, they're good.*'

Racetrack-goers were serenaded by the brothers' voices coming out of tannoy speakers dotted around the track. People threw them coins in appreciation; on the very first occasion they made £10, as much as Hugh made in a week. The following day, Goode invited the Gibbs back down to the track and asked the boys to sing him another song. What would he like to hear? Well, how many have you got? Twelve-year-old Barry Gibb told Bill Goode that he had written around 180 songs.

'They sang me an Everly Brothers song and I was absolutely amazed.' Sensing something special, Goode quickly got in touch with radio station 4BH disc jockey Bill Gates to check he wasn't hearing things. Goode wanted to sign the boys to a contract, but required a second opinion.

Like Goode, Bill Gates loved his cars. More importantly – as 'Swingin' Gates' – he was the most popular DJ in Queensland, the host of *Midday Platter Chatter* on 4BH. Gates was the only Australian DJ who could go to the States and get big-name interviews for 4BH to broadcast on their morning show, with stars of the calibre of Sam Cooke, Nancy Wilson and George Shearing. Bill Gates just happened to be driving a car in a charity meeting at Redcliffe. He heard the brothers' harmonies over the tannoy. He confirmed that Bill Goode wasn't hearing things: 'Even under such primitive conditions,' he recalled, 'their sound was remarkable.' Goode remembers Gates being 'pretty stoked . . . I asked him if he wanted to join in the [management] company and promote them and he said yes please.'

So Bill Goode introduced Barry Gibb to Bill Gates, whose sign-off just happened to be 'BG on BH'. Gates was quite taken aback by the older brother's brio and confidence. He also suggested a new name. It was goodbye to Barry and the Twins, goodbye to Johnny Hayes and the Blue Cats, goodbye to the Rattlesnakes. The trio renamed themselves for the fourth and final time at Redcliffe's speedway track: Bill Goode, Bill Gates and Barry Gibb – all the main players had the initials B.G. They became the BGs. It would take a while for an official spelling and house style to settle in, and later the name would be retro-fitted to stand for Brothers Gibb, but Goode and Gates were the first people – aside from their parents – to believe the brothers were a significant talent.

Straight off, Gates offered to record them. He recorded six songs onto a tape at the 4BH studio, including Barry's originals 'Twenty Miles to Blueland', 'Let Me Love You' and 'The Echo of Your Love'. Bill Gates played this acetate on his show every day until it was worn out. It says much for the isolation and obscurity of Brisbane that this didn't cause an instant sensation across Australia – remarkably it would be another three years before any of their music was officially released.

With Bill Gates as 'promoter' (he was wary of using 'manager' as even Barry was still only twelve) they played tent shows and agricultural expos where the stink and the heat got the better of more fragile souls than the young Gibbs. Australia was still so primitive that it had only begun its first TV broadcasts in 1956; when Brisbane got its own channel in 1959, Bill Gates was in like Flynn. There were Gibbs all over it, very quickly, in tartan waistcoats. According to Nancy Knudsen, the host of *Swinging School*, they looked filthy and swore constantly. Ten-year-old children swearing! She warned them once, she warned them twice, then she fired them. So, instead, their first TV appearance would be on Russ Tyson's *Anything Goes*, in March 1960. They sang current hits, and the biggest current hit was Lonnie Donegan's 'My Old Man's a Dustman', a weird music hall echo of the old country.

Soon they had their own local TV show, *The BG's Half Hour* (or *Cottie's Happy Hour* according to Robin in a 1967 *NME* interview) on Friday night. Child welfare stepped in, and instead of a weekly show it was made monthly. Barry's songs at this time were basic building blocks, his technique learned from the radio, and they were often country-based. There weren't any lost future classics, but, then, *he was barely a teenager*. It was mind-blowing that he even considered writing his own songs.

'I like to make up the tunes I sing. I get the words from romance magazines and stories my sixteen-year-old sister Lesley reads,' Barry told *Australian Women's Weekly*, which also wrote about the 'make-believe television studio which they've built in their house'. Maurice claimed that they had a 'different script every day and we're always changing the floor-plan and the sets'.

Bill Gates stood down in 1960, a DJ who had taken them as far as he could, but was smart enough to keep a share in the group. Hugh became their rather unwilling manager. ('They're my kids,' he must have worried; 'Who's going to listen to me?') The Bee Gees' national obscurity reflects how little TV mattered in Australia at the turn of the '60s – if this was the US then they'd already have been household names.

Teetotal Hugh could drive them all over Queensland. He began booking them into RSL (Returned and Services League) clubs, alongside dancing dogs, jugglers and comedians. They did some comedy. They sang more Lonnie Donegan hits from the old country – 'Does Your Chewing Gum Lose Its Flavour (On the Bedpost Overnight)'. They sang in dockside clubs, with sailors enjoying drinking contests as these underage artistes tried to get their attention. 'You might do two spots a night, two spots a show, five songs each spot, to a pretty heavy-drinking audience,' remembered Barry. 'So we saw things, we saw people sitting at tables having fights without standing up! And we'd do shows where water would pour in through the galvanised roofs. It was real *Crocodile Dundee*: it really was like that. But what a life.'

The baby Bee Gees were having fun.

Barry: 'We had very strong parents. Our father was always with us.'

Maurice: 'We had a great childhood. I always refer to the time when I was eleven, in the changing room of a stripper, and thinking to myself, *Will I be a normal child?* No! Most of the kids I went to school with I couldn't relate to.'

In 1959 the Gibbs moved to 12 Fifth Avenue, in the Brisbane suburb of Scarborough (in 1999, it would have a wooden sign that read Bee Gees Place), and then on to Orient House Flats on the Esplanade, a ten-minute walk from Humpybong State School where Barry first made friends with a fair-haired kid called Colin Petersen. The brothers were becoming the family breadwinners, and that income wasn't always enough. 'We were a family who had literally no money and we could get ten dollars a show,' Barry said. 'We had to earn money; it couldn't be done any other way. We probably rented twenty houses during the seven years or so that we were in Australia. I think, without over-emphasising it, my father just didn't pay the rent. We were that family in the middle of the night with the suitcases.'

'As kids, we never lived in one place for more than two years,' remembered Robin. 'As a result, we didn't really have a childhood.' It isn't too surprising that the brothers felt most secure in their own company. Their confidence and desire to succeed were pressurised by Hugh's struggle to make ends meet. 'In the early days,' Robin said, 'we practically had to work to live. Our family didn't have much money so I think they had to make it on us . . . My father was forty-one when we moved from Manchester to Australia.' To bring in more money, they began to tour further out in Queensland. Hugh sat in on drums. Mo started playing bass, Robin piano.

They had met British rock 'n' roller Tommy Steele when he was over in Brisbane, in February of 1960. There's even a rumour that he recorded Barry's 'Let Me Love You', but no tape has ever surfaced. By Christmas that year, the brothers were known well enough to indulge in the same family-friendly entertainment that would steer Steele out of the fevered world of British rock 'n' roll: panto. They appeared in *Jack and the Beanstalk* at the Rialto

Theatre, Sydney. By then, Barry was fourteen and had his first girlfriend – he started dating Ann Blackmore, and his parents let her stay over in Lesley's bedroom. They may have been singing 'My Old Man's a Dustman' in cute three-part harmonies on stage, but they were beginning to grow up.

What would they have heard on the radio in Queensland at the turn of the '60s? The Everly Brothers and Elvis Presley still beamed in magic from the USA, while Cliff Richard was the biggest British star. Robin became a fan of Cliff's backing group the Shadows, and moody instrumentals like 'Apache' and 'Man of Mystery'. Barry would recall loving Johnny Cash's 'Ballad of a Teenage Queen', Johnny O'Keefe's cover of the Isley Brothers' 'Shout', and Col Joye's 1959 top-three hit 'Bye Bye Baby'. Like O'Keefe, Col Joye was a genuine homegrown Australian rock 'n' roll star. Born Colin Jacobsen, he was solid, rugged-looking, but still a much gentler TV presence than the roughneck O'Keefe. Other local acts on the up were singing cowboy Reg Lindsey, the quiffed, saturnine Dig Richards and the teenage Billy Thorpe, who would become a major Australian star in the '60s and '70s. 'I wouldn't say they influenced us a great deal musically,' said Barry. 'Maybe they did in the sense of competition. We really wanted to get out and prove ourselves against those acts.' These acts were scoring Australian hit singles, though, and the Bee Gees had yet to even see the inside of a studio.

A stronger influence, according to Maurice, came from 'Dad's input . . . I would say the Mills Brothers' [influence] was professionalism. When you're on stage you smile, because if you feel like crap and you look like crap, people will feel like crap too.'

Hugh would always be down the back, grinning, just to remind the boys, 'because that's what the Mills Brothers did. And I think that's what he really wanted, for us to be a little Mills Brothers. I think the three harmonies was a beautiful sound.'

And still the Gibbs kept packing suitcases at short notice, moving on. In 1960, they had gone inland to Kallangur. Six months later they were in Nundah, near the airport, where the brothers shot a Goons-style version of *The African Queen* on their new Super 8 camera. By 1961, they were at a place called Cribb Island, now buried under Brisbane airport, then went to Cambridge Avenue, in Surfers Paradise, 50 miles south of Brisbane. It was warm, every day. And, though all three were still at school, for eighteen months they would have a residency at the local Beachcomber Hotel, playing to holidaymakers on the Gold Coast. Their sets were all covers, from their Lonnie Donegan numbers to Ray Charles's 'What'd I Say'. Hugh would be their guide through the choppy waters of grown-up, holiday-resort entertainment. 'My father knew exactly what those audiences wanted,' reckoned Maurice. 'Any bit of comedy would have them laughing their heads off. I was always the one who got suckered, always the straight man. Robin was the funny one, the cheeky little look. Barry was the older brother looking after us. It was always visual comedy, sort of Abbott and Costello.' It also sounded a lot like their real-life sibling relationships.

Barry left school in 1962, aged fifteen. He got himself a job as a tailor's assistant, but was fired after forgetting to hand over some money. If he was ever going to make it as a professional songwriter, he would need to force fate. Two things would happen that suggested he was more likely to make it in music than tailoring. First, he signed a publishing deal with Belinda Music after word had got around that he was a remarkably quick writer who could knock out songs to order. Secondly, that summer, Australian pop idol Col Joye played a show in Surfers Paradise, and his rehearsal room was a hundred yards from the Gibbs' house.

Like the Mills Brothers, Col Joye was always smiling. He had scored another three number ones since breaking through with 'Bye Bye Baby' back in 1959. Though his sound had become a little more countrified, less rock 'n' roll, he was the biggest name in Australian pop. So when he turned up for rehearsals, Barry collared him. 'We thought, this is the next step. If we can meet this guy we can sell him a song and we're on our way . . . Col came through and I said, "I'd like to sing you some of the songs we've written with a view to you recording them if possible." He said, "Oh, sure." I couldn't believe it!' Being from Sydney, Col was unaware of either the schoolboy songwriter or kiddie TV sensations the Bee Gees. He heard their harmonies and was shocked; the very next day, he recorded them in a church hall, using his own band's equipment. He still owns the tape, and it starts like this: 'My name is Barry Gibb, I live at 23 Cambridge Avenue, Surfers Paradise. My first song is "Let Me Love You" . . .' Col and his brother Kevin Jacobsen convinced Hugh and the brothers that they needed to move to Sydney to get more attention; Bill Goode and Bill Gates agreed to relinquish their share in the group's management. The boys were now, no question, providing their family's income.

They called time on their residency at the Beachcomber and arrived at 23 Colin Street, Lakemba, Sydney, in January 1963. It was some 500 miles south of Surfers Paradise. Sister Lesley's fiancé Alan Curtis was a comedian by night but a useful handyman by day – he built the brothers a rehearsal room out of an old tin shed, and a makeshift TV studio under the house. Baby brother Andy would remember the house on Colin Street, and how there were always three radios blasting music at the same time. He also recalled how Robin used to sing in the bath, developing what would become one of the most distinctive voices in pop – Andy thought he sounded like 'a quavering Arab'. The family had gone quite some time without a brush with death, and it was Robin's turn next. He was knocked off his bike in Lakemba by a delivery van – he had forgotten that the brakes on his bike weren't working and took a near-fatal turn down a steep hill. He stayed unconscious for two hours.

Col Joye had been right about the move to 'the Big Smoke'. Instead of cabaret turns in clubs and hotels, the Bee Gees now found themselves playing at Sydney Stadium between local rocker Johnny O'Keefe and Philadelphia's 'King of the Twist' Chubby Checker. Col himself had engineered the deal with local impresario and sometime A&R man Lee Gordon. It went well enough for the brothers to complete the tour with Checker and O'Keefe, through to the end of January 1963. They made more TV appearances, on former newsreader Brian Henderson's Saturday show *Bandstand*. They would become part of a family of local pop stars who were regulars on the show, very much a Sydney counterpart to Dick Clark's Philadelphia-based *Bandstand*: substituting for Chubby Checker, Dee Dee Sharp and Bobby Rydell were singers including Little Pattie, Judy Stone, Bryan Davies and Joye himself. The boys were also a regular support act on Col's shows across Australia, and he liked them enough to claim they were 'the only Aussie group good enough to make it overseas'. How frustrating it must have been, then, that the Bee Gees still didn't even have a record out. At least they had their own fan club, run out of her bedroom by big sis Lesley. That was busy enough for her to make an appearance in *TV Week* magazine, and having to apologise to fans for the delay in getting photos and membership cards out.

The Jacobsens' agency was securing them appearances on other TV shows, like *Sing Sing Sing* and *Saturday Date*, and club dates which brought in up to £20 a night, for a gruelling session. Backstage areas could be shared with strippers and bad-time drunks. 'We were like a dirty version of the Osmonds,' laughed Maurice years later. They could play up to five hours a night, and then Robin and Maurice would be back in school the next morning. The result was that they finally became a known name in every Australian state. And, eventually, Lee Gordon – who had taken the risk of throwing the three teenagers on in front of thousands of screaming Chubby Checker fans – convinced Fred Marks, owner of Festival Records, to sign them. Their first single would be released on Gordon's Leedon imprint. Both sides would be written by sixteen-year-old Barry Gibb.

4

SYDNEY

Radio station 2SM Sydney top ten, 3 May 1963

1. Little Peggy March – 'I Will Follow Him'
2. The Chantays – 'Pipeline'
3. The Shadows – 'Foot Tapper'
4. Cliff Richard and the Shadows – 'Summer Holiday'
5. The Cascades – 'Rhythm of the Rain'
6. Jay Justin – 'Proud of You'
7. The Exciters – 'He's Got the Power'
8. Gene Pitney – 'Mecca'
9. Roy Orbison – 'In Dreams'
10. Beach Boys – 'Surfin' USA'

Festival Records had been formed in 1952 after a merger between a company called Casper Precision Engineering and a record-pressing company called Microgroove Australia. Two years later, after the local EMI label had turned it down, Festival was smart enough to acquire the rights for Bill Haley's 'Rock Around the Clock'. Nobody at the company was much of a rock 'n' roll fan, but they could smell money in the new teenage sound and by the early '60s they had signed Johnny O'Keefe, Dig Richards and Col Joye, Australia's 'Big Three' rock 'n' roll acts. O'Keefe's 'Wild One' would become the first true Australian rock 'n' roll classic, covered in the US by the Crickets' Jerry Allison, in the UK by the Shadows' Jet Harris, and in the '80s by rebel's rebel Iggy Pop.

By 1961, Festival had been sold to someone with an even better nose for profit: News Limited owner and fledgling tycoon Rupert Murdoch. It was a shoestring operation, but the cracks in the creaking Festival studios at 52 Harris Street, Pyrmont, Sydney, would be papered over with Murdoch's investment, and he appointed his old assistant at News Limited, Fred Marks, as managing director. Marks twigged that Festival had to look abroad again to make the kind of money his boss craved, and so started to set up licensing deals around the world, flying to the States at Murdoch's expense. The deal that would safeguard the label's future was bringing in Herb Alpert and the Tijuana Brass's 'Lonely Bull' for $500. Not only was the song Australia's number-one record in November 1962, but this secured a connection with the freshly minted A&M label for years to come, including the catalogues of Alpert, the Carpenters, Burt Bacharach and Sergio Mendes. Between them, Murdoch and Marks ensured Festival Records would be Australia's biggest pop label in the '60s.

Local names didn't especially float Fred Marks's boat. When they cut their first single in January 1963, the Bee Gees were not a priority act for Festival Records. Their first single was recorded in downtime at the end of the day, on the cheap after

everyone else had gone home. It was engineered by the bespec-
tacled Robert Iredale, who was known for pushing and prod-
ding Festival's pop musicians; O'Keefe recalled him as bossy
and averse to anything 'noisy', though, given the limited gear
they were working with, Iredale was doing the best he could.
Col Joye was there to give the boys encouragement, and his
band the Joy Boys provided the Gibbs with backup.

That January, News Limited's *Sydney Morning Herald* was
breathlessly writing up Australia's eight-wicket win over England
at the Sydney Cricket Ground; Britain was freezing its extrem-
ities off during the coldest winter in living memory; and Cliff
Richard and the Shadows were dominating the radio in both
countries, just as they had done for the past few years. Festival's press department claimed the Gibbs' nocturnal recordings
were 'two great sides with definite Top Ten potential', but they
weren't about to give Cliff and the Shads a scare. Murdoch-
owned, the *Morning Herald* was happy to give the Gibbs some
space in the paper, though it was sister Lesley who they were
more taken with. She had just started working as a snake dancer
in Surfers Paradise, and they ran a piece which included her top
tip on how to avoid getting bitten: 'Clamp the snake's jaws with
sticky tape.'

The Bee Gees' debut was released in March 1963, on Festival's
subsidiary Leedon. 'The Battle of the Blue and Grey' was in the tradition of Johnny Horton's country-pop hits of the early '60s (most
specifically 'The Battle of New Orleans') and of Lonnie Donegan's
Anglicised takes on American folk yarns. (To give an idea of how
Australian pop culture time lagged behind, Donegan's final British
hit single had been back in 1962.) Barry sang from the perspective of a Confederate veteran, and the result wasn't a million miles
away from the skiffle sound of the Rattlesnakes in 1957. It wasn't

embarrassing, though neither was it outstanding nor anywhere close to 1963's cutting edge. It was convincing enough. The boys promoted it on *Bandstand*. The B-side got airplay too: 'The Three Kisses of Love' was actually the better song, a post-Everlys sound that shone a light on their harmonies. The plinkety guitar backing on 'Three Kisses' was weak, rather like Adam Faith's 'What Do You Want' on a Woolworths budget, but it was still a charming debut, especially given that neither Robin's nor Maurice's voices had broken yet. Barry was still just sixteen, though the press release said he was seventeen. There was no national chart in Australia yet; 'The Battle of the Blue and Grey' had to be satisfied with sneaking into the bottom end of the Sydney top twenty.

New releases from Britain in March 1963 had included the Tornados' rollicking sci-fi instrumental 'Robot', Tommy Steele's signature tune 'Flash Bang Wallop', and the Beatles' second single 'Please Please Me'. Seeing the light of day in America were the Beach Boys' 'Surfin' USA', the Chiffons' girl group finger-snapper 'He's So Fine', and Little Peggy March's frighteningly devotional 'I Will Follow Him', which would become a number one in both the US and Australia. Martha and the Vandellas' 'Come and Get These Memories', Doris Troy's tough 'Just One Look' and Barbara Lewis's jazzy, seductive 'Hello Stranger' pointed out new directions for R&B, now quickly morphing into soul, while Lou Christie's 'Two Faces Have I' introduced one of the wildest falsetto voices in history to the American top ten. In time all of these records would have a subtle influence on the Bee Gees' writing and style, but it wouldn't show just yet. Another new release in March 1963 was Peter, Paul and Mary's 'Puff, the Magic Dragon', a peculiar mix of kids' nursery singalong and narcotic epiphany, and this was the one that the Bee Gees introduced to their own repertoire. It may not have been their idea – you'd certainly hope not – but they knew their audience, and a cover of 'Hello Stranger' would only have led to abuse and bottle-throwing in the RSL clubs.

Slowly realising that news in the pop world was news worth printing, the *Sydney Morning Herald* reported changes at Festival Studios on 14 April 1963 – new upgraded microphones, tape recorders, limiters and 'frequency benders' bought with the money rolling in from sales of 'Lonely Bull'. Col Joye was one of the first beneficiaries, recording Barry's '(Underneath the) Starlight of Love' for the B-side of 'Put 'Em Down', making him the first artist to cover a Bee Gees song. The brothers' lives had hardly been changed by the sales from their first record, and they continued playing shows like the Lysaght's steel factory day out in Wollongong, the equivalent of a large summer fete. Appearances on *Bandstand* found them singing the Beatles' 'Please Please Me' and James Gilreath's 'Little Band of Gold' rather than their own minor hit. 'We went right back into the studio,' remembered Robin, 'and cut our second one, "Timber!", which did exactly what the title suggested.'

Released in July, 'Timber!' borrowed its tom-tom intro from the Everly Brothers' 1961 hit 'Temptation', before skidding into a breakneck-speed song ('My heart cries timber . . . / . . . 'cause I'm a-fallin' for you') with hasty string sweeps – at least the orchestration was a Bee Gee first. 'Timber!' was the happening sound of 1961, but unfortunately it was now 1963. The whole thing was all over inside one minute forty-four seconds; it was possibly the corniest record they would ever release. The chorus ended with a 'yeah yeah yeah' a matter of weeks before the Beatles would turn the phrase into a byword for contemporary pop, but no one would ever confuse 'Timber!' with 'She Loves You'. Again, the flip side was the stronger track and – again – it picked up some interest on its own. 'Take Hold of That Star' was a doo wop ballad in the classic tradition. Presumably it drew on the Mills Brothers as much as it did Dion and the Belmonts, but it was endearing and showed off the Gibb harmonies in a very pure way. Intriguingly the backing featured a Nashville piano sound reminiscent of Floyd Cramer, which helped to take the song away from its Sydney locale; 'Take Hold of That Star' was the side they decided to plug on *Bandstand*.

However, it wasn't doo wop but surf music that was massive in Australia that summer. In Hawthorn, California, was another harmony group centred around three brothers. The Wilsons – Brian, Dennis and Carl – based their vocals on the clean-cut sound of the Four Freshmen rather than the Everly Brothers, an unusual enough reference point to ensure the Beach Boys – né the Pendletons – stood out sonically. Similarly, their big brother Brian was a singer and songwriter. The major difference between the Bee Gees and Beach Boys at this time was that the latter had scored a hit with their very first record, 'Surfin'', and that by 1963 they were bothering the upper end of the *Billboard* chart.

Beach Boys aside, surf music was largely an instrumental concern, with groups attempting to create a two-minute representation of the thrills and terror of catching a wave. The futuristic rumble of the Chantays' 'Pipeline', Jan & Dean's Brian Wilson-penned 'Surf City', and Sydney group the Atlantics' 'Bombora' were all number ones in Australia, with the Surfaris' 'Wipe Out' just behind at number three, and Jack Nitzsche's 'The Lonely Surfer' at number nine. Further local surf hits came from dear old Col Joye's Joy Boys, who cashed in with their own top-twenty surf instrumental 'Murphy the Surfie'; Little Pattie's 'He's My Blonde-Headed, Stompie Wompie, Real Gone Surfer Boy'; and the Delltones' 'Hangin' Five', which had the lingo if not the vibe. The same could be said for Barry Gibb's 'Surfer Boy', a baroque ballad recorded by Noeleen Batley in the autumn of 1963. Barry was entirely unacquainted with a surfboard, yet this song was quite gorgeous, with plangent chords, a melancholy oboe counter-melody, and the kind of sympathetic arrangement noticeably missing from the Bee Gees' own 1963 singles.

The Gibbs would be on stage with a ballgowned Noeleen at the Sydney 2UW Spectacular, in Lane Cove National Park, in September 1963, where 40,000 kids saw them on stage with Col Joye, Judy Stone, Johnny Rebb and Lonnie Lee. This was an unwitting farewell to the sound of pre-Beatles pop – within weeks, even surf music sounded antique as the Mersey Sound conquered the world.

The Bee Gees were wholeheartedly taken in by Beatlemania. What they heard in 'Please Please Me', 'She Loves You' and 'I Want to Hold Your Hand' – whose Australian chart peaks of number nine, number three and Christmas number one showed a steady, inexorable climb – was the screaming roar of possibility. Their sound, after all, used almost exactly the same building blocks, yet while one group were conquering first the British charts, then the Australian charts, then the American charts with each successive release, the other had spent a single week on the Sydney hit parade. Maybe it wasn't just the undernourished Festival studio sound to blame. Maybe it was their age. The Gibbs never seemed to want to admit just how young they were. On 22 December 1963, Robin and Maurice left school, aged thirteen. Hugh must have somehow convinced the education authorities that they were just about to turn fifteen. With the Beatles as guiding lights, the Bee Gees intended to use this subterfuge to turn pro and take off in 1964.

First up, in February 1964, they released the Mersey-modern 'Peace of Mind' / 'Don't Say Goodbye'. Barry had by now become more of a potential pin-up than a child star – most of the 500 fan letters they received every week in 1964 were aimed at him – and so, for their third single, they became Barry Gibb & the Bee Gees. 'Peace of Mind' gave us more than an inkling of what was to come, with its shrieks of delight, fuzzy guitars and harmonies rising and uniting over a boss rhythmic backing. It was the first recorded Bee Gees song that doesn't sound like children playing music for grown-ups. It sounded teenage.

Inside the Australian music industry the boys seemed popular. King rocker Johnny O'Keefe invited them onto *Sing Sing Sing*, the show that he hosted; they were not only regulars on *Bandstand* and *Saturday Date* but also got to play 'Peace of Mind' on *Teen Beat*. Brisbane's Channel 9 offered them a half-hour special in April. Despite its clear, up-to-date Beatles influence, the single didn't sell.

Hugh and Barbara now uprooted the family again, first with a midnight flit to 8 Kent Street, Bronte, south of Bondi Beach, then in the autumn to Middle Cove, just north of Lane Cove. In February 1964, Jimmy Little's 'One Road' gave Barry his first top ten composition, at least in New South Wales. By this point a fourth Bee Gees single had come and gone, the echo-laden 'Claustrophobia', on which they were given twang-heavy backing by local group the Delawares. The lyric was daffy ('I get claustrophobia 'cause there's too many boys in your heart') but the production was worthy of Joe Meek, overloaded with reverb – it must have almost physically jumped out of transistor radios. It also featured a neat melodica solo from Robin, a mournful echo of the Beatles' harmonica. On the flip side, 'Could It Be' was a high-quality Beatles knock-off, with handclaps pinched from 'I Want to Hold Your Hand' and a melody that whizzed up the whole of *With the Beatles* in a blender. But even an appearance on new TV show *Thank Your Lucky Stars* couldn't help it.

They returned to the show in November with a very different sound. Festival's peculiar line of thinking was that the Bee Gees' lack of sales had to be down to Barry's songwriting. Kids don't buy records written by kids, right? Barry saw something to this logic, and was talked into recording Glen Campbell's 1961 hit 'Turn Around, Look at Me'; it must at least have chimed with his love of country ballads. Robin was less sanguine and blamed Festival for their low sales – how were they expected to bash out a hit single in an hour of downtime? The new direction made no difference. No one liked this adult-child version of the Bee Gees either. By the end of the year they were no further on as full-time musicians than they had been with the twins still at school a year earlier.

Maybe another house move – this time to Castlecrag, just north of Sydney – might be the answer to their problems? It at least provided alternative employment for the boys' stagnating career. All three brothers would spend most of 1965 working part-time in Automagic Carwash in the suburb of Edgecliff.

Spring 1965 saw Festival release another Bee Gees single that they hadn't written, this time a version of Arthur Alexander's 'Every Day I Have to Cry'. A slight song, it had been a minor hit for Steve Alaimo in America, a smaller one still for Dusty Springfield in Britain – and it wasn't about to turn the Gibbs' fortunes around. Still, for the twins, now fifteen, it provided a brace of firsts: it showcased the arrival of Robin's distinctive voice, as he ad-libbed wails over the end; and Maurice played organ on a Bee Gees record for the very first time. It wasn't a good record and it sold zilch, but it did feel like a true group effort. Over on the self-written flip side, 'You Wouldn't Know' was far more interesting, a slice of moody Mersey R&B that showed the group were keeping abreast of changes in the UK, even if Festival weren't.

As the boys rinsed out filthy sponges, scraped flies off windscreens and began to feel like chamois leathers were almost an extension of their arms, America at least seemed to get the appeal of Barry Gibb's songs. Hope remained strong, as a pair of fellow child stars recorded his songs. Jimmy Boyd cut 'That's What I'll Give to You', arranged and produced by Doris Day's son Terry Melcher, who gave it a fuzz guitar hook. And then there was future Vegas fixture Wayne Newton, who included 'They'll Never Know' on his top-twenty *Red Roses for a Blue Lady* album. This was an epic beat ballad, rather like Burt Bacharach's recordings with Chuck Jackson. It turned out that Melcher had been touring Australia with Newton, where he was given the songs by a surprisingly forceful Belinda Music – who clearly had more faith in Barry Gibb than Festival. Both these American recordings had polish and heft and stood in stark comparison to the watery Australian Gibbs releases.

In the Sydney suburb of Darlinghurst, meanwhile, a new group called the Easybeats were playing their first gigs by late 1964, with regular shows in the basement of the Courthouse Hotel, which had been ritzily renamed Beatle Village. The Easybeats' scene was entirely created by teenagers, and the band quickly found themselves a deal with a new local production company called Albert, who in turn signed them to the Australian wing of Parlophone. This meant the Easybeats' records not only sounded

Beatle-esque but appeared on the same black label, with its distinctive 45 logo. Their first single 'For My Woman' was top thirty; but in the spring of 1965 they were in the top three with 'She's So Fine', and the local press were talking about 'Easyfever'.

There was no Bee Gee Fever – not yet – but the Gibbs still managed to at least keep the local hospitals busy. Barry almost blinded himself after firing an air rifle at a wall. He wore a patch over his eye for Sydney's 1965 Royal Easter Show, where the Bee Gees had to play a soul-sapping twenty sets a day during a week-long residency. They continued to travel as far as they were able, attempting to reach places that hadn't been reached by their underperforming singles. A few weeks after the air rifle incident, when Hugh was driving them home from a show in Goulburn, their car overturned at 80 mph some 130 miles south-west of Sydney, and slowly skidded to a halt. There was an awful silence, then they climbed out of the car one by one, looked at each other, and burst out laughing; Barry had a broken rib, but they were otherwise completely unscathed. Robin recalls: 'Somehow, the word got back to Sydney that the Bee Gees had been killed. The radio stations started playing our records and reading out messages of sympathy. When we got home safe and sound, it was almost as if they were annoyed to see us after crying their eyes out for nothing.'

The Australian pop world already had a bad relationship with automobiles. In the early hours of 27 June 1960, Johnny O'Keefe had been returning to Sydney from Queensland when he fell asleep at the wheel of his cherry-red Plymouth Belvedere and crashed into a gravel truck – he needed ninety stitches to his face and body as well as reconstructive surgery to his gums and mouth. He wasn't alone: fellow Festival Records rocker Dig Richards had sustained serious injuries in a crash on Sydney Harbour Bridge; Lonnie Lee was off the scene for months after driving into a telegraph pole; Barry Stanton was almost decapitated after he drove under a truck; while Noel Weiderberg, singer with surf act the Delltones, died after his car overturned in the Sydney suburb of Brighton-Le-Sands. The Bee Gees had been incredibly lucky not to become another Australian road safety statistic.

This latest brush with death – all three brothers this time – would make them feel even tighter as a unit. With the American covers they were forced to record, and the self-sufficient Easybeats' painless rise to fame, the Gibbs needed to rally together; they became convinced that outside forces were holding them back, and you couldn't really blame them. The deal-making Fred Marks, the dead-eared Robert Iredale – these weren't people with much imagination. They only saw three scrappy kids, couldn't understand their in-jokes, didn't even really get the Beatles, and put less than their whole hearts into the Bee Gees project. It had been a while since a Bill Goode or a Bill Gates had walked into the brothers' lives and given them a nudge forward on the Monopoly board. Where was a life-changing Bill when you needed one?

In the summer of 1965, Bill Shepherd arrived at Festival as house producer and engineer. A square-jawed but kind-faced man, he had been born in Merstham, Surrey, in 1927. Shepherd had worked as orchestral arranger on *Idle on Parade*, the film that had turned Anthony Newley from a child actor into a pop star. More recently he had worked with Gene Vincent as well as producer Joe Meek, meaning he had been adjacent to hits like the Tornados' 'Telstar', a particular favourite of Robin's. But work in the UK had been patchy, so he decided to emigrate in 1965 and landed the gig at Festival. Straight away, he recognised the Bee Gees were something special.

It had been a full six months since their last trip to the studio. In the meantime, Maurice had played along to every single Beatles record on bass guitar, his newly adopted instrument. For their first session with Shepherd, Robin would be on organ, and Barry on rhythm guitar. The A-side would turn out to be 'Wine and Women', a maudlin waltz-time rocker – if such a thing were possible – with a clever if slightly confusing lyric. Essentially, this was the first record to sound identifiably Bee Gees, with Barry and Robin sharing a lead vocal and Mo's propulsive bass lines. There was a clear Beatles influence in the vocals and the melody, but the odd harmonies, the unexpected pauses and time changes, the universal but almost nonsensical lyric, the over-arching melancholy, the feel and atmosphere of a collar turned up against the rain . . . these were all Bee Gee traits that would remain. It was a major leap forward from 'Claustrophobia', and a ton more interesting than the two cover singles. Shepherd's production gave them punch, with a loud, distorted, low-end piano pushing the song along. 'Cars and buses and trams make a lot of noise / All my women have gone out with other boys': this may have given the impression that English was the Gibbs' second language. But it was evocative and autumnal – the words, music, overall sound and emotive pull worked together perfectly, and that was what counted.

Bill Shepherd, the Bee Gees and Hugh Gibb all felt like 'Wine and Women' had a good chance of finally breaking their chart duck. They weren't going to allow Festival to screw this one up. What's more, they saw a way in. By mid-1965 there was a national Australian chart, the Kent Music Report – if you were anywhere on this top-100 list then you suddenly had a platform; you were no longer isolated in your own city or state.

Robin later recalled the Gibbs' first attempt at gaming the pop charts: 'First of all, we found out the shops on the [Sydney radio station 2UE] survey – Walton's, Woolworths, about six in all. That was all we needed. You didn't have to sell many records to get on the actual Sydney record charts. We arranged for our fan club to meet us on the steps of Sydney Town Hall. It wasn't hard to rendezvous, because there were only six of them.' £200 meant 400 singles, enough to get them to number thirty-five. After that, airplay and momentum saw it go to number nineteen in Sydney, number twenty-five in Brisbane and number forty-seven on the nationwide Kent Music Report. 'It did an enormous amount for us, it made momentum for us in the country,' said Barry. 'Even if it was just one hit, it was something.'

And for a while, it remained 'just one hit'. 'I Was a Lover, a Leader of Men' was the all-important follow-up in November, and it did next to nothing. This wasn't any reflection on the song, which was terrific, neatly remodelling 'Wine and Women' while adding more wordless harmonies and a strange, mournful coda unconnected to the rest of the song. Festival simply didn't get behind it, and the single failed to chart at all in Sydney, Melbourne or Brisbane. But in Adelaide it went as high as number nine, and radio station 5KA gave Barry the 'Top Talent Award' – effectively songwriter of the year – purely for 'I Was a Lover'. This kind of formal recognition meant a lot to the confident but insecure Gibbs. On the B-side was 'And the Children Laughing', where Barry gave his barbed-wire tongue a go on a *du jour* protest lyric – an intriguing but failed experiment.

In spite of the single's failure, it was reckoned that there was enough noise around the Bee Gees to justify a first LP. True to form, Festival were too tight to record an actual album – why bother recording new songs when most of Australia had yet to acquaint themselves with the squeaky charms of the two-and-a-half-year-old 'Timber!'? And why think of a snappy title when you can call it *The Bee Gee's Sing and Play 14 Barry Gibb Songs?* (Yes, it's spelled 'Bee Gee's', right there on the cover.) There was a grand total of three new songs, with the rest being previously available on singles: 'How Love Was True' was reminiscent of the Beatles' 'Yes It Is' or 'This Boy', with some nice tremolo; 'To Be or Not to Be' was also Beatles-esque, this time channelling the raucous 'I'm Down'; and lastly there was 'I Don't Think It's Funny', Robin's first lead vocal, which was neither muckling nor mickling. Stood against other albums that appeared in the last two months of 1965 – *The Kink Kontroversy, The Four Tops' Second Album,* Dionne Warwick's *Here I Am,* the Byrds' *Turn Turn Turn,* Bert Jansch's *It Don't Bother Me,* and especially the Beatles' *Rubber Soul* – the album sounded awfully jejune.

If you were wondering how teenage Australia read the Bee Gees at this point, it's worth remembering they were still doing impressions on stage – Elvis, Rudy Vallee (one for the grand-parents) and local star Little Pattie (Robin in a blonde wig). They were closer to the Barron Knights than the Stones. But in March 1966, their startling, abrasive 'I Want Home' came out with its two-note guitar hook and fizzing break, a garage-punk single of the highest order. The lyric had a sexual urgency and some properly dynamic minimalism: 'Put on your dress, make it a blue one, everything's gonna be alright.' Sales were pitiful, though, and it has since become the rarest of their Australian singles. Worse news came when the homesick Bill Shepherd returned to the UK. Luckily for the boys, however, a Sydney businessman called Clyde Packer and a savvy pop producer called Nat Kipner had just started the Spin record label; they couldn't completely prise the Bee Gees from Festival's dead hand, but somehow negotiated a deal in which their records would come out on Spin with Festival handling distribution.

Nat Kipner had been born in Dayton, Ohio, and was just seventeen when he was stationed in Brisbane during the Second World War. He met and married local girl Alma Moore and carried her over the threshold and back to Dayton. In the early 1950s, they returned to Brisbane with their young son Steve, and Nat found work in the home appliance department of Queensland Home Furnishers. By the mid-'60s he was working for music impresario Ivan Dayman's Sunshine management company, and stepped sideways into record production; 1965's biggest-selling single in Australia was the Kipner-produced 'Que Sera Sera' by Normie Rowe & the Playboys. The fact he wanted the Bee Gees so badly suggested strongly that 1966 might hold some genuine promise for the brothers.

If their record sales were weak, it didn't mean the Bee Gees weren't still a decent live attraction. They continued to make a regular income from RSL clubs and beer barns, but in between shows at the Police Citizens' Boys Club in Wagga Wagga and the Lyndale Disco, Dandenong, they played the Sydney Hilton's Silver Spade room in March 1966, a prestige showbiz venue equivalent to the London Palladium. At the same time, a new TV show called *Six O'Clock Rock* – Australia's answer to *Ready Steady Go!* or *Shindig* – was launched, with host Johnny O'Keefe. The Bee Gees became regulars, grew their hair longer, played their instruments live, and never went back to the square world of *Bandstand*.

Nat Kipner next introduced the Gibbs to a forty-year-old producer called Ossie Byrne. He was already a Bee Gees fan and happened to have built a studio of his own, St Clair Recording Studio, just outside Sydney in Hurstville – it was primitive, using a pair of two-track recorders, but St Clair was much more amenable than Festival's set-up. Most significantly, Nat and Ossie gave the brothers as much studio time as they wanted. The studio was a former storeroom around the back of a butcher's shop – the control room with the tape recorders was the old 'cold room'. The brothers spent March, April and May 1966 doing sessions. 'We were in there day and night, and we could experiment for the first time,' remembered Robin. 'We felt great!' Other local musicians would pass by and drop in: Barry's old chum Colin Petersen, who was dating Lesley Gibb and drumming with Steve & the Board (Steve being Nat Kipner's son), had sat in on the session for the rocker 'I Want Home'; Vince Melouney, who had scored an Australian number-one hit as guitarist on Billy Thorpe and the Aztecs' version of 'Poison Ivy', came by too. Vince had the added credibility of having played guitar with the Beatles' Hamburg mate Tony Sheridan as well as the Joe Meek-produced Heinz and Screaming Lord Sutch when they had toured Australia – real pop stars from blessed England. Both Colin and Vince would become close friends with the Gibbs. Over cups of milky tea, Colin told the brothers he was set to move to the UK and look for acting work. But he also said he'd be happy to rejoin them on drums if they ever decided to emigrate.

The sessions at St Clair included both Mo's first composition ('Where Are You') and Robin's ('I Don't Know Why I Bother with Myself'), as well as the first Barry–Robin co-write ('Tint of Blue'). With time to stretch out, Mo learned to play the mandolin. The first single to emerge from the sessions, released in June 1966 on the new red-and-white Spin label, was 'Monday's Rain'. Fans and radio stations were taken aback by Robin's choked soulful vocal on the dirge-like A-side which disguised much of the lyric, reducing it to strange rhythmic noises – the title came out less like 'Monday's rain', more like 'mawn-eh reh-eh'. There was no detectable Beatles influence, and it was the most singularly Bee Gee thing they'd done to date. It was also the most uncommercial thing they had ever created. It flopped, and a second album was put on hold by Spin.

They brought in an apprentice butcher called Russell Barnsley to play drums on their next single, 'Spicks and Specks'; but he turned down the chance to join permanently, and Geoff Bridgford – briefly Petersen's replacement in Steve & the Board – became the new drummer instead, as it turned out for a matter of weeks.

Emigrating suddenly became a hot topic for teenage Australians. The Easybeats had shown it could work by signing a deal with United Artists and moving to London in June 1966; by the end of the year they would be in the UK top ten with the rabble-rousing weekend anthem 'Friday on My Mind'. The impetus for Petersen, Melouney and the Easybeats to get out of Australia and try their luck in England may well have been connected to an announcement by Australian prime minister Robert Menzies back in April. He claimed his government had received a request for 'further military assistance' from South Vietnam; young Australians would be conscripted to fight. Menzies reckoned a communist victory in South Vietnam would be a direct military threat to Australia, and 'must be seen as part of a thrust by Communist China between the Indian and

Pacific Oceans'. It later transpired that South Vietnam's prime minister, Phan Huy Quát, didn't make the request at all, and indeed had to be coerced into accepting Australian troops; he had simply sent an acceptance of the offer to Canberra, the day before Menzies announced the news to the Australian Parliament. Some 15,381 conscripted Australian servicemen would fight in Vietnam between 1965 and 1972. More than 200 would be killed. Communist China, of course, made no such moves on Australia, so the deaths were entirely needless.

Ossie Byrne continued to nurture the Gibbs. Through June and July 1966, they virtually took up residence at St Clair; Ossie produced most of these all-night recording sessions, some co-produced with Nat Kipner, while others saw the Bee Gees themselves operating the levers in the former cold room. Ossie had struck up a friendship with Hugh Gibb, and they talked about Ossie becoming the group's co-manager. He was ambitious on their behalf, and in June 1966 started the Down Under record label, distributed through Festival; it would only exist until October 1966, releasing thirteen St Clair-recorded singles, but the bulk of these included songs written by Barry, with occasional help from Ossie or Nat. Sixteen-year-old Mo wasn't far behind, with a rare burst of songwriting, all in partnership with Nat Kipner: the folk rock jangler 'Young Man's Fancy' was recorded by Bip Addison; and Anne Shelton (also sixteen, and not to be confused with Britain's former Forces' sweetheart) recorded 'Talk to Me', sounding like a seductive waitress in a café: 'Settle back, relax, have a cup of tea.'

'You are the most original group in Australia,' Ossie constantly reminded the brothers, even though 'Monday's Rain''s feeble sales seemed to indicate Australia didn't want them. What could be done? How about moving back to England, lads? Hugh was so cross at Ossie's suggestion that he threatened to confiscate the brothers' passports.

Barry, still just nineteen, then managed to throw another spanner in the works by flightily marrying his girlfriend, Maureen Bates. Maybe this was also preying on Hugh's mind, along with the notion that all of his sons, bar infant Andy, might be sent to fight the Viet Cong. He relented, and on 26 October 1966 *Go-Set* magazine mentioned 'the Bee Gees, who leave for England in February'. When they eventually left, Barry's bride Maureen wouldn't be with them; after being separated for four years, they would eventually be divorced in 1970.

One afternoon in the summer of 1966, Mo had picked out the super-basic, single-note piano line for 'Spicks and Specks', and Barry fleshed out the melody. The title was taken from a fictional band the brothers had invented. The lyric made the maudlin 'Monday's Rain' sound like a minor sulk: 'The sun in my life,' whispered Barry. 'It is dead. It is dead.'

'Spicks and Specks' again bore no relation to the Beatles, Col Joye and the Joy Boys, or the Mills Brothers. The St Clair studio piano – a pianola with its roll removed – played a mordant, repeated, single note. It laid out a bleak lifeless landscape – 'Where is the sun / That shone on my head' – and carried on building, repeating, until its final release when the title is sung out repeatedly by an anguished Barry over Robin's wordless wail. By this point, the song's theme – this being a 1966 pop song – has revealed itself to be lost love, but it still sounds nothing less than apocalyptic, its questioning emptiness closer to 'Where Have All the Flowers Gone' than 'Yesterday'. On the other side of the single was Robin's equally startling 'I Am the World'. Over furiously thrummed guitars, like a Greek film noir, Robin – almost inaudibly – sings, 'I'm the sun, I'm the falling rain / I'm the kind of man you can't explain,' before the song itself starts with a Roy Orbison-like Latin feel and Robin singing quite differently, as if the opening had been some kind of fevered aberration.

Without a doubt, this was their best single to date.

'Spicks and Specks' / 'I Am the World' was released in August 1966, both sides aided by the impact of trumpeter Geoff Grant towards the songs' climaxes. On 28 September, it sneaked into the Sydney charts at number thirty-eight, going on to spend nineteen weeks in the Sydney top forty, eventually peaking at number three. Reaction was so strong that *Go-Set* magazine would anoint 'Spicks and Specks' their Australian single of the year. Given that the competition included the Easybeats' beloved 'Friday on My Mind' this was quite something.

Spin hurriedly released a second album, initially called *Monday's Rain* but quickly retitled *Spicks and Specks*. Among the highlights was a song of Robin's called 'Jingle Jangle', which sounded closer to klezmer music than 'Friday on My Mind'. It was melancholy in the extreme, and a perfect canvas for Robin's tremulous, emotional voice. 'I think that came from our admiration for Roy Orbison,' remembered Barry. 'Robin loved Roy Orbison. And our father was always bringing records home. He had varied taste, strange taste, but he would bring home a Bing Crosby album, then the next day he'd bring home an opera, like *La Traviata* or *Tosca*. So I think there was something going on melodically that was being poured into us through Dad's records. The emotional melodies of opera, the romanticism, the sentimentality, which you get from Robin.

And you get it from me, too, but he was good at that, and he loved it.'

★

On 3 January 1967, with Ossie Byrne in tow, the Gibb family sailed for England on the TSS *Fairsky*. Before they left, they had written and recorded a truckload of Barry Gibb songs at St Clair for Jon Blanchfield ('Upstairs Downstairs'), Ronnie Burns ('Coal-man', 'Exit Stage Right'), Jenene ('Don't Say No'), Lori Balmer ('Who's Been Writing on the Wall Again'), and the Twilights ('Long Life'). Mo had also written the solid garage-punker 'Raining Teardrops' for Barrington Davis, a terrific single which would emerge on Spin while the Gibbs were still at sea.

What might have happened to their career if they hadn't returned to Britain on the *Fairsky*? Spin gave us an inkling, by lifting 'Born a Man' as a single from the new album just as 'Spicks and Specks' was getting released all over Europe. It's one of the weakest Bee Gees singles, an attempt at macho British R&B that seeks to swim in the same waters as the Animals' 'We Gotta Get Out of This Place' or Them's 'Gloria' but can barely keep its head above the water: no tune, no tension, just a few soulful growls that sounded perilously close to club singer parody. Given the alternative album tracks at their disposal, this suggested Spin wouldn't have had a clue what to do with the Bee Gees, even after they had finally scored a major breakthrough hit.

What's more, there was a whole third album's worth of material. Recorded at the same time as 'Spicks and Specks' and 'I Am the World' were twenty-eight new originals, plus thirteen more covers which were presumably cut to get the hang of Ossie Byrne's studio. Some were clearly experiments they never

expected anyone else to hear, like a faithful cover of the Lovin'
Spoonful's 'Daydream'. They had recorded 'Paperback Writer'
just a couple of days after the Beatles' single had been released.
Other tracks, like 'The Storm' and the gorgeous Barry ballad
'In the Morning', were clearly A-grade material which would
be mined not only by cash-in compilations in the future but by
other acts looking for a hit.

On 25 November 1966, just as 'Spicks and Specks' was peaking on singles charts across Australia, Hugh Gibb had written to
Brian Epstein's NEMS Enterprises in England. The Bee Gees
are planning a trip to London, he told them, and they would
need representation. 'The eldest boy, Barry, is acknowledged to
be the top songwriter in this country. At the time of writing they
have a hit record, Spicks and Specks, which has just reached the
no. 3 position in every state in Australia. We quite realise that
this does not mean much overseas, but considering the enormous size of Australia, this is considered quite a feat here.' Hugh
included some records and acetates of new Bee Gees songs. It
seemed a long shot. The Beatles management! But you could
dream.

In fact, Hugh's letter to NEMS would turn out to be the best
career move he ever made.

5

HENDON

'First of all, we had no idea what we were. If you think about it, we were not a rock group, we were not a pop group. We were three brothers who weren't really a band.'

                                                   – Barry

'We had good managers and plenty of luck.'

                                                   – Maurice

'Take care of the sounds and the sense will take care of itself.'

                                           – Lewis Carroll

Record Mirror UK top ten, 4 February 1967

1. The Monkees – 'I'm a Believer'
2. Cat Stevens – 'Matthew and Son'
3. The Move – 'Night of Fear'

4. Rolling Stones – 'Let's Spend the Night Together' / 'Ruby Tuesday'
5. Tom Jones – 'Green Green Grass of Home'
6. Jimi Hendrix Experience – 'Hey Joe'
7. Paul Jones – 'I've Been a Bad Bad Boy'
8. Four Tops – 'Standing in the Shadows of Love'
9. The Who – 'Happy Jack'
10. The Seekers – 'Morningtown Ride'

Waiting for a chance. Waiting for a change.

On the *Fairsea*, while heading to Australia, the brothers had played for other passengers in exchange for passage. On the *Fairsky*, sailing back to England, Barry and Robin spent much of their time writing a book of short stories called *On the Other Hand*. They were still playing live to entertain their fellow passengers, still playing 'Twist and Shout' and 'Puff, the Magic Dragon', but this time they had a far better reception, from kids familiar with smash hit 'Spicks and Specks'. They also carried on songwriting, creating songs that would eventually appear on *Bee Gees' 1st*, their third album, but so titled because it would be their first international release. At a stop-off in India, Maurice bought himself a sitar, a sound the Beatles had introduced to the teenage western hemisphere a year earlier on *Rubber Soul*. Maurice had a go. He sold it as soon as the ship docked; maybe they didn't need to shadow the Beatles' every move. During the journey the brothers discovered that 'Spicks and Specks' had gone to number one in Sydney and New Zealand. Hopes were high. But on arrival in the UK, on 6 February 1967, they spotted another group – 'absolute Beatles lookalikes,' Barry remembered – standing in the murk of Southampton dock, waiting to take a boat in the opposite direction. 'We went down the steps, and there in the

fog was this group. Heaven knows what they were doing there,'
he laughed. 'And they said, "Go back to Australia, there's nothing happening here. They won't sign groups anymore."' Having
left Sydney just as seven years of back-breaking effort was finally
paying off, the Gibb family must have felt a mild sense of panic.

What to do next? They kicked their heels in a rented semi-
detached house in Hendon, north London. The freshest faces
on TV and voices on the radio belonged to the Monkees, a fictional American group who lived together on North Beechwood
Drive in Hollywood, together with a unicycle, a candelabra and
a grinning showroom dummy. The Bee Gees all lived together,
too, only with their mum and dad. There was nothing out of the
ordinary about the Bee Gees' house, on a nondescript street in
a nondescript suburb of London. It had a privet hedge in need
of a trim. The metal gate was painted bottle green. The front
door was painted pillar-box red. The front room had dark wood
furniture redolent of radio shows *Hancock's Half Hour* or *Life with
the Lyons*, the hits of the previous decade. There was no central
heating and there was condensation on the windows, perhaps
because this three-bedroom semi in Hendon was full of shouty,
tearing-round-the-house, Anglo-Australian Gibbs while the
weather outside always seemed to be frosty. In the hallway sat
the telephone, a wartime relic in black and chunky Bakelite, as if
Carlton-Browne of the F.O. might call up at any moment, bark-
ing instructions at Hugh. Except it never seemed to ring.

Sunny Gardens Road was one of those endless streets of
identikit semi-detached houses that webbed up every town in
England in the 1930s, before the war and then the green belt

scheme stopped their spread. It also had a haunted name – because the sunny slopes of the 1920s were long gone, buried under houses, sheds, garages, tarmac and pebbledash. And things had got a whole lot worse in the 1960s when Britain's first motorway, the M1, was built alongside its northern end, with all the noise and dirt and dust of people and cars heading into and out of London at a steady 70 mph, skirting the blankest part of Hendon's suburban anonymity.

But the Gibbs didn't stop to worry about whether they'd made the right decision by moving. After all, even Sydney didn't count for that much anymore. The Australian music industry had moved en masse to Melbourne, flush with the transatlantic success of the Easybeats, whose 'Friday on My Mind' had still been at number seven in Britain when the *Fairsky* departed. Melbourne was eager to build recording studios that could compete with London and New York. A new generation would quickly emerge, with groups like the Twilights and the Strangers, who planned to explore the limits of four-track studios and create world-class records. Nothing stayed the same. You had to keep on moving; it made sense to keep the suitcases on top of the wardrobe for easy access.

Who even knew the Bee Gees were in Hendon? One of the old St Clair studio gang – drummer-turned-wannabe-actor Colin Petersen – knew. He had rented a van to pick the Gibb clan up in Southampton when the *Fairsky* docked, on that foggy, Dickensian evening in February 1967. He had even found them their furnished Hendon home; Hugh had been smart enough to ask him to do as much in advance of the trip. But Colin couldn't find work either. Barry and Hugh were taking the Northern Line down from Hendon Central every morning, walking the streets of London's West End, knocking on doors, pinning most of their hopes on Eddie Jarrett of the Grade Organisation, who managed Australia's biggest export, folk-pop act the Seekers. Having already registered a brace of UK number ones in 1965, and the *Junior Choice* favourite 'Morningtown Ride' over Christmas 1966, the Seekers' recording of Jim Dale's 'Georgy Girl' – a film theme no less – was currently climbing to number three on the UK charts. Jarrett had worked wonders for the Seekers. Could he find work for the Bee Gees? No, he couldn't: 'He painted a very black picture about the possibility of touring,' said Hugh.

It probably felt like an age before the telephone rang in Sunny Gardens Road, and when it did it wasn't Eddie at the other end of the line. The boys were all out, so Barbara took a note; someone called 'Stickweed' had called. It may have felt like forever, but they had been in England for less than a week.

Robert Stigwood's background was in theatre. He had been born in Adelaide in 1934 and apparently hitchhiked all the way to the UK in 1955, ending up in Norwich. By the start of the '60s he had set up Robert Stigwood Associates – RSA – with an office at 41 Charing Cross Road, which provided models for TV adverts. The British class system had combined with the theatre world to ensure that agencies were extremely snooty about commercial TV, thinking of it as a cash cow for actors but barely deigning to converse with it. So Stigwood only had to be polite to the TV ad people and they flocked to him. He started handling actors in TV shows. *Emergency Ward 10*'s soft-eyed John Leyton would turn out to be Stigwood's ticket to the music business. Leyton and Stigwood teamed up with independent record producer Joe Meek, and the combination of Meek's maverick studio skills and Stigwood's nous sent

Leyton's 'Johnny Remember Me' to number one in Britain in 1961. By an odd coincidence, Stigwood had met arranger Bill Shepherd when they recorded a version of Gene Vincent's 'Temptation Baby' at Olympic Studios for the soundtrack of a pop-sploitation film called *Live It Up!*; Shepherd would soon be off to Sydney, but their paths would cross again. Mike Sarne was another handsome singing actor on Stigwood's books; he duetted with Stigwood's secretary Wendy Richard for the novelty hit 'Come Outside', another number one in 1962. Ruthless and unruffled, Stigwood fell out with Meek after he poached the boyishly bobbed Billie Davis from Meek's grasp in 1963, and quickly saw her reach the top ten with a cover of the Exciters' 'Tell Him'. He also managed comedians Spike Milligan and Frankie Howerd; he liked to have fun while he was amassing money.

At the end of 1964, RSA went bust. Stigwood had badly mis-judged the rise of the beat groups, a youth movement he wasn't yet equipped to understand, and in the coming age of the mop-top his ad revenue from Brylcreemed models started to fail. Still, bankruptcy couldn't curb his gift of the gab, and the Robert Stig-wood Organisation – RSO – quickly obtained the funding to start up in 1965. A year later he launched a record label called Reac-tion, with distribution by Polydor. He poached the Who from Shel Talmy. He acquired, he accrued. He then tried to coax the Small Faces away from their manager Don Arden, only chang-ing his mind after Arden's heavies dangled him by the feet from a fourth-storey window.

Very quickly, Robert Stigwood had become a big wheel, and like every other music business operator he dreamed of getting his hands on the biggest music entertainment money-spinner there was – the Beatles. The dream seemed a little closer when

Brian Epstein's management company NEMS Enterprises merged with RSO on 13 January 1967.[1]

Stigwood and Epstein were both gay men in an age when that could lead to prison. Both were in thrall to the fast-evolving cultural possibilities of the 1960s, but in most ways they couldn't have been more different. Epstein loved the idea of running his own theatres; he was in talks with BBC DJ Brian Matthew about building one in Bromley, Kent, a tidy modernist structure that the conservative local council were making a fuss over. Epstein was modest, in both his ambitions and his manner. He dressed impeccably. He was quiet and likeable. Stigwood – with his crisped hair and bullfrog voice – was loud and uncompromising; he wanted, above everything else, above any considerations for his charges, to be very rich and famous. The plan for NEMS was that Epstein would step down by the end of 1967, exhausted after more than four years at the very top of the tree. Stigwood imagined, understandably, that this would leave him well placed to become the next Beatles manager.

Epstein may have been cool to the marketing strategies of Stigwood – as were the Beatles, who apparently couldn't stand him – but the Bee Gees were not.[2] Stigwood would quickly shape not only the public's perception of the brothers, but the brothers' perception of the outside world. They would repeat and amplify Stigwood's approach until they believed it to be hard fact. Many times, it would be difficult to tell how much of what he made available to the press was true, but some of

---

[1] The initials derived from the Epstein family's Liverpool-based North End Music Stores.

[2] Paul McCartney threatened that the Beatles would only ever record out-of-tune versions of 'God Save the Queen' if Epstein stepped down to allow Stigwood to become their manager.

it demonstrably wasn't. His cleverness was in making great claims that – even in the digital age – are tricky to prove or disprove. Brian Epstein was an aesthete and a kind man. Robert Stigwood may not have been an aesthete, and almost certainly wasn't a kind man, but he was assuredly a smart one.

At the beginning of 1967, the German-owned Polydor record label was a very minor player in the UK pop field. Its only top-ten hit to date had been Helmut Zacharias's 'Tokyo Melody' way back in 1964, an instrumental celebrating that year's Olympic Games. Roland Rennie worked for Polydor, where he acquired the rights for its releases – he had done a cheap deal with Spin Records in Australia that meant 'Spicks and Specks' landed on his lap one day in January. He liked it very much and set about contacting the group in Australia to see if they might want to come to Britain and promote it. By pure coincidence and with no appointment, Barry Gibb bowled into the Polydor office the following day, telling Rennie, 'You need to sign us.' Maybe Barry came over as a little gauche, but he was also charming, and what's more he was handsome. Rennie quickly realised the group required representatives with more clout than Hugh Gibb and Ossie Byrne, and decided to let a fellow Australian try to break these arrivistes – 'The group needed some management,' Rennie would later recall, with considerable tact. He had met Robert Stigwood a couple of years back, when they were both working with EMI. Coincidentally, Stigwood's interest had already been piqued when he had heard one of the acetates that Hugh had sent to NEMS from Australia. And so, when Rennie called Stigwood about the Bee Gees on the Monday, he jumped at the chance. On the Thursday, Stigwood phoned Hugh Gibb in Hendon. On the Friday, he gave the Bee Gees an audition in the basement of the Brian Epstein-owned Saville Theatre; they played with Colin Petersen sitting in on drums.

Stigwood was so hungover at the Bee Gees audition that he had to be helped to his seat. He didn't look up once. The Gibbs went through their whole *Fairsky* act, comedy shtick, lousy covers, plus a few originals like 'Spicks and Specks' and 'I Can't See Nobody', which must have sounded as if they had arrived from a parallel world. Stigwood sat there in silence, and possibly thought he was hallucinating as they played 'Puff, the Magic Dragon', only to follow it with their latest evocative pen-portraits, 'Gilbert Green' and 'Town of Tuxley Toymaker'. Then he croaked, 'Come to my office at six.' On the Friday night, 24 February 1967, Robert Stigwood signed the Bee Gees to a long-time recording, publishing and management deal. Any lawyer in the music business would have cautioned the brothers against the conflicting interests in handing so much of their career over to one person. But they had gone from nowhere, from penniless Aussies in a Hendon semi, to within touching distance of the Beatles inside forty-eight hours. Who could blame their eagerness to sign?

'Robert had the foresight and the vision to see what we could become, not what we were,' said Barry years later. 'And it went from there. I can't believe it ever happened . . . there we were, without really a self-identity, loving the Beatles, being entranced by the Beatles and the Hollies and the Fortunes, and the people that really had great harmonies, and being influenced by those people. "Go Now", the original Moody Blues. The original Pink Floyd, "See Emily Play". The Kinks, and Ray Davies and Dave Davies. And us being in the middle of *that world*, suddenly being signed to the Beatles' company.'

Talking to Alexis Petridis in the 2010s, Barry could still recall the utter shock, the unbelievable truth that the Bee Gees were no longer playing RSL clubs, as they had for years and years, but were placed right into the heart of the twentieth century's greatest pop culture explosion. 'This was the most colourful time in Britain. The colours are still vivid for me, and witnessing all of that, seeing the Beatles wandering around the office . . . you have to imagine what this was like. This was crazy, you know? The people we worshipped, we were signed to their company. And Robert Stigwood was the guiding light. Brian didn't have time, and Robert saw something. I don't think it was necessarily us standing there singing – he saw the potential in the songs. He saw that, maybe in another five years, we could really be something.'

Stigwood later said the very first thing he had heard by the Bee Gees was Robin's 'Jingle Jangle', one of the acetates lying around at NEMS. 'Astounded,' he said. 'Some of the best harmony singing and composing I had ever heard. I was absolutely knocked out with their writing. I thought it was sensational. The boys had been barely sixteen years old when the songs had been written, so I figured that if boys of that age had been able to turn out material of that calibre, they must have immense potential . . . it would be very difficult for them to go wrong.' He might have rethought that judgement when the brothers told him they wanted to change their name from the Bee Gees to Rupert's World. Stigwood diplomatically said that if the first single bombed, he'd think about it. Barry later admitted it would have been 'like changing your name from Charlie Shit to Fred Shit'.

After the boys first walked into the NEMS office, receptionist Molly Hullis remarked to Stigwood that she thought their look 'very out of date'. Stigwood took note, immediately giving them £300 and sending them off to Carnaby Street. They came back with clothes that he deemed 'unacceptable'. They looked very much like newbies, kids from a nowhere town, out of their depth in pop's international capital. 'We couldn't have been greener,' said Barry.

'Spicks and Specks' was positively reviewed by the *NME* on 4 March 1967 – they thought it was 'a bit dated' but 'very good indeed'. On the same day, they visited IBC Sound Studios at 35 Portland Place for the first time – for the next five years it would become a second home to the brothers. The session was booked for 'Town of Tuxley Toymaker', which they were giving to Billy J. Kramer, a NEMS act now signed to Stigwood's Reaction label. Given their less-than-hit-filled career in Australia, this was an incredible vote of confidence. The quietly spoken Kramer had scored international hits, and a brace of UK number ones in the peak Merseybeat era. He had been in the top twenty as recently as 1965, but now needed a shot in the arm from the new kids on the block. It was a fine record, but it didn't sell. Soon after, they recorded 'Gilbert Green' with another NEMS-managed Merseybeat figure, Gerry Marsden, who was just going solo from the Pacemakers. This was a tale of a loner who stayed in his attic composing his masterpiece, which you heard a snatch of on the song's coda. It was considerably more complex than anything they had written in Australia.

The first Bee Gees session proper would be in Polydor Studios, effectively a converted cupboard in an office block at 19 Stratford Place, where they worked on demos that included a minor-key, folkish tune that didn't yet have a lyric. According to Barry there was a power cut. They sat on stone steps, next to an old goods lift with metal concertina doors. They liked the echo of the lift shaft and, using their powers of improv, came up with a lyric for the minor-key song about being buried underground, giving it the eye-catching title 'New York Mining Disaster 1941'.

Stigwood loved it. They would record a version with strings and a tolling bell with Ossie Byrne at IBC Studios a few days later, but when it came to the crunch they decided the production should be stripped back. This was their first Polydor single, and all you heard was what sounded like an acoustic guitar that seemed to come through the window of an abandoned shack, a deathly bass drum from some pagan ritual, and a lone cello. On top of this were the brothers' tight, almost Celtic harmonies – they still sounded like they came from the north-west of England. It was the unlikeliest, gloomiest, most minimal debut hit by a major act since Elvis Presley's 'Heartbreak Hotel'. It was eerie in the extreme, ripe with claustrophobia and real death.

They worked fast. They had an unfailing confidence. As Barry recalls:

I've seen Paul McCartney interviews where he talks about 'Here, There and Everywhere' being influenced by the Beach Boys, so it was okay: wait a minute, they're influenced by someone else, too. Even Frank Sinatra had an idol: it was all okay, it was all relative. Emulating someone else, or trying to do something like someone else is not such a bad thing, it's okay. It takes you somewhere else. We learnt that real early. It's okay. The Beatles were influenced by Little Richard and Chuck Berry and people like that. We began to realise, okay, just enjoy. Be creative and don't worry if something doesn't sound completely original. Don't worry about it. So we went from making ten, fifteen demos in Stratford Place, the old Polydor building, with Roland Rennie as the president, to making a real album at IBC on Portland Place, which we just drove through, in about March, April '67.

★

Word of Stigwood's new charges moved quickly to America, where there would be a tug of war between pop giants Capitol (home to Frank Sinatra and the Beach Boys) and Atlantic (Ray Charles, Aretha Franklin, the Modern Jazz Quartet) – Brian Epstein favoured Capitol because of the job they had done for the Beatles; Stigwood wanted Atlantic Records because they had recently signed Cream, the blues rock power trio he also managed. Atlantic boss Ahmet Ertegun later said he thought the group had an 'originality and brilliance rarely heard on record'. Other key Atlantic players Tom Dowd and Jerry Wexler had heard them independently, and both were desperate to sign them as the label moved on from its traditional R&B base into the white rock world.

Under Stigwood's auspices, things came together in a matter of weeks.

By late February 1967, the Bee Gees had become a five-piece for live shows. The loyal Colin Petersen, by now a flatmate of 'Wine and Women' producer Bill Shepherd, became the official drummer; Vince Melouney, who, at Maurice's invitation, had borrowed Easybeat Harry Vanda's guitar to play on 'New York Mining Disaster', also became a full-time Bee Gee. Stigwood's mate Dick Ashby became their tour manager; he'd previously worked for Ronnie Wood's R&B band the Birds, another Reaction act who had just split up. The group's first show outside of Australia would be at the scenester-heavy Cromwellian, a club on west London's Cromwell Road, and in attendance was the sphinx-like Ahmet Ertegun.

Between 7 March and 21 April, now happily reunited with Bill Shepherd, they recorded *Bee Gees' 1st* at IBC. Shepherd delivered career-moulding orchestral arrangements – the brothers asked for strings and he provided them, no holds barred. He shaped their sound, effectively becoming a member of the group. The multi-tasking Maurice took on bass, piano, harpsichord and Mellotron, the new miracle string machine which emphasised both the richness and melancholy of their songs. Mo was also encouraged to arrange by former guiding light Ossie Byrne. By now, Ossie was the Bee Gees' ex-manager, surplus to requirements. The rate of progress was phenomenal.

Shepherd's arrangements would become integral to the Bee Gees' records, making them stand apart from the largely blues-influenced groups emerging in 1967 London. Barry reckoned it was the lack of the possibility of ever using strings and harps and woodwinds in Australia which made them decide to go so orchestra-heavy once they were in Britain; he also noted the result was 'a world-class album'.

It seemed like everything was falling into place as the nascent five-piece became the talk of the town. But not everyone was ready for this mournful, string-laden, future pop sound. On 1 April, they supported Fats Domino and Gerry and the Pacemakers at the Saville Theatre. The audience was largely made up of Teds, all there to see Fats, and they flat out hated the Bee Gees.

One aggrieved Ted threw an egg at Robin. It hit him on the chest, dribbling down his shirt as he sang 'I Can't See Nobody'.

A few weeks later, on 14 April 1967, 'New York Mining Disaster 1941' was released, and it equalled the Easybeats' feat of reaching both the UK and US top twenties, an extraordinary achievement for a group that had released nothing but dud singles in Australia for so many years. 'THE MOST SIGNIFICANT NEW MUSICAL TALENT OF 1967' screamed Stigwood's full-page *NME* ad for it. If he had been happy to trickle 'Spicks and Specks' out, letting it sink or swim on its own, he turned the publicity full on for this haunting piece of baroque neo-folk. Maurice called it 'a total rip-off of the Beatles', doing it an odd disservice, though there was no doubt it was influenced by *Revolver*'s three-minute experiments. Jerry Wexler at ATCO, the American label that Stigwood had signed the Gibbs to, claimed he sent out white labels of the single to radio stations with nothing but a note that said the group's name started with a B and ended with an S – who could that possibly be? None of these records has ever surfaced, but it became a good anecdote. What's more, the Gibbs believed it to be true. 'To us it was an honour,' said Mo, 'to actually think we were as good as the Beatles.'

Where the Easybeats had failed with their follow-up single, and quickly faded from Anglo-American prominence, the Bee Gees had an ace card up their sleeve. Back in March, Barry had been at the Waldorf Astoria Hotel in New York, his first time in the city. He was introduced to one of his favourite soul singers, Otis Redding. Inspired, he went back up to his room and wrote a song for Redding that same evening called 'To Love Somebody'. Penny Valentine, one of the most acute pop writers of the day, understood it completely in her *Disc and Music Echo* review:

Of course, after 'New York Mining Disaster' I was bound to be a little disappointed by the Bee Gees' follow up record, which bears none of the remarkable hit-you-straight-between-the-eyes distinction and none of the strong story line. But in its way this record is a far more commercial proposition and equally as good. What I particularly like about it is the lead singer's voice. He sounds as though he's carving and cracking his way through the lyrics meaning every little bit . . . Like the record very much indeed.

Released in July, it was a failure in Britain, where its bare blue-eyed soul – as Valentine suggested – was maybe too much of a sharp swerve from 'New York Mining Disaster''s folk drone for listeners to take. But in the US, it was another top-twenty hit and quickly became something of a standard. 'Other groups all raved about it,' said Robin, with cheerful, childish big-headedness.

Bee Gees' 1st followed a few weeks later on 14 July 1967. Klaus Voormann designed the cover, just as he had for the Beatles' *Revolver. Klaus Voormann!* Could they believe this was happening to them?

Among its fourteen (like *Rubber Soul* and *Revolver*) tracks, the variety of styles and the unchained promise revealed on *Bee Gees' 1st* bore out Stigwood's faith in them. Aside from melancholic chords and baroque arrangements, the lyrics on *Bee Gees' 1st* were an arresting mix of evocative, grounded, transporting, and plain nonsense. But words mattered to the Bee Gees, the very sound of them, and they understood how that sound could accurately communicate an imprecise feeling. The Gibbs got inside language and used it for feel rather than explicit meaning.

Take 'To Love Somebody' with a lyric that is stoical, but close to angry. 'I'm a man, can't you see what I am?' sings Barry, still a teenager. 'In my brain I see your face again' is a classic Gibb lyric – the syntax is slightly out, nobody else would have kept that line as it was; they'd have changed it to something more conventional like 'in my mind'. But 'in my brain' is perfect, and suggests something more intense – he doesn't want to think about her, but what haunts him is completely beyond his control.

By comparison, 'I Can't See Nobody', Robin's highlight on *Bee Gees' 1st*, is stumbling, surrendering and morbid, the singer wading through a marsh of fixated emotion. From the very beginning, Bill Shepherd throws you into a well of loneliness. The string arrangement is vast and all-encompassing, but never close to treacly. It is one of the most intense records of its time, ranking alongside Scott Walker's 'Big Louise' in its colossal and total seclusion.

On 'I Can't See Nobody', the protagonist admits that he found pleasure in melancholic solitude, even before his paramour turned his life upside down: 'I watched the falling rain and listened to the sweet birds sing.'[3] Barry is fighting his infatuation on 'To Love Somebody'; he's cross with himself, impatient with the object of his affection. Robin's song is all fatality and quite without hope.

A harpsichord comes in after the second chorus as the strings hold back for just a couple of lines; this opens a window on the gloom, but only succeeds in pulling the song towards the baroque, shifting it in time, with Robin now sat alone in some timber-panelled drawing room. Finally, the brass intervenes as if it's walked into the wrong song, or maybe – after the three

---

[3] For many years, before listening to live versions of the song, I heard this line as 'I listened to the secret sea', which ratchets up the loneliness a little further. But that lyric is just in my brain.

brothers have engaged in a brief moment of 'baby, such a long time' primal-scream abandon – it just wants to shake Robin up and snap him out of his sepia reverie.

The Mellotron – the complex, primitive sampler that had been introduced to the world on 'Strawberry Fields Forever' just three months earlier – would be used to full effect on 'Every Christian Lion Hearted Man Will Show You', the most adventurous production on *Bee Gees' 1st* and a psychedelic masterpiece. It begins with an ominous low hum before the three descending notes of the Mellotron come in followed by faux Gregorian chanting. Then a bright guitar chimes in, and Colin Petersen blasts the roof off the darkness with dense, splash-heavy drumming. 'For every child / Is thinking of something wild,' sings Barry, and again you are reminded of just how young these industry veterans were. Their Mancunian years were re-emerging in this song, not just in their vocals, but in some more intangible way – Joy Division's 'Decades', the final track on their 1980 album *Closer*, would borrow 'Every Christian Lion Hearted Man''s heart-sink Mellotron chords. They suited the damp and the red brick.

There was playfulness on *Bee Gees' 1st*, too: the baroque 'Turn of the Century'; the psychedelic whimsy of 'Red Chair Fade Away' and 'Cucumber Castle'; and their latest pen portrait, 'Craise Finton Kirk Royal Academy of Arts', on which the line 'his wavy hair continues not to grow' may or may not have been about Robert Stigwood, much as the Beach Boys' 'She's Going Bald', released a few months later, may or may not have been about Mike Love. Maybe the most representative track on *Bee Gees' 1st* was 'Holiday'. Rarely has a song had a more misleading title. As teary as 'I Can't See Nobody', it was much more oblique: 'Millions of eyes can see,' cried Robin, 'yet why am I so blind? When the someone else is me, it's unkind.' In America it was rushed out as

'To Love Somebody' began to fall down the singles chart, giving them a third top-twenty hit within six months.

On 4 July, Stigwood threw an expensive, all-day press party on a yacht. Brian Epstein was furious. Not only had Stigwood failed to okay it with him first, but the entire shebang had been charged to NEMS. He also hated that Stigwood constantly referred to the Bee Gees as 'the next Beatles'. The day after the shindig on the yacht, Stigwood announced the Bee Gees' first film – it would be called *Lord Kitchener's Little Drummer Boys*, and would be scripted by Mike Pratt, who had co-written Tommy Steele's early hits with Lionel Bart, and would go on to star in comedy crime series *Randall and Hopkirk (Deceased)*. The Beatles hadn't made a film in two years; Stigwood was intentionally stepping on their toes.

The Beatles' latest single in the summer of 1967 was 'All You Need Is Love' and, of course, it was number one all over the world. It was a jaunt, a simplistic message wrapped up as something rather more significant thanks to a debut performance broadcast from Abbey Road on the first live global television link. It had the air of an impromptu party piece, with snippets of 'La Marseillaise' and 'She Loves You' bouncing across the room like funny-face balloons. But it was a weak record by Beatles standards, and just the other side of their career peak. *Sgt Pepper's Lonely Hearts Club Band*, released that April, had been such a cultural high-water mark that it was impossible to follow and, in tandem with the simplistic message of the chorus, the mumbled nothingness of the lyric on 'All You Need Is Love' ('There's nothing you can do that can't be done') left it a place marker at best. It rode out the summer, but from now onwards the air would be slowly escaping from the Beatles' balloon.

'All You Need Is Love' began to slide down the chart in September, the month the Bee Gees released their third UK single,

'Massachusetts'. Just after they recorded it, Maurice had bumped into Brian Epstein as he came out of his office at NEMS. Eppie turned and put his hand on Mo's shoulder. '"Massachusetts" is going to be the world's number one,' he said gently. 'It's beautiful.' Two days later, he was dead.

'I had this line in my head,' Robin remembered. 'All day. "The lights all went out in Massachusetts." Later that night I mentioned it to Barry and he said, 'Yes, I know. I've already got the tune for it.' So we did the rest of it together.'

The telepathy between the brothers was now at its peak. On 'Massachusetts', they channelled their own rootlessness – no one has ever felt homesick for the entire state of Massachusetts, any more than the Gibbs felt homesick for the regional district of Greater Manchester. But the song was broader, vaguer, and more effective for it. 'It's not talking about people going back to Massachusetts,' said Robin in 1967. 'It represents all the people who want to go back to somewhere or something.' It was about a sense of belonging.

In late 1967 and 1968, the UK chart profiles of the more adventurous likes of Cream, the Who and the Kinks were nosediving, nudged out by singers of flowerpot ballads like Tom Jones, Engelbert Humperdinck and Vince Hill. This shift is usually blamed on the closure of the pirate radio stations that November, but this is a myth. In fact, the trend had begun with Jim Reeves' 'Distant Drums', a number one all the way back in autumn 1966, and intensified when Jones's 'Green Green Grass of Home' spent seven weeks at number one shortly after, at one point preventing a Val Doonican single from reaching the top. Ballads went on to outsell psychedelia, soul, or any other genre in 1967, with Petula Clark's 'This Is My Song' and Humperdinck's 'Release Me' and

'The Last Waltz' all reaching number one. Certainly, 'Massachusetts' followed the weepy nature and draped orchestration of these records, but it still felt youthful, quite separate from Humperdinck's adult concerns. Lyrically, it was smart enough to put an autumnal full stop on the 'Summer of Love'. Even the Beatles were still engaging in the flowery, technicolour dreamwork of *Magical Mystery Tour* that autumn, and wouldn't retreat or reconsider until the following spring with '50s throwback 'Lady Madonna'.

The common ground between the Beatles and Humperdinck – kings of 1967 pop, and as far apart as can be – was in their maximalist arrangements; the Bee Gees discovered the middle ground that kept both opposing wings happy. The teenage Gibbs had pitched up in Hendon as unknowns at the start of the year. By November, with 'Massachusetts', they were top of the pile, and dishing out lessons to their musical heroes on how to take pop forward.

6

HITHER GREEN

Record Retailer UK top ten, 14 October 1967

1. Bee Gees – 'Massachusetts'
2. The Move – 'Flowers in the Rain'
3. Engelbert Humperdinck – 'The Last Waltz'
4. Traffic – 'Hole in My Shoe'
5. Keith West – 'Excerpt from a Teenage Opera'
6. Box Tops – 'The Letter'
7. Frankie Vaughan – 'There Must Be a Way'
8. Diana Ross & the Supremes – 'Reflections'
9. Procol Harum – 'Homburg'
10. Small Faces – 'Itchycoo Park'

In six months' time, if the family had stayed in Manchester, Maurice Gibb would have been sitting his A levels. If only he'd applied himself at school, got his head down and stuck at it, he might now be getting ready to sit his mocks. He might be revising about oxbow lakes. Instead, he was about to sink his fifth scotch and Coke and trying not to stare at Jane Birkin and her ridiculous, impossibly long legs. He wasn't a Casanova, didn't ever want to be one. Besides, there was Lulu, right at his side, with her impossibly big eyes. Everything seemed unreal, super-sized. He went to the bar to buy John Lennon a drink; he opened his wallet and saw his own Australian Beatles Fan Club membership card. Ridiculous. Impossible. He wasn't yet eighteen years old.

Brian Epstein's death in August had meant the deal between RSO and NEMS was off. Stigwood walked away with an alleged £500,000 payoff. If he wasn't going to be the Beatles manager anymore, he would try harder yet to develop his own Beatles. Cream were big, getting bigger, the power trio forming a foundation stone for hard rock, but that's not who Stigwood had in mind. Eric Clapton laughed about it through clenched teeth – the Bee Gees, better than Cream? Did Stigwood really think that? He did. The Bee Gees were his new Beatles. Talking to the *NME*'s Keith Altham, Barry was quick to cool his manager's claims: 'We're not another Beatles and we've never pretended to be. There will only be one Beatles and you cannot hope to emulate what they have achieved in a lifetime.'

Still, they were giving their heroes some serious competition. 'Massachusetts' had gone to number one within four weeks of release. It got so big, so quickly, that Maurice was almost apologetic. 'We thought it would be fun to write a number like Engelbert or Tom Jones,' he had told *Music Maker* in November 1967. 'After all, they do get the number ones. We are much more thrilled about "World", which isn't released yet. Now, that is great. A lot more work went into it than "Massachusetts".'

★

Lulu and Mo's first date had been to see the Pink Floyd at the Saville Theatre on 1 October. Lulu had told her mum she was dating the handsome one from the Bee Gees, and her mum was thrilled – she had assumed Lulu meant Barry, who was the group's real Casanova in its first flush of fame. Barry, though, had met Linda, who worked on *Top of the Pops*, someone whose Scottish colouring, with her contrasting black hair and pale skin, made her perfect for black-and-white telly.

Robin, meanwhile, had overcome Molly Hullis's reservations about the brothers' old-fashioned dress sense. He was now seeing the NEMS receptionist, and it quickly became quite serious. She took him down to Hastings to meet her parents and they approved. It was Sunday 5 November 1967: fireworks night. They got the train back to London at 7.43, as Robin had arranged to meet Robert Stigwood and pick up a tape of a new song called 'Sinking Ships'. Mrs Hullis had made them some bread pudding for the journey back. They were travelling through the suburbs of London when they heard loud noises outside – maybe a kid had thrown a firework at their window, Molly thought.

Hither Green wasn't a name anyone outside of south-east London was that familiar with until that night. It was as suburban and uneventful as Hendon, without even a successful amateur football club to call its own. It had a lost twin – Further Green – which had been swallowed up by the expansion of Catford in the Victorian age. It had a clock tower, quite an ugly one, and that was about it. Apart from being a railway junction with a large goods shed, Hither Green was a nowhere place.

Going over the junction at speed, heading towards London, Robin and Molly's train ran over a broken rail just before Hither Green station. It began to shake. Robin reached for the emergency cord but was thrown down by the vibrations. 'It felt as if we were going over great boulders,' he told the press the next day. 'One minute we were in the luggage rack, the next we were on the floor.' The train was on its side, sliding along the track. Robin and Molly were near the front of the train, sitting in a first-class compartment to celebrate the success of 'Massachusetts', and that may have saved their lives. In the second-class carriages behind them people were tossed like rag dolls. When the train finally came to a halt, Robin and Molly climbed out of the broken window and walked along the side of the overturned train, offering to help people, not realising they themselves were injured and covered in blood. 'I was lifting very badly injured people about three times my weight out of the compartments,' said Robin. With fragments of glass in his hair and his mouth, sat on the disfigured train carriage, he turned to Molly and joked, 'All this just to get to Battersea fun fair.' But when he got to the hospital, he couldn't stop crying from the shock.

Fifty-three people died in the Hither Green train disaster; unsurprisingly the horror of that night would remain with Robin for the rest of his life. In the late '90s he recalled how 'people had to be amputated on the railway line, and I was talking to them as they were being injected. It was like a scene from World War One . . . I didn't sleep for a long, long time afterwards. I went through a guilt trip of feeling people were hurt, so why wasn't I?'

The following day, Molly went to work at NEMS as if nothing had happened – clearly in shock, she was sent home. Robin threw himself into work immediately, writing a song called 'Really and Sincerely' the very next day.

'And of course it rains every day.'

The artist Dan Graham once noted that Ray Davies had been born on the summer solstice. This, Graham thought, explained the essence of 'Sunny Afternoon', 'Lazy Old Sun', 'Waterloo Sunset', 'Sitting in the Midday Sun', and a host of other Kinks songs, in spite of Davies's rather misanthropic reputation. Graham was an acute pop observer and might also have known that Brian Wilson of the Beach Boys was born on the cusp of the summer solstice. Certainly it's hard to think of a more sun-worshipping songwriter than Wilson, again in spite of a personality that led him to steer clear of the beach, at one point spending three years in bed.

Robin and Maurice Gibb were born on the winter solstice. The Bee Gees were the negative to the Wilson brothers' positive, the binary to the Beach Boys – and if this ever got ambitious, crowd-pleasing Barry down, then he'd have to blame the moon rather than his brothers.

No sooner was 'Massachusetts' out of the top ten than 'World' was released. This was the song Maurice had talked of so excitedly to the press. It wasn't hard to see why – from the off it was a full group effort, with Maurice's pounding one-note riff and heavy use of the sustain pedal, distorted and compressed until it sounded like a dozen pianos at the same time. Then a silent break, and Barry's voice sang 'Now . . .', as a reedy, buzzing-bee Mellotron faded in behind him: 'Now I've found that the world is round / And of course it rains every day.'

Like their harmonies, the words in the Gibbs' songs had an internal logic, and with 'World' it stretched to a philosophy. They never seemed embarrassed by their lyrics, which they always said were in the service of the melody. Often they worked as colouring, a shade that matched the melody or the arrangement, and the purple-shades-of-evening 'World' was a good example. The single's flip side, the psychedelic oompah pop of 'Sir Geoffrey Saved the World', opened with the line 'Ev'ry day's Saturday', which similarly summed up the song's sunniness just so.

Robert Stigwood detached himself from NEMS in November 1967. With a reborn RSO he aimed to be involved in film and television on an international level – first up, the Bee Gees would be starring in *Lord Kitchener's Little Drummer Boys*, with filming to commence in Kenya early the following year. Before that, they would turn on the Christmas lights on Oxford Street, with help from *Bonnie and Clyde* actress Faye Dunaway; free soft drinks and cigarettes were handed out to the crowd. With Robin presumably still in shock, having received no counselling, the Bee Gees agreed to play a benefit for the victims of the Hither Green disaster later the same night. The previous week they had headlined on the Saturday of a weekend-long event called Hippy Happy Festival in Rotterdam – Friday's headliners were the Jimi Hendrix Experience, Sunday's were Pink Floyd, both figureheads of future rock and quite some company to keep. As if this flurry of activity wasn't surreal and eerie enough, Barry was interviewed in that week's *NME* about their next single, which was planned to be 'Sinking Ships'. With either a total lack of tact, or as an actively malicious sibling dig, he explained how it was 'all about life and death. It has a connection with disasters like plane crashes. This must sound a bit sick, but it's really not – you'd have to hear the record.'

They returned to the Saville Theatre, where just months earlier they had been pelted with eggs by psych-resistant Fats Domino fans. This time they played with a thirty-piece orchestra and cemented their place at the top of the year-end polls: best new group in the *NME*; most promising new group in the USA's *16* magazine; a Best Pop Stars award in Holland; and a similar one – called the Golden Otto – from Germany's *Bravo* magazine, which gave second place to the Beatles and a bronze medal to the Monkees.

As 1967 came to a close, the Bee Gees appeared on *How on Earth*, a live ITV broadcast from Liverpool's Anglican cathedral, where Robin sang their specially composed 'Thank You for Christmas' and upset Mary Whitehouse by seeming too long-haired – lion-hearted he may have been, but not visibly Christian enough. Stigwood bought each Gibb a Rolls-Royce for Christmas, and then flew all five Bee Gees back to Australia to see their families. They had travelled over on the *Fairsky* in January as gawky kids; in December they returned, internationally famous and looking five years older.

Horizontal had been seven months in the making by the time it was released in February 1968. Fans often retain a soft spot for a debut album, and over the years ahead *Bee Gees' 1st* would remain a firm favourite, but *Horizontal* was a more uniform set, browner, more muted and fuzzier-edged in tone, much like its sleeve. As a band, they had had time to gel. Over the previous autumn, Vince Melouney and Colin Petersen had been constantly threatened with deportation as their work visas had expired. Stigwood had organised a stunt involving an elephant and a protest outside home secretary James Callaghan's house; eventually, Callaghan announced the two non-Gibb Bee Gees could stay in the UK. This affair seemed to bind the five-piece closer together. Vince's blues-rock guitar flashes had been prominent on 'World', and Colin's splashy playing was perfect for their psychedelic pop tendencies, giving many of the songs a heady whoosh. 'Massachusetts' and

'World' opened each side of *Horizontal* but were not typical. Side one, track two, was Robin's impossibly pretty 'And the Sun Will Shine', one of their songs that had an inexplicable structure and no apparent forebear. It started with Robin singing the chorus, an optimistic melody over a simple guitar line, but once again the lyrics were riddled with vague but ominous meteorological metaphors: 'And the clouds will break into tears. You should be here standing so near to me.' The verse then plunged off a cliff, with an almost klezmer-like melody, leaving Robin exposed even as strings and drums attempt to keep his head above water. And then, just as you've given up hope for him, the backing drops out – 'Then I wake up,' he sings over a bird-like woodwind trill. 'Then I grow up.'

'The Earnest of Being George' was essentially Vince and Colin creating a Jimi Hendrix Experience-like backing with only Mo's wobbling electric piano and some whip-crack percussion for support. Having toyed with Hendrix, Vince then sounds closer to Peter Green of the fast-emerging Fleetwood Mac on 'The Change Is Made', one of Barry's chest-baring soul numbers ('Oh Lord, Lord, I've been a good man') and a rare nod to late '60s blues rock, a genre the brothers would otherwise swerve. 'Harry Braff', a character sketch about a racing driver, had been one of the first songs recorded for the album the previous summer, and it showed. It's a terrific song, ending with a burst of harmonies, brass ad-libs and Colin's oceanic cymbals. But the fact it was identifiably a few months older than something like 'Really and Sincerely' showed how much their writing, even their personalities, had changed since they arrived in London.

Robin's 'Really and Sincerely' was three minutes of restrained terror, its structure based on icy fear. There's an old accordion, like a Jacques Brel relic from the port of Amsterdam, and Robin's tremulous voice trying to make sense of his surroundings: 'My mind is open wide, I'm on the other side.' As the song fades, Bill Shepherd tries to inject some hope into the proceedings – a brass fanfare, a harp, a swirl of violas – but Robin still sounds utterly lost: 'Turn me down. Turn me down,' he sings, as if he is attempting to lower the volume not only on the din that surrounds him, the cacophony of fame and its noisy demands, but on his own life. Quieter. He wants to be quieter. Maybe he wants to disappear completely.[4]

Horizontal was released just as 'Words', a most florid ballad, became their fifth UK-based hit single. 'World' and 'Words' had been recorded at the same time the previous October, their first session without Ossie Byrne, whom, unlike arranger Bill Shepherd, they had simply outgrown.[5] Surprisingly – given their comparative legacies – both singles were similar-sized hits at the time. Both made it into the UK top ten; both were number ones in Germany. But 'Words' was much the more straightforward record, with Mo's heavily compressed piano taking it away from mere chintz. Barry sang softly with heavy vibrato, a style he would employ more and more with the passing years. In 1968, it would be sung by Georgie Fame and shoehorned by Robert Stigwood into a none-more-swinging-London movie called *The Mini Mob*. A couple of years later, Elvis Presley would be singing 'Words' on stage in Las Vegas. It was that kind of instant standard. Elvis's band gave it a strong, funky backbeat, and Rita Coolidge would give it a West Coast

---

4 An earlier version with Robin singing over Maurice's signature piano sound is maybe more desolate yet; it was released on the deluxe *Horizontal* CD in 2008.
5 Ossie would stay in the UK as a producer for other acts, notably melodic prog-rockers Cressida.

sheen in 1977, but it was Boyzone's milquetoast version that eventually took 'Words' to number one in Britain in 1996. Neil Young liked the melody so much that he took it wholesale for his 1974 recording 'Deep Forbidden Lake'.

'Words' was about pointless arguments, which the siblings were well used to. Its distinctive piano sound, which Mo would effectively trademark, emerged when he was messing about in the studio at IBC. 'Everyone had gone to lunch. I started playing about with the knobs in front of me. When I played the tape back, I had all these incredible compressed piano noises. Mike Claydon, who engineered all our records, said, "What the hell was that?" It was just compression, but he didn't know what to call it then, I think he called it "limited" . . . It made the piano sound like forty pianos at the same time and very, very thick. It was very beautiful.' The sound was unique to IBC because the compressor/limiter was a hand-made one-off. According to IBC engineer John Pantry, responsible for two British psychedelic classics with the Factory's 'Path Through the Forest' and 'Try a Little Sunshine', it had been purpose-built by 'a guy called Denis King'. Maurice owed Denis King a heavy debt.

For almost a year, they had hardly had time to catch their breath. Since 'New York Mining Disaster' became an international hit they had been a constant presence in the UK top twenty, with at least one single in there from September 1967 to April 1968. All three Gibbs were now rich and very famous. All had met their future wives. The twins were still just eighteen. The title track of *Horizontal* had a chorus that ran 'This is the start of the end' – and it was uncomfortably prescient. Having achieved everything they'd been aiming for since they first harmonised on their parents' bed in Keppel Road, the brothers could probably sense that the toppermost of the poppermost was a hard place to relax and enjoy oneself; Maurice claimed that he owned six Rolls-Royces, because he didn't know what else to spend his money on.[6] Adam Ant would later recall how his early '80s heyday as Britain's biggest pop star went by just like that – he'd never had time to stop and think and enjoy himself. In 1968 the Gibbs were in a similar place and still they kept working, kept writing. Their manager drove them relentlessly, but they had set this pace for themselves when they were proper kids and weren't equipped to slow down.

At the very start of the year, after their family Christmases in Australia, the Bee Gees had been set to take a short break in Istanbul on their way back to London. Robin and Barry ended up sedated, in an Istanbul hospital. 'It was supposed to be a holiday but there were people waiting for us to arrive,' Barry told the *NME*. 'Press and television people wanting us all the time . . . Not that we mind interviews,' he quickly added. 'It's great that someone is taking an interest in you.' A week later they were in the studio working on songs for *Idea*, their third album in less than a year. There were side projects, too: the *Lord Kitchener* movie rumbled on; and a self-scripted TV special called *Cucumber Castle*, named after one of the softer songs on *Bee Gees' 1st*, was set to be filmed in January 1968 but was then put back due to Barry and Robin's exhaustion. Roland Rennie, the Polydor man who had first put Robert Stigwood in touch with the Bee Gees back in 1967, added to their heavy release schedule by announcing he would issue the 1966 *Spicks and Specks* album internationally. Stigwood was apoplectic – this

---

[6] Barry would later roll his eyes when this was brought up in an interview with Alexis Petridis of *The Guardian*: 'Maurice was the master of exaggeration. It never went away. Maurice only had one Rolls-Royce, but he loved expanding everything that happened to him.'

old stuff will confuse their fans, he roared at Rennie – but Rennie was quite within his rights after doing a deal with Festival. 'Their talent is rare, precious and beautiful,' Stigwood bibbled, and unintentionally gave Rennie a title for the collection. *Rare, Precious and Beautiful* sold well enough to make the top twenty in Germany, where 'Words' had just given them their third number-one single in a row.[7]

No one would ever take the curious 'Jumbo' to number one. A hurriedly released sixth UK single, it had no intro to speak of, certainly not compared to the instantly recognisable 'Words', 'World' or 'Massachusetts'. Its verse had drums on the off-beat, maybe as a nod to ska, though it was near impossible to dance to. There was no obvious chorus, either – the song seemed to head straight from a Mellotron-led bridge back into the verse. It was an underpowered exercise in laurel-resting. When it quickly became clear that 'Jumbo' wasn't going to be another major hit, the single was switched to a double A-side, with Robin's lush ballad 'The Singer Sang His Song' promoted to equal weighting. A clip was shot for 'Singer' with the boys standing in line onstage, Robin to one side, smiling beatifically, his hair at its most spaniel-like. This was interspersed with footage of a young, very 1968-looking couple chasing each other around a park – the girl looks a little like P. P. Arnold, the guy looks a little like Keith West, both modish names in the spring of 1968. It didn't really help the single.

The usual Gibb half-truths were employed to explain the single's failure. It had been Vince's idea, apparently. Stigwood shouldn't have listened to Vince. And he should have known

---

[7] Two more volumes of *Rare, Precious and Beautiful*, mopping up every previously released Australian recording, would be issued before the decade was out.

better than to release a guitar-heavy single. No matter that the successful 'World', a few months earlier, had been considerably heavier. The only explanation for 'Jumbo''s A-side status was as a way of breaking into the expanding rock market in the States, where Stigwood's other charges Cream were already huge. Falling between stools, it was just a poor choice of single, and they didn't need to over-explain or point fingers.

In Britain, 'Jumbo' stalled at number twenty-five; in America, the single didn't even reach the top fifty, but it disappeared so fast there that no one seemed to notice it even existed and it didn't harm their growing presence one jot. Back in January they had visited Los Angeles to do some press, and to play a pair of shows in Anaheim – their first in America – with the same full orchestration they had used at the Saville Theatre. 'We've done a half-hour concerto, which we're about halfway through,' Barry told the press. 'It's the type of thing the great geniuses like Beethoven used to do. Half an hour. It's a challenge to ourselves, to see if people will say "That's nice" or not.' It may have been sleep deprivation talking, but we'll have to assume he was serious.[8] Their support acts in Anaheim were the super-soft harmony act Spanky and Our Gang and the organ-led, proto-stoner rock Vanilla Fudge. For now, the Bee Gees were one of the very few acts who could walk a tightrope between these two wings of contemporary pop.

Reviewing the shows for *16* magazine, editor Ann Moses raved:

---

[8] It's possible Barry was talking about one or more of the orchestral instrumentals that appeared on *Odessa* in 1969, though none touched ten minutes, let alone thirty.

The Bee Gees made their American debut at the Anaheim Convention Centre and gave Los Angeles THE greatest pop show it has ever witnessed! The LA audience, which is usually rudely blasé (to the point of booing Jimi Hendrix on the Mamas and Papas concert last summer), showed their appreciation and complete admiration by giving the Bee Gees a standing ovation at the close of their second show!

Among the cheering audience, Moses noted, were 'Peter Tork, the Mamas and Papas, John Barbata of the Turtles, Dewey Martin of the Buffalo Springfield, and Tommy Smothers'.

Somehow their 1968 itinerary also allowed time for their first tour of Germany, supported by Procol Harum. Molly remembered police with guard dogs and guns at the shows. After a show in Switzerland, Mo recalled how fans 'crushed the car', with the terrified band having to hide from sight on the floor of the vehicle. When the car lurched forward in an attempt to get away, a girl was thrown through a plate-glass window. The Gibbs returned to their hotel convinced she was dead.

Vince Melouney, slightly detached from this mania, wrote 'Such a Shame' about the potential misunderstandings and petty jealousies that were starting to bloom in this hothouse situation: 'All that I hear doesn't feel right . . . / I listened and I heard but don't tell me.' The threat was vague, but he was clearly unhappy. The lyrics were veiled enough that the song made it onto *Idea*, released in September 1968, without being vetoed. 'Everything was falling apart,' Vince would tell writer Andrew Sandoval in 2006. 'That's what the song's about. It mentions Stigwood in the lyrics.' That June, in Nassau, Colin Petersen married Brian Epstein's former assistant, Joanne

Newfield. Vince was his best man, and Vince's wife Diane was the couple's bridesmaid. No Gibbs were present, nor was Stigwood. Blood was thicker than water – the non-Gibb Bee Gees could hardly have felt more othered.

Idea would be trailed by one of their best-loved singles. The fall-out from 'Jumbo' had meant that the next single would receive ten times as much effort. 'I've Gotta Get a Message to You' would in turn become their second UK number one and their first single to crack the top ten in America. They had apparently written it with Percy Sledge in mind – his 'Take Time to Know Her' had been a story song, and his biggest hit in two years, in the spring of 1968. That was about a romance going wrong and a mother's unheeded advice. 'I've Gotta Get a Message to You', meanwhile, was sung by a prisoner on death row: 'Well, I did it to him / Now it's my turn to die.' It was very matter of fact, with no real back story. Percy Sledge, presumably flattered, if confused, went on to record the song as a single in 1970. Barry stated his position to the press on capital punishment: 'The nominating of the moment that a man's life is going to be taken, the long wait, it's terrible. Much more cold-blooded than the average murder. I don't see how execution can be justified.' As it battled for the number-one spot in the UK in September 1968 with the Crazy World of Arthur Brown's horror-movie-on-45 'Fire' and the Beach Boys' 'Do It Again', a plea to turn back the clock to the early '60s, it was safe to say the boundless positivity of 1967 had gone. 'I believe that the moment we're born, we're dying,' argued Barry, 'and there's no use going through [life] looking miserable.'

If there was any bad feeling within the Bee Gees camp, any perceived Stigwood favouritism towards Barry, it hadn't reached the press. Not yet. The eagle-eyed would spot that Barry was edging closer to the front in band photos, which had been unusually democratic in 1967 – even Vince and Colin had occasionally been front and centre. Their wild fraternal telepathy was still there, though. Barry explained how he had been on a break in Los Angeles but 'found it to it be phoney, and I wasn't enjoying myself', and so took a plane elsewhere. Meanwhile Robin had gone to the other side of the world for a break, to India, but he had also got bored and changed his mind. So he flew to Rome . . . where he bumped into Barry at the airport.

Still, Robin had an itch that the current Bee Gee schedule wasn't scratching. He went to IBC Studio A in June 1968 and recorded a bunch of new songs, only a couple of which would end up as Bee Gees recordings. The master tape is a peculiar listen, with Robin playing guitar and rattling through them in one take, only pausing to introduce each song, in the style of early wax cylinders. 'The Band Will Meet Mr Justice' was Dylanesque, with the odd very Bee Gee line ('And now it's started raining, the band can stop complaining'), while 'The People's Public Poke Song' was closer to Syd Barrett's more naïve work on *Piper at the Gates of Dawn*: 'Roger the cat had a patch on his stomach that was shaped like a hat.' At the end of the take he mumbles that he's 'been flying for two nights, bear that in mind'. Barry's motto that everything they recorded should be a potential A-side flies out the window with these recordings; the tape ends in the middle of 'Heaven in My Hands', with Robin saying, 'We'll leave that as it is, I don't have much voice to do any more.' The tape suggests he was already looking towards solo work.

This could have been an act of self-preservation. Barry's head had been turned by the number of people in LA telling him he could be a movie star. In August 1968, he mentioned to the press, quite casually, that he was going to leave the group to work in films. Stigwood's office denied the story, taking a rather aloof position that suggested ongoing irritation between band and management: 'I think he will feel differently when he's had a rest,' said Stigwood. 'I can't let him go this year . . . Barry said more than he really meant. Although he hasn't seen the script yet, he has the starring role in *Lord Kitchener's Little Drummer Boys*. That will please him.' Maybe he was trying to sound paternal but, interviewed while filming an album-length TV special for *Idea* in Brussels, Barry felt patronised: 'I have said that I shall be leaving the Bee Gees and I stand by that. I shall fulfil all existing commitments. The group scene is not an everlasting thing.' His decision to include 'Swan Song' as the closing track on their next album, *Idea*, was probably quite intentional.

In the meantime, the brothers also found time to write three songs for an aborted Pippi Longstocking film – two of them, 'Treacle Brown' and the strongly atmospheric 'Four Faces West', were given to eleven-year-old Australian Lori Balmer. She recorded them in July with a classic Bee Gees backing and a Bill Shepherd arrangement. It's a rare but very lovely single. A third track, 'Chocolate Symphony', was marked down for inclusion on *Idea*. Barry also managed to write a hit single for another old pal from Brisbane, Trevor Gordon, and his fierce-voiced Skegness-born mate Graham Bonnet. 'Only One Woman' could easily have been included on *Idea*, a booming, overwrought rock/soul ballad with Barry's unmistakable leonine touch. He christened the duo the Marbles and they briefly seemed a big deal in Britain when 'Only One Woman' reached number five in November 1968, keeping records like 'All Along the Watchtower', 'Hey Jude' and Joe Cocker's 'With a Little Help from My Friends' company in the top ten.[9]

Robin's apparently poor health was now being used by Stigwood as an excuse for cancelled American shows. It's hard to know how much of this was based in reality; Molly later said 'there was no "nervous exhaustion". It was just a thing Robin did for the group, a way out of the tour.' As the group's sensitive soul, Robin's Chatterton tendencies were to the fore when the Gibbs came into contact with high commercialism. Barry and Robin were both asked to write jingles for Coca-Cola in 1968: Barry came up with a chirpy woodwind-led tune ('Sitting in the meadow, frolic in the grass'), but Robin's was morose and better suited to meths-drinking. It opened with the line 'Another cold and windy day' before the drink's obliterating powers were extolled: 'I open up some Coke and smile. And then my mind's free, for a while.'

Before *Idea* was in the shops, Stigwood had already decided that their next long player should be a concept album. With this in mind, the group spent much of August 1968 in the studio in LA. A year later Maurice claimed it was to record an album that was 'originally going to be called *The American Opera*. Each song was going to help build up the history of America, from the beginning to the end.' At the time he reckoned they recorded 'a load of rubbish' as they couldn't get the sound they wanted. No matter, the beginnings of their sixth album were already well under way by the time their fifth, *Idea*, was released in the UK in September.

---

[9] A second Bee Gees-penned single, 'The Walls Fell Down', very similar to the first hit, would make the top thirty in early 1969 before the two split.

Idea was another very strong collection, reaching number four in the UK album chart in October 1968, their highest placing to date, and making them real contenders in the brave new world of album-oriented rock. The title track was a tour de force, with Mo's urgent pounding piano leaning on the Stones' 'We Love You', taut, effective playing by Vince on his Gibson, and one of Barry's most powerful vocals. Barry said he wanted 'to do something with more aggression, with more energy' – the song sounded like it was powered by springs. 'Let There Be Love' and 'When the Swallows Fly', meanwhile, were both emotive Barry epics, crimson red romances: 'I've got to give you my life,' he sings on the magnificent 'Let There Be Love', though it is Robin who gets the plum moment, elevating the song as it comes out of the middle eight with a heart-tearing unexpected leap, and almost choking on the emotion: 'Let there be love, so I can be loved by you / In Paradise Avenue . . . oh yeah.'

'Down to Earth' opened with crashing, near atonal piano chords before Robin delivered one of the most enigmatic opening lines of any Bee Gees song: 'Hello there. Is there any air?' It also (surprisingly) featured alto sax, and some prime Gibb philosophy: 'You can see if you stand on your chair that there's millions and millions and millions and millions of people like you.' Barry's 'Kilburn Towers' – more likely to be referencing a pair of circular modernist buildings on Sydney's north harbour than the turreted Victorian villas of north-west London – was hazy perfection. It also contained arguably Vince's finest moment on a Bee Gees record; as the guitar break doubles with Bill Shepherd's strings coming out of the second chorus, the hairs on your arms stand on end. The lyric is like a lonelier version of 'Cracklin' Rosie', sung from the perspective of a street drinker: 'We drink and we swill / 'Til the early hours'. It was neatly at odds with the melody and the dream imagery of the opening verses ('I am a bird . . .') and it was quite beautiful.

On the closing track, 'Swan Song', Barry was trying hard to write a standard. Why not? He wasn't a teenager anymore. He was all of twenty-one. And it's a hell of a lot more appealing as a final bow than 'My Way': 'This is my last chance / A chance to show the world that I am strong.'

For many, the standout track on *Idea* was Robin's enigmatic 'I Started a Joke'. It would be released as a single everywhere but the UK, where 'I've Gotta Get a Message to You' curiously wasn't followed up at all. It became their biggest US hit to date, reaching number six as 1968 turned into 1969, and was the kind of song that raised questions among the heads: '. . . I finally died / Which started the whole world living.' The idiosyncratic Robin Gibb lyric was about understanding your place in the world – would it be better off if I wasn't here at all? 'I Started a Joke' had been the last song recorded for the album, a late addition that would bump the similarly lush 'Chocolate Symphony' from the final running order.

Robin must have been annoyed that a song still regarded as one of his best loved wasn't released as a single in his homeland. What could Stigwood have had against it? Instead it was given away to a simpering balladeer called Heath Hampstead, a name so beyond parody it would have been struck out from an *Austin Powers* script; it was released on Polydor (so *they* thought it was good enough to be a single) and it flopped. Maurice, trapped between simmering arguments, had admitted on returning from the States: 'We had a couple of arguments while we were away. I forget what they were about. When I saw Barry at Mr Stigwood's, he didn't seem to be on speaking terms. He didn't say hello, let's put it that way.

I definitely don't want to split. I hope the five of us keep together and remain good friends.'

But Vince would drop a bombshell just as *Idea* was released: he was leaving. He may not have been too visible, or vocal, but clearly he had played a major musical part in the Bee Gees' first run of success, and indirectly kept Barry and Robin's egos in check. There were chunks of contemporary pop – certainly at the progressive end of the spectrum – that the Gibbs tended to shun. But not Vince, and he would go on to leave his mark, albeit in a smaller way than the brothers, in the '70s. In November 1968, he told the *NME* that he 'never really felt 100% a Bee Gee, because the talent I have doesn't come up to the standard of the Gibb brothers. I don't think I am adding as much as they are.' What did the brothers make of this sad news? In 2006, Vince would confess to Andrew Sandoval: 'I didn't get on with Hughie Gibb. He was always treating me like an outsider. It never spilled out into an argument with the lads or anything like that. It was just a thing between Hughie and me. I thought: "I've always been friends with the Gibb brothers and Colin, I don't want to be part of this anymore." After a while I didn't have a life.'

Hugh and Barbara Gibb. Remember them? Though he had moved into the background, Hughie had remained a constant figure on tour with the boys even after Stigwood signed them, but he was smart enough to let the experienced wheeler-dealer take the reins. Still only fifty-two, Hugh now decided it was time for him and Barbara to settle down, at least for a while, and they bought a house in the solid commuter belt suburbia of Gerrards Cross, Buckinghamshire. Things were stabilising for them – no more moonlight flits – just as the earth beneath the brothers was buckling. Three days after Vince officially left the group, Robin and Molly married at London's Caxton Hall on 4 December. Robin was eighteen. 'I probably wasn't suitable to be married to anybody,' he would later confess. Their honeymoon had to wait, naturally, for some more recording sessions, and songs for the new concept album that was now going to be a double called *Master Peace*. 'There won't be any sound effects,' said Barry, as if to calm fans who might have worried about something too experimental. 'Just ballads with an emotional message,' Barry assured them. All very normal, he was saying, nothing to look at here. Just a week later, *Disc and Music Echo* announced the album would now be called *Odessa*, and the eight-minute title track would be released as a single in January, which rather undercut Barry's milky assurances. The news stories, like the Bee Gees' schedule, seemed endless. Everyone needed a holiday, including the Polydor press officer.

Robin and Molly finally got away for their honeymoon on New Year's Eve 1968, renting a chalet near Geneva. It was nothing more than a wooden hut – no telephone, one tiny stove. They woke to a terrific noise which turned out to be an avalanche: 'The snow came down in a solid sheet. With it came half the mountain.' Robin burrowed his way out of the door and went out for help, with the snow up to his neck. Just as there seemed to be a real danger of him dying of hypothermia, he was spotted, then pulled out of the snow with a chain tied to a truck. Back at the chalet, he shared a raw egg with Molly: 'There was nothing to cook with. I can tell you it was the nicest thing I've eaten in my life,' he said. They survived, just about, into 1969.

7

ODESSA

1. The Seekers – *Best of the Seekers*
2. Cream – *Goodbye*
3. Beach Boys – *20/20*
4. Original Soundtrack – *The Sound of Music*
5. Herb Alpert and the Tijuana Brass – *The Beat of the Brass*
6. Diana Ross and the Supremes – *Join the Temptations*
7. The Seekers – *Live at the Talk of the Town*
8. Engelbert Humperdinck – *Engelbert*
9. Scott Walker – *Scott 3*
10. Bee Gees – *Odessa*

By 1969, the Bee Gees weren't just a constant presence on the chart, but an audible influence too. Their rainy, melancholic, orchestrated sound had been partly responsible for the Moody Blues' reinvention, from lightly baroque R&B to full-on symphonic balladry, on the tremulous 'Nights in White Satin' and concept albums like *In Search of the Lost Chord*. There was a strong Bee Gees flavour to new records by acts who would become giants in the following decade: Elton John's single 'Lady Samantha' could easily have been written and sung by Barry; Peter Gabriel later said that, in order to impress producer and Bee Gee fan Jonathan King, Genesis's 1968 debut single 'Silent Sun' had been a direct attempt to mimic the Gibbs' songwriting. David Bowie's first hit, 'Space Oddity' in the summer of 1969, would be smothered in Mellotron, with a verse that was so indebted to early Bee Gees that its opening line may as well have been 'In the event of something happening to me in outer space.'[10] Likewise, the first albums by Yes and, to a lesser degree, King Crimson (the *Horizontal*-like Mellotron workout on 'In the Court of the Crimson King') had the clear stamp of the Gibbs.

The Bee Gees had inadvertently founded the string-driven wing of progressive rock – they were ancestors of the Moody Blues, but Yes even more so, and also Queen – only to be quite left out of the histories. The brothers never saw the group as either psychedelic (in spite of the evidence on 'World') nor as part of prog (in spite of *Odessa*), and their name would rarely be mentioned subsequently in discussions of either. Why was this? Possibly because there was seen to be an intellectual seriousness to a group like Yes, even if it was only so much dressing up. Singer Jon Anderson had grown up in a terrace house in Accrington, Lancashire, not dissimilar to

---

[10] Bowie's collaborator at the time, John 'Hutch' Hutchinson, said: '"Space Oddity" was a Bee Gees type song. David knew it, and he said so at the time, the way he sang it, it's a Bee Gees thing.' Marc Bolan later added: 'I remember David playing me "Space Oddity" in his room and I loved it . . . he said he needed a sound like the Bee Gees, who were very big then.'

the Gibb home on Keppel Road in Chorlton, and had prosaic dreams of playing for local football club Accrington Stanley. In a red-brick industrial small town, it wasn't hard to understand why he would also create dreamscapes in his lyrics, with drifting clouds and starship troopers heading into the heart of the sunrise above nearby Pendle Hill.

One other possible reason for their omission from the conversation was the Bee Gees' reliance on arrangers and orchestration, which was by 1969 largely being discarded by both singer-songwriters – now looking to the sparer sounds of Laurel Canyon – and rock groups, who became more self-contained, inspired by the post-psych, roots-digging Rolling Stones. Still, the Mellotron used by Yes and the Moody Blues was essentially an affordable substitute for strings and woodwinds. There's no doubt that the Bee Gees fitted into this softer progressive streak, but both their outsider goofiness and Barry's conservative professionalism meant they would not be absorbed into the music's written history, even though they understood better than most how 'Puff, the Magic Dragon' and a yearning for the land of Honalee were the secret forgotten roots of prog.

Yes were one of a new wave of rock groups who were proving you didn't need a hit single to push an album, and it was album sales the industry now craved as the profit margins were so much greater. In 1969, with the Bee Gees' stock high among their peers, it made both commercial and artistic sense to follow this trend. The year would see a massive shift from the sales of 45-rpm singles to 33-rpm albums. Changing hardware habits meant teenagers were now more likely to buy a stereo hi-fi than a mono Dansette record player with its party-friendly spindle for stacking 45s. Stereos were designed for concentrated listening, in twenty-minute spells, and to album-based acts like Jethro Tull, Ten Years After or King

Crimson. The received wisdom was that rock music had gravitas and pop was for kids; Stigwood decided the Bee Gees needed to follow Cream into the 'rock' camp, and *Odessa* would be their ticket to the ball. The irony is that *Idea* had been a huge hit album, while their 1968 singles had almost all done likewise. They had a foot in both camps, so why move the furniture?

Robin certainly took this gambit seriously. 'Odessa (City on the Black Sea)', 'Black Diamond' and 'Lamplight' were all like condensed Hollywood epics, with scripts pulled from the pages of obscure nineteenth-century tales known only to Robin Gibb. Stigwood wanted to follow another recent trend, too: the epic single. Richard Harris's 'Macarthur Park' (June 1968), the Beatles' 'Hey Jude' (October 1968) and Barry Ryan's 'Eloise' (November 1968) had been groundbreaking and hard to avoid, stretching the notion of what a pop record was, with multiple sections and groove-cramming length. Robin's seven-minute-long 'Odessa (City on the Black Sea)' told a story of a shipwreck, and a sea captain who had 'left himself a lonely wife in Hull' to end up floating on an iceberg in the North Atlantic. He imagines writing letters home, possibly picturing his wife with a new paramour ('You love the vicar more than words can say / Tell him to pray that I won't melt away'). These fleetingly comedic moments make the intensity of the chorus almost unbearable. Bill Shepherd's arrangement made the 'Warsaw Concerto' seem like a fuss about nothing. It was described by Stigwood as the greatest thing they had ever done.

This introduction to *Odessa*'s velvety richness was certainly the epic Stigwood craved. Would it be the single, or would they plump for a more solidly guaranteed AM/medium-wave radio hit? It had to be Stigwood's call. It always was. 'Robert makes the choice about which songs to release as singles,' said a guileless Barry in *Melody Maker*.

Barry, meanwhile, carried on writing songs – great songs, love songs – one at a time. 'Melody Fair', 'First of May' and 'Sound of Love' were all potential hits, but none had any clear part in a concept album, lyrically or sonically. He had written several of his *Odessa* songs (including the Band-inspired Americana of 'Marley Purt Drive' and 'Give Your Best') in the summer of 1968, before Stigwood had announced they were working on a concept album called *The American Opera*, and presumably he wasn't going to ditch this gold just because their manager was baiting the press with promises of conceptual derring-do.

Meanwhile Maurice came up with the oboe-led 'Suddenly', a gorgeous tune that was quickly covered as a single by Mike Batt, but again it was a standalone tune that didn't fit a narrative arc. His 'Seven Seas Symphony' was much more in keeping, something he'd had on the back burner for some time and an impressive piece of light music, closer to Rachmaninov than anything in the top twenty or the Gibbs' back catalogue.

The verse on Robin's extraordinary 'Lamplight' had the air of a forgotten national anthem, a stirring tune that could have been designed to keep the Ottomans at bay in Hercegovina. Hand out the arms and ammo. The chorus was a more straightforward swoon, its lyric suggesting love in a time before electricity. It was grandiose, there was no doubt, and given the records that would be sitting above it when it rested as a B-side at number six on the singles chart, maybe its grandiosity would have made it a better choice of A-side: of those singles, Engelbert Humperdinck was still sat in a taverna, mooning over lost love on 'The Way Love Used to Be'; there was a proper old-school flowerpot from 61-year-old Donald Peers, called 'Please Don't Go'; while Peter Sarstedt's Franglais monster 'Where Do You Go To (My Lovely)?' was at number one. But in its intensity and unguarded soulfulness, albeit a soulfulness of non-specific eastern European descent, 'Lamplight' had more in common with the record at number two, and soon to be number one: Marvin Gaye's 'I Heard It Through the Grapevine'.

Shunning both Robin's 'Odessa (City on the Black Sea)' and 'Lamplight', Stigwood decided that Barry's' First of May' should become the Bee Gees' first single of 1969, released in February, with 'Lamplight' on the B-side. As a result, 'First of May' can get the side-eye from Robin devotees but, really, it was a marvellous piece of work. 'When I was small and Christmas trees were tall' was an impossibly good, scene-setting opening line, and Mo's compressed piano led beautifully into Bill Shepherd's string swell on the second verse. Talking about *Odessa* specifically, Barry said at the time, 'Don't look for meaning in the lyrics – there isn't any.' But, not for the first time, he was surely being disingenuous, trying not to scare off the squarer demographic in their fan base. 'First of May' is extraordinarily evocative, deeply resonant, and it doesn't let up. It detailed a non-specific love affair, probably in childhood or adolescence, possibly set in the Edwardian era (Robin would surely have approved of that). It reached an unexpected anti-dramatic climax, with a cappella Barry left alone at the end of a long tunnel, gradually disappearing into the distance, fading to black, mournfully singing, 'Don't ask me why but time has passed us by / Someone else moved in from far away.' It can cleave my heart every time I hear it. I can't think of another single that ends this way, and DJs must have hated it.

Barry would say that, musically, the best times in his life had been before the brothers ever became famous: 'There was no competition, it didn't matter who sang what. When we had our first number one, "Massachusetts", Robin sang the lead, and I don't think he ever got past that; he never felt that anyone else should sing lead after that. And that was not the nature of the group.' Robin clearly did not think 'the nature of the group' should be dictated by his big brother or Robert Stigwood. The song Stigwood had called a 'masterpiece' – phoning him in the middle of the night to tell him so – would be sidelined, as just an album track. When he learned that 'First of May' was to be the next single, Robin lost his rag and quit the group.

'There's fame and there's ultra-fame, and it can destroy,' Barry would say in 2020. 'You lose your perspective, you're in the eye of a hurricane and you don't know you're there. And you don't know what tomorrow is, you don't know if what you're recording will be a hit or not. And we were kids, don't forget.'

Robin's decision to leave the Bee Gees went down very badly. Stigwood cast aspersions on his mental health. 'I don't think Robin is at all well at the moment, and he is not capable of making decisions.' You would think Robin's family might have offered some support, but instead he was castigated for stepping out of line. His mum Barbara made him sound like either a pre-Raphaelite eccentric or a member of the Bonzo Dog Doo Dah Band: 'He's a fanatic about his food,' she told the press. 'He always inspects his knife and fork to make sure they're clean. He has got beautiful hands and really looks after them. His nails are long and slender. He uses his hands to express himself; if you cut them off he couldn't talk. He wears suits all the time; he'll never wear anything casual, even in hot weather.' Dad Hugh was no help either: 'Robin had some feeling against Robert Stigwood for some reason. I don't know what it was. I don't understand it all.' Picking at a scab, he carried on: 'When it comes to anything physical, he can't be bothered. If there was a wallet on the ground with £100 in it, he'd walk over it rather than bend down to pick it up. Another thing about him – he always thinks he's right.'

When it was released in March 1969, the packaging of *Odessa* – like *In the Court of the Crimson King*, or the White Album, or *Electric Ladyland* – was instantly eye-catching. It had a gold-embossed, red flock gatefold cover; the fibres involved in its production caused rashes among workers at the printers, Ernest J. Day & Co. A bigger problem with *Odessa*, though, was that the group were not happy with it. They didn't hate it; they just felt it was half-cocked, a blend of ephemeral songs ('Edison'), pretty, potential hits ('Melody Fair'), and more portentous work like 'Seven Seas Symphony', 'Black Diamond' and the title track. If the whole album had kept up this level of greatness, *Odessa* would have been their crowning triumph. Some still believe it is.

'*Odessa* . . .' sighed Barry, years later. 'I remember Robin and I arguing through the trade press. We just didn't understand that we were brothers. Sending messages to each other through the press was stupid, but we didn't know that. We thought, everyone should know we're fighting.' And at the time, he was unflinchingly rude about Robin: 'I wouldn't say he's slow – I'd just say he was dead.'

Barry had also made his feelings known on *Odessa*'s 'You'll Never See My Face Again', which may not be about Robin but with the bad feeling around at the time it's hard to imagine 'it makes me laugh, you've got no friends' would be about anyone else. Robin was the least sociable of the brothers, after all. Barry was tight with flamboyant characters like *Jason King* actor Peter Wyngarde and shiny blonde pop singer David Garrick, who was handed the middling Gibb song 'Maypole Mews' as a single in 1969. Mo meanwhile was making the scene with Oliver Reed and Peter O'Toole by night; he would wake up with a hangover to see his next-door neighbour Ringo Starr pottering around in his shed with a new Moog synthesiser. The two talked about building a tunnel under the garden fence so they could drink whisky and create mad synth music in their garden sheds without Lulu or Maureen Starkey finding out. The only known recording by the pair – not that it is ever likely to be released – is called 'Modulating Maurice'.

Barry and Maurice had studio time booked on the day Robin officially walked out on the Bee Gees – why waste it? They cut 'Tomorrow Tomorrow', which Barry had initially written with Joe Cocker in mind – it was way tougher than any single they had cut since 'World' in late 1967, with a fast verse/slow chorus structure that took a few listens to click. The lyric, meanwhile, was bullish – 'Tomorrow every one gonna know me better. And tomorrow, every one gonna drink my wine' – like a variant on Frank Sinatra's then-new 'My Way'. 'Tomorrow Tomorrow' was rushed out as a single to prove the Bee Gees were still a going concern without Robin, but did poor business, stalling at number twenty-three in the UK and number fifty-four in the US.

Sister Lesley suddenly found herself having to step in as Robin's replacement for a show at London's Talk of the Town, a prestigious booking that had recently led to hugely successful live albums by both the Seekers and Tom Jones. She described the split as a 'brotherly spat', suggesting the Gibbs thought tough love was the way to bring Robin back into the fold. A new mother of twins, poor Lesley had to rehearse in his place just three weeks before they were due to play.

'I secretly became the fourth Bee Gee,' she remembered. 'It was amazing. I know Robin watched it and he said he felt very choked up about it. I couldn't sound like Robin, of course, but our harmonies as Gibb family members sounded very much the same. He said he loved my performance, but I told him if you feel like that, why don't you just come back then?'

In 1960s Britain, it was virtually unheard of for women to take any prominent role in the music industry, unless they were behind a microphone.[11] Music was produced by men to be consumed by women, on the general assumption that they were all either schoolgirls or housewives. For a successful group to consider swapping a male vocalist for a female vocalist was unheard of, and says something for the Bee Gees' gentle, unconscious gender fluidity. The only other British group of the era to do anything similar were the Kinks – Ray Davies' wife Rasa was brought in to add high vocal parts on hits like 'Waterloo Sunset', 'Sunny Afternoon' (the chorus of which she also had a hand in writing) and – most audibly – 'Death of a Clown'. This was not a coincidence. The Bee Gees and the Kinks were arguably the least overtly masculine groups of the '60s, in spite of the regular fist fights. Gender confusion would eventually lead the Gibbs to both glory and near-destruction in the '70s.

Lesley Gibb, though, wasn't interested in remaining a Bee Gee. Unlike her brothers, neither fame or even music held her interest much.[12] She regarded the Talk of the Town show as

---

[11] A hat-tip here to writers like Lesley Duncan, uncredited producers like Dusty Springfield, journalists like Penny Valentine and TV producer/label owner Vicki Wickham who managed to successfully swim against the tide.

[12] Lesley loved animals more than showbiz, and would go on to become a Staffordshire bull terrier breeder back in Australia, marrying a salesman called Keith Evans, and raising seven children.

a one-off – 'I loved it on the night' – and that was enough to satisfy her curiosity.

In the meantime, Robin was developing his own peculiar way of recording. He had bought a Rhythm Ace drum machine in Soho, a wheezing contraption that sounded both futuristic and antique at the same time. Robin either played piano or organ to the drum machine's accompaniment, then asked his new pal, arranger Kenny Clayton, to do the orchestration. Maurice helped his twin brother out on bass and piano at a session at De Lane Lea Studios in March 1969. They cut four songs including the intensely melancholic 'Janice' ('I'll write your name in black-hearted skies') and the waltz time 'Saved by the Bell', which had a lyric so minimal it sounded like it had been written as a dare. Barry learned that Maurice had played piano on it, and was withering: 'I don't see how Robin can go ahead with this single in view of this fact. As for it being a commercial hit record, I've heard it and frankly I just can't agree.' It was probably just as well that Colin Petersen kept his involvement a secret.

Unique, foggy ('Now I walk down our grey lane'), and reminiscent of a broken-down fairground, 'Saved by the Bell' went to number two in Britain when Polydor released it as a solo single, only kept from the top of the pile by the Rolling Stones' 'Honky Tonk Women'; it was a number one in Ireland and did equally well on the Continent.

Robin was now setting out his own strange territory. There was a song about Winston Churchill called 'The Statesman'. He had also 'completed a book called *On the Other Hand* which is to be published soon', reported the *NME*, as 'Saved by the Bell' climbed the chart. 'It's a collection of poems and stories, all very classical. I'm a great admirer of Dickens.' In the few weeks between leaving the Bee Gees and hitting the chart with 'Saved by the Bell' he wrote more than a hundred songs, and set about work on a Christmas special. 'I'm also doing the musical score for a film called *Henry the Eighth*,' he told *Fabulous*, 'and I'm making my own film called *Family Tree*. It involves a man, John Family, whose grandfather is caught trying to blow up Trafalgar Square with a home-made bomb wrapped in underwear.' There was more: 'I've got an uncle called Brian Pass who was 21 when he went missing in Burma in 1952. I think he's probably in East Germany or Russia. He was the sort of person who'd answer back . . . I'm thinking of getting a private detective.' There was a book about 'early England, and one about how England would have been if Hitler and Germany had won the war.' And more: 'I'm planning an overland trip from Tangiers to Timbuktu which is something I've always wanted to do.' Of course it could have been the amphetamines talking, but he'd clearly given all of this some thought. Robin Gibb was still only nineteen years old.

Barry must have been furious; Stigwood too. Scared of losing ground to the renegade Gibb after 'Tomorrow Tomorrow' had flopped, RSO took action – Robin was now prevented from recording as a solo act by lawsuits. That wasn't all. His parents attempted to make him a ward of court, a legal move usually brought to protect children. But Robin Gibb was a married man. His wife Molly, having survived both a major train crash and an avalanche with Robin, felt they were perfectly capable of taking care of themselves and being a stable family unit without the needs of court orders. Robin, meanwhile, was straight into the studio recording instrumentals as 'The Robin Gibb Orchestra and Chorus', which he thought might get him out of his legal bind: 'To Heaven and Back', an epic commemoration of the moon landing recorded in June 1969, was made with arranger Kenny Clayton and a 43-piece orchestra. 'It is an entirely instrumental piece, with the choir being used for "astral effects",' claimed the *NME*. It would remain unheard and unreleased until 2015, as would 'Ghost of Christmas Past', which took a chunk of Dickens' *A Christmas Carol* and set it to brass and choral music reminiscent of the soundtrack to *The Lion in Winter*, a historical movie released the previous year. (It's a safe assumption that Robin would have held *The Lion in Winter* in higher regard than the 1968 movies aimed more at people his age, such as *Planet of the Apes* or *Bullitt*.)

Astonishingly, the next Bee Gees single also went to number two in Britain. The country ballad 'Don't Forget to Remember' was as sentimental and trad as 'Saved by the Bell' was ornate and eerie. Maurice described it as 'Jim Reeves-ish', which suggested they had quickly abandoned Stigwood's notion of becoming a serious albums band. Barry was no fool, though – this country ballad was straight down the line, and it put the Bee Gees back on an even keel after 'Tomorrow Tomorrow'. Listening to both 'Tomorrow' and 'Don't Forget' from a distance, it becomes quite clear that they both signified the Bee Gees' future directions – country and blue-eyed soul – but, just for the moment, Robin's baroque visions would be the more commercial proposition.

The remaining Bee Gees, now two members down, resurrected their movie star plans.[13] Barry announced, to Stigwood's surprise, that he was to play the part of Claude while Maurice would be Wolf in a film adaptation of *Hair*. The long-dormant *Lord Kitchener's Little Drummer Boys* was finally dropped, with Barry

---

[13] Briefly Barry and Maurice found a replacement for Robin, a singer called Peter Mason who was introduced to them by Dave Dee. He would get to sing on one session, which included 'Don't Forget to Remember', and go clothes shopping with Barry (he still owns the suit) before Robert Stigwood blocked his joining the group.

saying: 'I thought it would be a catastrophe . . . it reminded me too much of the Beatles' *Help!*' They did finally begin filming the much-delayed *Cucumber Castle* in late 1969, with guest stars Vincent Price, Eleanor Bron, Spike Milligan and the young Andy Gibb, but then had to start from scratch after Colin Petersen was abruptly fired by Robert Stigwood. Having had the temerity to question the amount he was being paid, and then whether Stigwood's position as both manager and paymaster was ethical, he was shown the door shortly after filming began. Though he was sore, and sued Stigwood – saying that he was as much a part of the Bee Gees as Barry or Maurice – the dust would eventually settle; Colin moved into management himself, handling singer-songwriter Jonathan Kelly. And then there were two.

Stigwood relented and agreed to release Robin from the Bee Gees contract. He was now free to sign a management deal with Vic Lewis of NEMS, with former *NME* news editor Chris Hutchins becoming his day-to-day manager. Of the myriad new songs Robin recorded, the most ear-popping was the episodic 'Hudson's Fallen Wind', over twelve minutes long, about a farmer who watches a storm destroying his land and killing his livestock. It was a five-part suite, beginning with a mock-Shakespearean spoken intro ('This is a tale of a storm worse than hail!') that led into a lengthy strummed acoustic guitar section, with wheezy drum machine, Kenny Clayton's strings slowly building, and details of the farmer's mundane plans for the imminent future. A peculiar, solo synthesiser melody then came in as the farmer's day-to-day life faded into history. Supernatural blobs of sound are the calm before the literal storm, which Clayton's arrangement renders genuinely frightening. The final section is the aftermath, the death and destruction, a eulogy from Robin for the farmer: 'He sat by a table and cried in his rum . . . / The cobwebs hung heavy and dreary.' It's not really a spoiler to say that the farmer dies before the song is over. It was never going to have a happy ending.

There was often a sense of access on Bee Gees' recordings to information portals that much of '60s pop missed. Robin read a lot – probably more Asa Briggs than Tom Wolfe – and watched a lot of movies, both new and old, which would feed into his music just as fluidly as the Beatles, or the Impressions, or folk music. This was almost a proto-Bowie move – he absorbed it all, digested it lightly, and through his unique Robin Gibb filter out came idiosyncratic results such as 'Hudson's Fallen Wind'. It remains a remarkable and a very singular piece of work.

By letting go of Robin, Robert Stigwood showed that he still believed Barry to be the heart of the Bee Gees. Barry and Maurice now aimed to set up a new label. The label would be blue and white, of this at least they were certain. It might be called Lemon, though that did sound a bit like Apple, which worried them. They thought about BG, or GB, or Diamond. They settled on Gee Gee. Former Ikette and Immediate Records singer P. P. Arnold, whose 'The First Cut Is the Deepest' had been a UK top-twenty hit in 1967, recorded an album for the label in June and July 1969 – which would eventually be released, decades later, as *The Turning Tide*. They were also trying to decide what the next Bee Gees single should be, another country ballad called 'Sweetheart' or the dreamy, regretful 'If I Only Had My Mind on Something Else' (note how Robert Stigwood only seemed to be responsible for choosing the singles when they turned out to be hits). In the end, they plumped for the latter in the US and the bouncy bubblegum 'I.O.I.O.' everywhere else in the world.

Even Robin's second single had made the top twenty in Germany, something it didn't come close to doing anywhere else. Sounding like a state funeral with just one mourner in attendance, 'One Million Years' was over four minutes long, but it took that long just to get through two extraordinarily drawn-out verses and choruses. DJs must have choked at the opening line: 'I'm dead, my life's been sold. All my years are cold.' Could it have been less commercial? The number-one record in Britain at the time was the Archies' 'Sugar Sugar'. With his legal battle concluded, and Christmas less than a month away, the morbid 'One Million Years' wasn't anyone's top priority and it failed to chart at all. The perky yet still rather morose 'Weekend' on the other side ('Hello, I'm down, take me for this weekend / I'm yours to borrow tomorrow, good friend') would at least have had a better shot.

'Weekend' would turn up on *Robin's Reign*, the solo album that was completed in October and released the following January. After the myriad news stories, it was slightly disappointing, and it seems unlikely Robin would have chosen the final track listing: 'Hudson's Fallen Wind' was frustratingly reduced from its original twelve-minute length to a three-minute excerpt, and retitled 'Farmer Ferdinand Hudson'; there were no astral, orchestrated instrumentals, nor were there the promised allusions to Dickens or Shakespeare. The drum machine was still there, smothered with balalaikas on 'August October'. The standout track was the frosty 'Lord Bless All', which featured nothing but a church organ and a choir made up of multi-tracked Robins. The closing 'Most of My Life' suggested he wasn't entirely happy with his lot: 'The friends that I thought I had were never there / You look for love, but you don't know where.' Dressed in vintage military uniform on the cover, with his eyes not looking fully engaged with the camera, it was a hard sell for Polydor.

(Interestingly, it wasn't Robin but Maurice who said in a 1969 interview: 'Dressing up in period costumes does something to you. You feel like the person you're supposed to be playing. Errol Flynn admitted in his autobiography that he couldn't act. He simply found he could be convincing when he was dressed in period costumes.' Look at the covers of *Robin's Reign* and the self-titled second album by the Band, also recorded in 1969, on which they affect the look of nineteenth-century prospectors, and wonder if they weren't trying to channel a similar energy.)

By late 1969, Barry and Maurice were talking about a twelve-part TV series of *Cucumber Castle*, with different episodes set in different historical periods. They finished the accompanying album and readied it for release in the new year. If *Robin's Reign* had a peculiar, rather off-putting cover, it seemed his brothers were desperate to outdo him. *Cucumber Castle* saw them decked out in suits of armour gazing into the middle distance. The deeply silly cover hardly suited an album which, with Maurice's piano and Barry's keenness for a lush, occasionally Spector-esque production, was more fully realised than anyone might have expected. The brothers' talents were perfectly merged on the heartbreaking 'I Was the Child', an alternative take on the 'First of May' tale; 'Then You Left Me' featured a soulful rasp from Barry and a near-whispered chorus; and best of all was 'I Lay Down and Die', a thunderous blend of Mo's hammered piano, kettle drums and another magnificent Barry vocal: 'I lay down and die / The whole world joins in.' Sadly, possibly because it already included a large number of ballads, they decided against including the heart-stopping 'Every Time I See You Smile', which featured a high, emotional Maurice lead and some spoken interjections from Barry that are pathetic in the truest sense. On top of this were the two contrasting singles, Barry's rueful 'If I Only Had My Mind on Something Else' (US number fifty-two) and the cheeky 'I.O.I.O.' (UK number forty-nine but top ten in Germany, Austria, Holland and New Zealand). The flip side of both was the Euro-country sway-along 'Sweetheart', which was catchy as hell and would later give Engelbert Humperdinck a hit in 1970.

After the shenanigans of the previous twelve months, press fatigue had set in. The album was largely ignored. Reviewing it in the *UCLA Daily Bruin*, Harold Bronson wrote: 'The group is less committed on this latest release; there are no outward attempts to drag the listener into the heavy emotional text of the song.' The intensity remained, but the rich orchestral sound of *Odessa* had left with Robin. 'We wouldn't claim to be very profound thinkers,' said Barry, 'but we have always carefully considered the words of our songs, and we have put many of our deepest beliefs into them.'

With the '60s fast ebbing away, all three brothers were uncomfortable and unhappy, too proud to pick up the phone, too down to work out where they could go next. Mo was also having problems at home. He drank more. Barry smoked more. Robin took uppers and couldn't stop writing, ever wilder creations, most of which no one else would hear in his lifetime.

Barry left the Bee Gees – though there was not really any group left to leave – in December 1969, saying he was 'fed up, miserable, and completely disillusioned'. Plans for the Gee Gee record label were shelved. The hastily concocted *Best of Bee Gees* was on the album charts around the world at Christmas and appeared to be an obituary.

8

NOWHERE

Billboard US top-ten singles, 3 January 1970

1. B. J. Thomas – 'Raindrops Keep Fallin' on My Head'
2. Peter, Paul and Mary – 'Leavin' on a Jet Plane'
3. Diana Ross and the Supremes – 'Someday We'll Be Together'
4. Creedence Clearwater Revival – 'Down on the Corner' / 'Fortunate Son'
5. Steam – 'Na Na Hey Hey Kiss Him Goodbye'
6. Led Zeppelin – 'Whole Lotta Love'
7. Jackson 5 – 'I Want You Back'
8. Shocking Blue – 'Venus'
9. Neil Diamond – 'Holly Holy'
10. Bobby Sherman – 'La La La (If I Had You)'

BEE GEES

Record Mirror UK top-ten singles, 3 January 1970

1. Rolf Harris – 'Two Little Boys'
2. Kenny Rogers and the First Edition – 'Ruby, Don't Take Your Love to Town'
3. Blue Mink – 'Melting Pot'
4. Cuff Links – 'Tracy'
5. Bobbie Gentry and Glen Campbell – 'All I Have to Do Is Dream'
6. The Archies – 'Sugar Sugar'
7. Elvis Presley – 'Suspicious Minds'
8. Dave Clark Five – 'Good Old Rock and Roll'
9. Stevie Wonder – 'Yester-Me, Yester-You, Yesterday'
10. Harry J All Stars – 'The Liquidator'

'Do you know what was really strange? When the Beatles broke up, it was like so did everybody else. The Beatles had such a powerful pull on the whole culture, that even their breaking up meant that you should break up too. So that affected us as well: the Beatles have broken up, everyone wants to be an individual; everyone wants to be a pop star in their own right. So at a subconscious level, let's break up too.'

– Barry Gibb

1 January 1970, the day after the '60s. Where were the Bee Gees? They were quite visible on the UK album chart with *Best of Bee Gees*. There it was, with its mustard-coloured cover and murky image of them on a boat, somewhere in some docks. Maybe they had retreated to Southampton, and were ready to take the *Fairsea* back to sunny Australia.

In real life, the group didn't exist. The album looked like a gloomy tombstone on a career that now seemed tarnished by bitchiness and in-fighting. Like many totems of '60s British pop – the Beatles, Manfred Mann, Herman's Hermits, Freddie and the Dreamers, the Swinging Blue Jeans, Dave Dee, Dozy, Beaky, Mick & Tich – the Bee Gees broke up as the new decade began. The three brothers would independently write and record over ninety songs in 1970 but between them ended up releasing just two, the A- and B-side of Barry's solo single 'I'll Kiss Your Memory'. Robin spent the first day of the 1970s at the bijou Recorded Sound Studios near Marble Arch recording 'A Very Special Day', a dreamlike, contemplative piece that revolved around minor piano chords and an Edwardian setting, with war just around the corner: 'People danced, like in a story from Bernard Shaw.' This was subject matter he would repeatedly return to over the next few months. To lighten the mood he also cut 'Sky West and Crooked', accompanying himself on acoustic guitar and singing 'I spent years as my father's apprentice, he was a dentist in East Derbyshire.' The title was presumably taken from the rather unsettling 1966 Hayley Mills film. Robin wouldn't pause for breath. 'I wrote three songs one night in my mind,' he told *NME*.

Returning from Australia just before Christmas, Maurice had been rather surprised to hear Barry had left the group. So Maurice was now the Bee Gee. He shrugged; he had already begun recording away from Barry, with Lulu's brother Billy Lawrie, also at Recorded Sound – twins will be twins. Mo had also made merry with Lulu on ITV's Hogmanay show in Scotland, before turning up on a short-lived BBC panel show called *So You Think You Know the New Laws?* He seemed to be keeping himself busy. With a hatful of his own songs in the bag, he wasn't going to let his big brother spoil his fun; the first *NME* of 1970 revealed the country jogger 'Railroad' was to be his first solo single. But Maurice never thought the Bee Gees were really over: 'Barry was bored and said the wrong things in the wrong way,' he told *NME*. He came across much like his neighbour Ringo, similarly in denial that the Beatles had disintegrated. The two of them worked together, drowning their sorrows on the old Gene Austin standard 'Bye Bye Blackbird', which would end up on Ringo's *Sentimental Journey* album.

Lulu was busy, all the time. Maurice was kicking his heels, much of the time. In the studio with Billy Lawrie, he recorded some lovely things, including a film theme without a film, complete with ambient rain noise, called 'Journey to the Misty Mountains'; the pair's 'Give Me a Glass of Wine' was atmospheric in a different way, somehow melding Burt Bacharach and Neil Young while remaining unmistakably Gibb. Neither song would see the light of day. In February, much to his surprise, Mo found himself on stage, rehearsing for a show about music hall star Marie Lloyd. *Sing a Rude Song* was written by the wit and bon viveur Ned Sherrin, who described it as 'Stigwood's therapy for keeping Maurice interested . . . he needed to be kept with something in his mind. So I think that was the main reason for Robert's investing in it . . . it wasn't *quite* his metier.' According to Sherrin, 'Maurice was a bit lifeless on stage,' so he encouraged his co-star Barbara Windsor to 'give him one . . . brighten him up a bit. She did, but unfortunately it had no effect, it didn't get any better.' Mo didn't want Babs' saucy attention, and he didn't really want to be making a solo album. Come April he took time out from *Sing a Rude Song* to appear on *Top of the Pops* performing 'Railroad', a doleful country ballad that suggested a case of the jitters – he already had better, more adventurous stuff in the locker. Anyone who bought it and played the B-side, 'I've Come Back', would discover a tremendous mix of West Coast self-reflection ('It's hard to laugh when you know the score') and chamber-pop orchestration. But there he was, at Television Centre, singing this weary trudge of a song to an unappreciative audience while Jimmy Ruffin broke hearts with 'Farewell Is a Lonely Sound' and kind-faced Dana sat at number one singing with naïve wonder about 'sailboats and fishermen, things of the sea' on her sweet-toothed number one 'All Kinds of Everything'. On tour in Australia the following year, Mo would recall his nine weeks in *Sing a Rude Song* as 'the worst part of my life'. His solo album was set to be called *The Loner*: 'I was under a great depression at the time.'

Robin had begun work on a second solo album – which would become known as *Sing Slowly Sisters* – in early January 1970. It wouldn't be released in his lifetime – tapes and acetates of the abandoned material would circulate among fans for decades; even now, no one is quite sure which of the twenty-one solo songs he recorded in 1970 were intended for the album. February saw Robin take his solo turn on *Top of the Pops*, performing the Viennese whirl 'August October'. His studio comrades on *Top of the Pops* that day included Jethro Tull doing the freak-folk 'Witch's Promise', John Lennon roaring through 'Instant Karma' and the sparkly trouser-suited Bobbie Gentry's husky take on 'Raindrops Keep Falling on My Head', while Pan's People danced to the record at number twelve and climbing fast, the Jackson 5's 'I Want You Back'. 'August October' failed to tickle the public despite a BBC Radio 1 session for Johnnie Walker and an appearance on Granada TV's *Lift Off*, the ur-'70s pop show presented by Ayshea Brough. It staggered up to number forty-five before falling off the charts.

Years later, in a BBC Radio 4 interview with Pete Paphides for a series called *Lost Albums*, Robin would explain how it was 'important to paint pictures with songs . . . like making films with music and sound and voice and atmosphere'. Even in the Bee Gees catalogue, it's hard to think of a better example, or a more evocative song, than 'Sing Slowly Sisters'. Given the dearth of anti-First World War songs written at the time, it felt like Robin was trying to correct a historical wrong.[14] 'Here are my hands / Keep them warm for me', from the departing soldier to his girl-friend, expressing love in the most difficult circumstances, is one of the quintessential Gibb lines.

In April 1970, Robin recorded three songs intended as the scar-let centre of *Sing Slowly Sisters*. None of them featured drums or guitars. 'I think the human state is predominantly sad,' he once said, and both 'I've Been Hurt' – with its full woodwind section and cellos – and 'Irons in the Fire' are pastoral and tragic. The latter was powered by harpsichord and strings, intensely baroque: 'Oh my hair's grey / And I watch another day / Passing by the arcade of my age.' Robin seemed to be going further back in time. 'Without your voice, I'm a helpless choice,' he cried: 'Why am I still alive?' The more mistily optimistic 'Cold Be My Days' name-checked both Peel Castle and Snaefell on the Isle of Man, as well as the Warwickshire town of Shipston-on-Stour, where he, Molly and Barry had ridden horses in happier times: 'Damp be the dew on a long summer's night.' It felt like something unearthed rather than written. All three songs were deeply contemplative, ten-der, and drenched in loss and longing. 'I have had my share of shame . . . please don't share my name in vain.'

---

[14] An honourable mention here for another: the Zombies' stark and unnerv-ing 'Butcher's Tale' from 1967.

There were perkier numbers, like 'Life' ('You must be my wife – that's life!') and the country-ish 'Engines Aeroplanes', which suggested an outside influence on Robin's artistic vision. 'Everything Is How You See Me', with its *Magnificent Seven*-like opening, was an attempt at straight pop, though lines like 'She's sarcastic and she's so kind' were always going to put off White Plains, Edison Lighthouse or the Marmalade's Radio 1 fan base. This was especially true of 'Return to Austria', which, in demo form, ran to eight minutes and consisted of no more than Robin singing and playing a harmonium over his wheezing drum machine. It was darkly gripping and hypnotic. This was closer to outsider art than pop, the sound of a musician very much on the furthest edges, though the shorter finished version of 'Return to Austria' blurs its deep sadness. With its implication of the wider loss of the First World War, it was also a companion piece to both 'Sing Slowly Sisters' and 'A Very Special Day'. There were more militaristic drum rolls on 'C'est la Vie, au Revoir', which featured the bleakest lyrics of the album: 'All the trees around me ignored the sun and died / Grass and reeds around me quietly apologised.' It could have been sung to his homeland. Or to his family. His brothers. 'You made me feel like a king, where did I go wrong?' It was almost revelling in defeat.

The last brace of solo songs that Robin would record until the early '80s were both quite upbeat, and more convincing chart contenders than 'Return to Austria'. 'Anywhere I Hang My Hat' was a delight, with the odd mournful sob breaking through the bonhomie ('So anyone can come and use my phone / Anywhere I hang my hat is home') while 'Loud and Clear' was a jollier rewrite of 'I've Been Hurt', sharing its melody but losing its curtained drawing room atmosphere. Whether they were intended for the *Sing Slowly Sisters* album, or a single beyond, is open to conjecture. The *Saved by the Bell* set, released in 2015, finally allowed fans to assemble their own versions of the lost album.

So how about bored big brother Barry? He had begun his own solo work in February, but was keen to continue promoting Bee Gees material with Maurice. Indeed, he seemed to backtrack on the split almost as soon as he'd announced it. The first Barry solo single would be 'I'll Kiss Your Memory', which was so enervating it made 'Railroad' sound like 'Love Grows (Where My Rosemary Goes)'. Released in June, Barry sat by his phone waiting for the expected call from *Top of the Pops* – it never came. To rub in the indignity, Colin Petersen's new band Humpy Bong appeared a few weeks later performing 'Don't You Be Too Long'. Their singer Tim Staffell had just left a band called Smile to jump on the Humpy Bong-wagon; Smile would replace him with a market-stall trader called Freddie Bulsara and change their name to Queen. Barry may have been seething, but Humpy Bong's *TotP* victory was the definition of pyrrhic.

Like his brothers, Barry set to recording a solo album that would only be destined for the vaults. Songs for *The Kid's No Good* have aged pretty well, though it lacked any real identity. Its gospel-fed opener, 'Born', didn't pull its punches: 'I was born to be needed, born to be free / Born to be loved, born to be me.' 'One Bad Thing' was prime 1970 bubblegum, in Bobby Sherman or Pickettywitch territory, and it would go on to be covered by a bunch of people, from their old Australian pal Ronnie Burns to Irish showband the Freshmen; 'Peace in My Mind' and 'Mando Bay' similarly sounded like high-quality Tin Pan Alley songs of the early '70s, suitable for one and all, devoid of a specific Bee Gee flavour. The anti-war 'What's It All About', meanwhile, drew on Bob Dylan for its delivery, which was novel for a Gibb. The album's real high-light was the gorgeous 'The Victim', which musically drew on Burt Bacharach and didn't need much reading between the lines: 'For who can mend a broken heart / When's there's no one else around, to show me how.' The sentiment, and that line in particular, would be reclaimed a few months later on a new song, in very different circumstances.

While Barry was sat by his phone, Robin and Maurice had pondered the non-appearance of their respective solo singles on the top forty, and wondered if the albums they were working on separately, *The Loner* and *Sing Slowly Sisters*, were going to similarly fall on stony ground. They decided to see what they could do together, just the two of them, away from their big brother's influence. In semi-secrecy, Mo invited Robin along to a session at Recorded Sound on Sunday 7 June 1970 with Australian drummer Geoff Bridgford – whom they had briefly worked with in 1966 – and arranger Gerry Shury. They must have missed each other badly, as the relief was palpable on a song called 'We Can Conquer the World', slightly reminiscent of Badfinger's Beatles-esque powerpop only with added Mello-tron. It is one of the key songs, and performances, in the Bee Gee oeuvre. The chances are Mo came up with the uplifting music, with its George Harrison-like arpeggios, while Robin wrote the lyric. Like Barry's 'The Victim', it couldn't have been more heart-on-sleeve: 'When my sailing ship went out into the open sea / I hoped one day you'd be back with me,' he sang, in a soulful voice he had hardly used since 'I Can't See Nobody', back in their earliest days in London. The same session also produced two more songs, Mo's swamp rocker 'Lay It on Me' and Robin's darker 'Distant Relationship', which were good enough to convince them to get back together a couple of Sundays later;

on 21 June they recorded another five songs, three of which ('Come to the Mission', 'Bluebird', 'Whistle Me') were linked to form a suite. Almost no one has heard these songs, but archivist Andrew Sandoval describes them as 'obviously impressive, with no real counterpart in the Bee Gees' catalogue'. The next time Robin and Maurice were back in the studio, in August 1970, the tape box would read 'Bee Gees'. Their solo albums were quietly shelved. Suites of songs about the First World War and journeys to misty mountains were sidelined. Barry's *The Kid's No Good* and Maurice's *The Loner* remain unreleased more than fifty years later.

To Mo's relief, *Sing a Rude Song* closed in July after a nine-week run at London's Garrick Theatre. He then leapt straight into work on a film soundtrack. *Bloomfield* is a peculiar movie about an ageing Israeli football hero – in 1970, few outside Israel could name a single Israeli footballer, let alone one of George Best-like ability and magnetism. The only explanation for this peculiar storyline was that Israel, whose international football standing was somewhere below that of Zaire and Northern Ireland in 1970, had qualified for that summer's World Cup (they would draw 0–0 with Italy, 1–1 with Sweden, and lose 2–0 to Uruguay before flying home). Somehow the producers convinced Richard Harris to both direct and star in it, with Romy Schneider as his girlfriend. Harris contacted his drinking buddy Maurice, and he and Billy Lawrie used the title track of Mo's solo album as the gorgeously airy acoustic theme tune. Pye issued 'The Loner' on a single under the name the Bloomfields. It was considerably more enjoyable than the film.

It was also a lot lighter in mood than the legal meetings the brothers had to attend that summer. The eventual reconciliation between the three would largely arise from sitting in offices listening to legal ins and outs about the Robert Stigwood Organisation's plans to go from a privately held company to a public one. They each had their own advisers. The twins were still just twenty years old. What the hell were they doing there? Who needed this shit? It gave them an excuse to chat together about Barbara Windsor and Humpy fucking Bong and even about getting back together. Stigwood probably guessed this might happen – nobody's fool, he knew that the value of RSO's shares would be far higher with a three-piece Bee Gees back on the roster. For their part, the brothers decided it was probably easier to reunite as a trio than to figure out how to divide their stake in RSO.

This is Barry's take on what happened next:

Robert went public and RSO went public, and Robert needed us to be back together, because we were one of the assets of the company. There was no great desire in it. Not personally, I don't think so. Because there was still a lot of out-of-controlness with everybody, you know? How many groups have you seen that way? Everybody's talking about the Beach Boys . . . Robert said, 'We need to be together.' He sent Robin to see me, and – boy, and then . . . it was difficult. Yes, it was difficult. Because we weren't really communicating at all.

  On the day he came to see me, Linda and I were then living in Kensington, in a three-storey townhouse. I was halfway through a song called 'How Can You Mend a Broken Heart' when Robin walked in. And this is the truth: I said, 'Oh, sit down,' and we started talking and trying to communicate, and I said, 'Well, I'm working on this song, do you want to do it with me?' That's why

Robin sings the first verse, and I sing the second verse. Because I wasn't willing to give the whole song up, and because he wanted to be a part of it. So, I'm singing the choruses, Robin's singing the first verse, and that came about literally because that's how it happened. We did two songs. Maurice had done *Sing a Rude Song*, and so he came back. He came to Kensington, and we all talked. Robert was trying to make a film called *Lord Kitchener's Drummer Boy* [*sic*], which Spike Milligan was going to do the script for, and so this was Robert's way of bringing us back together. Do the songs for this film. We'd never done songs for a film. So this was his way of creating something which never occurred, except we got to meet Spike Milligan. Which is great for anybody.

Reuniting to get out of stuffy business meetings wasn't quite as romantic a reunion as Richard Burton and Liz Taylor passionately patching up their differences. Barry suggested he could still do solo work. Robin's manager suggested something similar. But by October they had decided to abandon all their solo projects, as well as working with outside acts. 'Besides, promoting other artists is a drag,' Barry told Australia's *Go-Set* magazine, 'as any record producer will tell you. One day they're bad tempered, the next day they've got a sore throat, and so on and so on.' Well, that told poor P. P. Arnold. Her album was also shelved.

Barry, now once again the spokesman, told the press that a reunited Bee Gees would be serving up 'simple melodic ballads put over with a lot of feeling, *à la* Roy Orbison'. It was interesting that he regarded Orbison's work as 'simple' when, to many, though it was undeniably beautiful and powerful, it also felt death-haunted, eerie and complex. Anyway, that's where they were apparently heading. Stigwood's tatty 1967 contract was pulled out of a filing cabinet; the *Sydney Morning Herald* reported that he had bought Robin's management contract back from NEMS for £50,000.

By 12 November, the Bee Gees were back together on *Top of the Pops*, as a trio once more, singing a blend of chamber-pop and soulful Americana called 'Lonely Days'. They had written it at their very first reunification writing session.[15] Barry sang, 'Where would I be without my woman?' as a statement of personal strength in a time of fraternal instability. As it had been on 'Marley Purt Drive', 'Tomorrow Tomorrow' and much of *Cucumber Castle*, his vocal was loaded with self-assurance and masculinity. Big brother would guide the errant cubs back into the pride.

Still, 'Lonely Days' was an oddly underdeveloped recording, with a gorgeous Maurice piano line allied to some very sloppy handclaps, a lyrically monotonous chorus and a full orchestral flourish that suggested something exciting was just around the corner – though it only occurred around five seconds before the song rapidly faded. In the UK, it sold a little better than their solo efforts, but *TotP*'s help still couldn't nudge it higher than number thirty-three. Fellow guests on the show that week included

---

[15] They would also go on to claim that 'How Can You Mend a Broken Heart' was written the very same day, and it may well be true, though Barry has since said he started it alone, and finished it with Robin. Why they wouldn't have also recorded that for their comeback album is a mystery. It's probably a case of misremembrance.

debutants T. Rex playing a new entry at number thirty called 'Ride a White Swan' that was part rockabilly throwback, part mystical futurism. Dave Edmunds played another '50s-derived thing, a cover of Smiley Lewis's 'I Hear You Knocking' – it was outside the top thirty, but would shoot to number one in a couple of weeks. Both were notably not 'simple, melodic ballads'.

An album would be rushed out called *2 Years On* (even though they'd only been apart as a trio for just over a year), and 'Lonely Days' was probably the best thing on it. Barry had a sweet song called 'Portrait of Louise'; Robin turned his 'Distant Relation-ship' into an elegy for his recently departed father-in-law called 'Sincere Relation'; and Mo revived his swampy soul number 'Lay It on Me'. Robin's extraordinary, autobiographical 'I'm Weeping' was the only true standout: 'My parents were poor, our house was so cold.' It anticipated the ambivalence to post-war redevelopment that would run through James Bolam and Rodney Bewes' TV show *Whatever Happened to the Likely Lads*, only with less laughs: 'Now I'm twenty-one, the street where I lived is blown up and gone.' But one song didn't make an album and *2 Years On* was quite underwhelming. 'Strange and immature,' Barry called it shortly afterwards. No one seemed that bothered about the smiling Bee Gees, together again, now apparently living in perfect harmony. Britain had moved on. Their reunion was a damp squib.

9

TRAFALGAR

US *Billboard* top ten, 30 January 1971

1. Dawn – 'Knock Three Times'
2. George Harrison – 'My Sweet Lord' / 'Isn't It a Pity'
3. Bee Gees – 'Lonely Days'
4. 5th Dimension – 'One Less Bell to Answer'
5. Lynn Anderson – 'Rose Garden'
6. King Floyd – 'Groove Me'
7. Dave Edmunds – 'I Hear You Knocking'
8. Elton John – 'Your Song'
9. The Osmonds – 'One Bad Apple'
10. Barbra Streisand – 'Stoney End'

America at the turn of 1971 was not in the same musical place as Britain. There was no bopping elf at the top of the chart, no sign of professional old fella Clive Dunn with the icky 'Grandad', nor McGuinness Flint's scrumpy-flavoured singalong 'When I'm

Dead and Gone'. While the rest of the world had heard 'Lonely Days' and turned away, the US had bought into it completely. It went to number three on *Billboard*, number one in *Cashbox*: this was the biggest American hit the Bee Gees had ever had. Maybe it really did feel like two years on, as the US had largely ignored *Odessa*, and certainly not paid any attention to 'Don't Forget to Remember', *Cucumber Castle* or *Robin's Reign*. To Americans, the Bee Gees seemed to have disappeared as teen idols and returned mature, bearded, a weightier prospect altogether.

In reality, they were still trying to find their way back home. Maurice and Barry had issued an open apology to Robin for things that had been said – but those things could not be unsaid. Much of the brothers' late '60s drama was probably related to Robin's ongoing trauma after Hither Green, but this wasn't mentioned by anyone. It also didn't help that all three brothers now had a different drug of choice – pot for Barry, uppers and downers for Robin, alcohol for Maurice – which meant that, while still being on the same fraternal plain and still being able to finish each other's sentences, they would always be slightly out of sync with each other.

What a bunch of contradictions. They thought they were a self-sufficient group, but consistently showed this was not really the case. They were grown up (Barry, once again, was now their boss) but they were still little more than children, with hardly any formal education. They thought of themselves as both inside and outside of pop; they wanted to be mentors, hit songwriters to the stars – as they had been since their days in Australia – but never fretted about their image. They were rude and tactless when talking about other groups – Mo ill-advisedly and unin-formedly had a pop at John and Yoko in 1971, complaining: 'They say power to the people but then charge enormous sums for seats at their concerts' – but would always admit they were in the Beatles' shadow.

The biggest contradiction in the group was between masculine Barry and Robin, always the gentler, more feminine presence. Sometimes Barry was visibly trying to be the leader; in the early 1970s he seemed to be channelling *The Onedin Line*, growing a beard and looking more like a sea captain than a contemporary pop star. A grown-up tick was his use of the word 'woman' in his lyrics – it had been there from the off, from 'One Minute Woman' in 1967 and 'Only One Woman' in 1968, and it would echoed by the deeply male Deep Purple in 1971 with 'Strange Kind of Woman'. But Robin would always sing 'girl' rather than 'woman'. In 1971 he was also singing 'my dearest, sincerest' like a poet of old, combining this with his ever-longer, wavier hair and his strange, effete stage presence. Maurice just played pool with Ringo and let the two of them get on with it.

Meanwhile, out in Gerrards Cross, Bucks, youngest brother Andy, thirteen years old, was finding life with his mum and dad pretty dreary. He decided to liven things up a little: 'I was moving about with my own gang, skinheads, wearing steel-toed army boots and kicking in shop windows. The main thing was football matches. You'd take a hammer into the stadium . . . we were really very nasty.' The family's peripatetic life didn't seem to be his choice: 'As far back as I can remember we always moved. We never stayed in a house more than eight or nine months . . . I never had a good day at school ever in my life.' He would be picked on by classmates for being a junior Bee Gee; in reality, he hardly saw his brothers.

The period between *Odessa* in 1969 and *Mr Natural* in 1974 would be an extended period of brotherly reconciliation, reflected in sometimes confusing, but always strangely fascinating albums. They lived out their rapprochement in their music. You can draw parallels with Fleetwood Mac's work between the loss of founder and mentor Peter Green in 1970 and the arrival of Lindsey Buckingham and Stevie Nicks in 1975. Or with Pink Floyd's albums between Syd Barrett's breakdown-led departure in 1968, after *Piper at the Gates of Dawn*, and 1973's *Dark Side of the Moon* – all were a necessary way of the bands getting over a shared trauma and slowly uncovering a way forward. The Bee Gees' albums from 1970 to 1974 found them struggling through relationship issues, addiction issues and just trying to work out what they were even there for. At every turn they would bluster, proclaiming their new album their best ever and how all their personal problems were behind them. They didn't seem to understand that we could hear the songs and tell what was going on – not in great detail, but everything was painted in darker tones than it had been before or would be again.

As ever, music was their therapy. Barry may have consistently talked about the simple ballads they wrote for the biggest audience, but no one listening to the five Bee Gees albums that emerged in this period could miss the strange remapping of their internal relationships.

2 Years On had been thrown together, patched up, too hasty – audiophiles even note how the sound pales alongside the Bee Gees records released immediately before and after. A few months after it was released, Mo described it as 'just an experiment to find out whether all of the tensions which caused the original break-up had gone, so we were all a bit wary about giving our best on that album. Gradually, the tensions and hang-ups disappeared and, as a result, the whole scene's back together again as it should be.'

With hang-ups declared gone, the Bee Gees began their first full American tour on 12 February 1971, at the Palace Theatre,

Albany. They were supported by the Staple Singers, whose unexpected assault on the American chart was just a few months away, first with the deathless 'Respect Yourself', and then the gospel funk slow-churner 'I'll Take You There' giving them a surprise number-one hit in early 1972. It seemed an unlikely pairing, but *Billboard* raved about it, calling their New York Philharmonic Hall show 'incredible . . . impeccably perfect'.

Guitarist Alan Kendall was Vince Melouney's live replacement, fresh from prog rockers Toe Fat; he never became a fully fledged Bee Gee, but would still be playing with them thirty years later. Drummer Geoff Bridgford – for unknown Gibbish reasons – did become the official fourth Bee Gee for a while, and would crop up in a bunch of photos. Maybe it was because he was Australian, like Vince and Colin, or maybe because he had a similar beard and bearing to Barry which made them look like a balanced four-piece. Either way, he temporarily left Tin Tin, the Australian band he had been working with, who were led by Nat Kipner's son Steve.[16] But there was no Alan or Geoff when the Bee Gees appeared on Johnny Carson's prestigious *Tonight* show in March 1971, as beloved entertainers, alongside George Burns and Della Reese. It was the three brothers. They wanted to make that clear. They presented a united front.

The start of 1971 also saw them working on another film and, what's more, one that actually made it to the cinema. *Melody* was a coming-of-age story set around Hammersmith and Battersea, which

---

[16] Tin Tin would enjoy a decent 1971 with a US top-twenty hit produced by Maurice, the baroque and dreamy 'Toast and Marmalade for Tea'.

were then still solidly working class, the latter riddled with photo-genic railway arches that housed auto businesses. The screenplay was written by Alan Parker, responsible a decade later for *The Wall*, soundtracked by Pink Floyd and a dark analogue to *Melody*'s spring-set joy. Both movies shared Victorian school settings but there were no jackboots in *Melody*, just sad-eyed Mark Lester mooning over cute, buck-toothed eleven-year-old Tracy Hyde while his schoolmate Jack Wilde dispensed advice (unsurprisingly sage advice, considering he was already seventeen). An absolute treat, *Melody* became a huge hit in Japan, where the soundtrack album went to number one and both 'In the Morning' and 'Melody Fair' became hit singles. For kids on the brink of teenage, *Melody* resonated. School was rubbish, girls were great, and everything felt brand new.

Before the year was out, the group would be talking of more movie projects: 'a comedy western with music called *The Bull on the Barroom Floor*' for NBC, with new boy Geoff Bridgford play-ing the sheriff, which was to be made by the production team behind *I Love Lucy*. There was also *Little Lord Fauntleroy*, another film starring Mark Lester. But these projects went the way of *Lord Kitchener's Little Drummer Boys*.

3 June 1971 saw the Bee Gees back on *Top of the Pops*. There had been a peculiarly long gap in single releases after their North America-conquering 'Lonely Days' back in January, and as they pulled up at the White City studio they must have felt confident in the new single, 'How Can You Mend a Broken Heart'.[17] It was a peach, simple and heartfelt, leaning into Crosby, Stills and (fellow Mancunian) Nash's mellow harmonies. Surely Britain was

---

[17] The gaps in their 1971 discography were partly plugged by the Dutch arm of Polydor belatedly releasing *Idea*'s 'When the Swallows Fly' as a single, while Japan released 'In the Morning' and 'Melody Fair'.

now ready for the return of their soulful balladeering? The show breezed along. Blue Mink's brassy bubblegum 'Banner Man' made light of the heavy session musician talent in their line-up. Mungo Jerry's 'Lady Rose' was a breezy jug band workout with unfeasible sideburns and too-tight tie-dyes. Tami Lynn's 'I'm Gonna Run Away from You' was five years old, but had been reissued thanks to plays in the discotheques of northern England, where demand for the mid-'60s Motown sound would remain high years after the relevant musicians had moved onto differ-ent sounds. Stevie Wonder was a case in point, and the crowd – mostly girls, mostly in hot pants – danced as he sang his hyper-optimistic take on 'We Can Work It Out' over the closing cred-its. The mournful Gibbs also had balladeering company, though. Brewer and Shipley sang the acoustic 'People Love Each Other', a song so winsome it might have floated away if it wasn't pinned down by its chorus harmonies. And Gordon Lightfoot was there too, singing 'If You Could Read My Mind', which was lyrically opaque and haunted enough – 'just like an old-time movie about a ghost from a wishing well' – to have graced the shelved *Sing Slowly Sisters*. But as an instant standard – right there, before the viewers' very eyes – 'If You Could Read My Mind' still couldn't go any higher than number thirty in a Britain besotted with Bolan and bubblegum. Neither Brewer and Shipley's nor the Bee Gees' singles even reached the top fifty.

Of course it bothered them that their homeland had moved on, and seemingly thought of the Bee Gees much as it regarded Herman's Hermits or the Tremeloes or the Searchers, as relics of the '60s. Robin took it personally. 'Look at Free,' he complained, the 'All Right Now' hitmakers having temporarily split just as their single 'My Brother Jake' was released. 'Free break up and their record goes straight to the top of the hit parade. When we broke up the whole industry sort of forgot that we existed.' To the British media the slow, messy Bee Gees disintegration, and their hurried rebuilding, felt stage-managed, and of course the Gibbs only had themselves to blame. But Robin's pain was eased by 'How Can You Mend a Broken Heart''s performance in America; a couple of months after their *Top of the Pops* appearance it outstripped even 'Lonely Days' and spent four weeks at number one, dislodging maybe 1971's most totemic American single, James Taylor's 'You've Got a Friend', in the first week of August.

Their ninth album, *Trafalgar*, would be issued in September. This was healing music. The cover, a period painting of ships with the title written on a scroll, suggested something of heft; it looked like a record for the ages. In the early '70s, this type of album cover signified something serious, or underground, like Bakerloo's solitary self-titled album on Harvest, or Fire's *The Magic Shoemaker*; these albums shared an intangible magic, gatefold sleeves, concepts, something beyond mere top-forty pop. The weight of the scroll text did not lie, *Trafalgar* was most certainly a heavy album, though not because it included Bakerloo's blues-rock guitars or Fire's poetic interludes. It was aural therapy for the brothers, and it never got above the speed of a funicular railway, slowly making its way up the steepest hill in Scarborough (and *Trafalgar* is definitely a funicular in rain-washed Scarborough, rather than Barcelona, or San Francisco). *Trafalgar*'s songs suggested constant rain noise, the browns and greys of London in 1971. Unlike the technicolour Bee Gees of the '60s, there would be no Vince or Colin to rein in the brothers' maudlin tendencies. It was all about mood. For anyone who dismisses the years between their '60s pop psychedelia and their '70s R&B pomp, the sumptuous understatement of *Trafalgar* is an essential port of call.

'A lot of people are going to think that the album has a general historical feel running through it because, apart from "Trafalgar" there are other tracks like "Waterloo", but I'm afraid that it's slightly misleading because none of them have any bearing on history at all.' There goes Barry undermining the group's work again. Just pretty ballads, is it? The Bee Gees' inability to understand their own mystique, or even what made their music special, was sometimes breathtaking.

'These boys are completely uneducated,' Stigwood rationalised in a *Rolling Stone* feature. 'They don't even know how to spell. They write lyrics spelled out phonetically. It's their poetry . . . the simple poetry of the words appeals to the public.' Robin had a more romantic, artistic way of putting it: 'It's like a spiritual thing when we write. We know what the other one is thinking, as if we had a language between us.'

The lyrics on *Trafalgar* showcased the Gibbs at their most peculiar, as violators of the English language ('Ten hundred people roam through the place I call me home'), who still somehow found a hard-to-pinpoint truth in their lyrical obscurity: 'I am the searcher of my fortunes, I've got my right hand on the wheel / We've got to dig for buried treasures.'

The *Bloomfield* soundtrack hadn't scratched their Israel itch hard enough, and they wrote a whole song about the country, a strangely unconventional thing to do in 1970. Maybe they were celebrating the ceasefire after the years-long War of Attrition with Egypt? Who knows. 'Take me into your arms,' sang Barry in his most open-hearted voice: 'Make me feel your goodness.' It's hard to work out quite what he had in mind here, though the sentiment would become more relatable a few months later, when the Munich Olympics brought the horrors of Black September.

The album was riddled with wonderful songs. 'The Greatest Man in the World' ('cos I can say I got the greatest girl') was one of Barry's finest valentines, with Bill Shepherd's string swell at the end worthy of John Barry. Mo came up trumps with 'It's Just the Way' – a touch of Lennon in the vocal, a touch of the Jimi Hendrix Experience in its feel, with a chorus based around a 'Wild Thing'-like guitar riff. Mo was striking some kind of instant '60s nostalgia zeitgeist (in 1971!), as Badfinger's Beatles/Who mash-up 'No Matter What' hit the top five, obscure Frankie Valli and Elgins and Tams reissues made the UK top twenty, and Beatles solo singles flooded the charts. Mo's title track was something else, echoing the sleeve, reaching deep into the muted, melted melancholy that made the Bee Gees so special. 'I rolled into the smoke, and there I lost my hope,' sang the protagonist on 'Trafalgar'; by the time the album comes to a close, this character was 'Walking Back to Waterloo'. There were flashes of history, a feeling of homelessness. Nothing specific, but the mood of *Trafalgar* is heavily clouded; the suggestion of feeling lost in London, or lost in general, permeates the entire album. Robin, naturally, creates the album's deepest deeps. Still singing from inside his 'One Million Years' tomb, 'Remembering' ('when you were my wife') was a very ornate thing: 'That's the way it was, now we live separately . . . / But now I feel as good as if I were dead.' 'Dearest' was a full-blown Victorian parlour ballad, closer to 'After the Ball' than 'After the Goldrush', while 'Lion in Winter' had an almost painful chorus, with Robin sounding as if he was intentionally shredding his throat in the most wildly over-emoted performance of his life – it's oddly enthralling, pulling you along with a death-march drum that dominates the minimal verses. Similarly, it's hard to credit Robin wrote 'When Do I' for himself, as the range on the vocal line is uncomfortably ambitious – again, it's fascinating, with the pristine arrangement at odds with Robin's vocal on the chorus, dropping into an octave that's beyond him. When he sings 'I wonder if I know where I fit in', he anticipates the gargled sound of the Wedding Present's David Gedge.

But it wasn't just Robin. The opening verse of Barry's 'Don't Wanna Live Inside Myself' defied airplay: 'I went walking through a graveyard, where the darkness is my friend.' The Bee Gees may have been back together, but *Trafalgar* wore its unresolved issues on its sleeve. It's one of their very best albums. It sold well in loyal Australia and the States too, thanks to 'How Can You Mend a Broken Heart'.

Heads down, they were back in the studio in the autumn to record a standalone single with a hypnotically repetitive chorus called 'My World'. Like many of their songs, you have to wonder if there was some kind of in-joke at play: 'My world is our world / And this world is your world / And your world is my world / And my world is your world is mine.' Vocals were stacked, Bill Shepherd pulled out all the stops, and both the UK and US agreed it was a number-sixteen hit. Maybe the arranger was fighting for his job, because the Gibbs had decided they would sever ties with Bill after six highly eventful years. They would record one more album in Britain, and then see what America – which in 1971 loved them a lot harder than the UK – could offer.

What had happened to Vince Melouney since he quit the group in late 1968? After losing money managing one-hit wonders Ashton, Gardner and Dyke, he had returned to Australia and put together a band called Fanny Adams. They then worked with an American singer called Donna Gaines, who had been in the German production of *Hair*, and Vince produced Gaines' minimalist funk revival of the Jaynetts' atmospheric girl group classic 'Sally Go Round the Roses'. It only came out in the UK and it wasn't a hit, but it sounded much closer to the pulse of British pop in 1971 than anything the Bee Gees recorded that year. It didn't earn Vince any more than kudos, but he had made the first great record by a future legend. Donna Gaines would marry a man called Helmuth Sommer in 1973, changing her stage name to Donna Summer. She would cross paths with the Bee Gees many times as the '70s rolled on.

Three members of the radical political group the Weather Underground – Ted Gold, Diana Oughton and Terry Robbins – had been killed in the basement of a Greenwich Village townhouse in 1970. The trio were working in their own bomb factory, and something went horribly wrong. Their immediate neighbours were Dustin Hoffman and theatre critic Mel Gussow; both of their houses were badly damaged. Gussow said the FBI report suggested that, 'had all the explosives detonated, the explosion would have leveled everything on both sides of the street'. In the days after the explosion, police combed the site of the collapsed building and found dynamite, detonators, timing devices and four completed bombs. The following year, the Bee Gees held a press conference for *Trafalgar* in New York that would be disrupted by a bomb threat. Barry told the press he wasn't scared, then cryptically added, 'Death couldn't be any worse than living.'

The Bee Gees weren't given to overt political statements; they loved music, all of it, and they just wanted to be inside it. Still, after the oddly apolitical 'Israel' in 1971, the events in New York were probably in their minds when they came up with one of their most idiosyncratic songs, one which also echoed Barry's nihilistic quote. It was called 'Paper Maché, Cabbages and Kings' and had the air of a nursery rhyme, a deceptively ghoul-ish one like 'Oranges and Lemons': 'Don't be scared / You're better off than nothing.' It ended with a calliope spinning round, ever faster, to the words 'Jimmy had a bomb and the bomb went bang / Jimmy was everywhere.' The song would appear on 1972's playful *To Whom It May Concern*.

One listen to *To Whom It May Concern*, and it was safe to assume the brothers had recorded it for themselves – they were seeking to re-establish the family, in the only way they knew how. The photo of them on the back cover was from 1963. The gatefold had a cartoon pop-up centre with all of their entourage pictured, but no one is named – which meant something to the Gibbs yet couldn't mean much to anyone else (the pop-up also excluded Vince Melouney and Colin Petersen, which seemed rather mean). They were quite self-absorbed, fully self-contained, happy to bring in family and friends as an almost commune-like musical aggregation. Swap Bill Shepherd's orchestration for fiddles and penny whistles and it could have been an Incredible String Band album. This tight-knit approach is a very appealing way of mak-ing pop music, but it can also be commercially limiting. *To Whom It May Concern* – so titled, Maurice explained in an unguarded moment, 'because we didn't know who the hell was going to buy it' – was another healing record for the brothers, much like the Beach Boys' 1968, post-breakdown album *Friends*. It cast aside *Trafalgar*'s heavy overcoat. Songs like 'Paper Maché', in spite of its lyric, were among the lightest things they had recorded in some time. It's easy to see why it has become a fan favourite – for forty minutes you can immerse yourself in Gibb World and hear the three brothers all pushing each other while still remaining comfortable in each other's presence, not caring about a specific direction, happy to be in the moment. In that respect, the album is also, like Harry Nilsson's slick, dark-humoured but always somehow light-filled *Nilsson Schmilsson*, a very 1972 record.

To Whom It May Concern also included their first UK top-ten hit in three years and one of their all-time greatest songs, 'Run to Me'. 'Now and then, you need someone older,' the brothers sang, with Robin and Mo still all of twenty-two years old. Presumably they were setting themselves against the new wave of teenage idols, notably Donny Osmond and David Cassidy, who both rose to prominence in Britain at the turn of 1972. Osmond was cute but literally a child. His voice had yet to break when he recorded his first UK number one, 'Puppy Love'. Cassidy was something rather different, with a lustrous mane of hair and a look in his eye that hinted at something a little less innocent than Donny's toothpaste smile. His breathy whisper on debut British hit 'Could It Be Forever' was not unlike a more burnished version of Barry's soft voice, the one that had melted America on the chorus of 'How Can You Mend a Broken Heart' a few months earlier. 'Run to Me' was an act of self-preservation, a twenty-something answer to Cassidy's upstart romanticism, as well as a bear hug of a song.

Recorded in early 1972, *To Whom It May Concern* tidied up odds and ends, cheerily waving goodbye to IBC Studios, and to Bill Shepherd. Geoff Bridgford also bade farewell, and drummers Chris Karon and Clem Cattini filled in. For the first time in years, it sounded like the brothers were having fun in the studio. There was room on the oboe-led 'Never Been Alone' for Robin to declare: 'I've never climbed a tree / But that's natural for me.' 'I Held a Party' ('and nobody came') nabbed its intro from John Barry's theme from *The Persuaders*, harpsichord and all: 'Maybe I drank an excess of my drink.' You can picture Robin, feet on the table, hungover on a Sunday morning, switching on the telly at 12 for Brian Walden's *Weekend World*, with its unlikely theme tune of Mountain's 'Nantucket Sleighride'.

The album certainly didn't feel in competition with 1972's touchstone albums like Rod Stewart's *Never a Dull Moment*, Don McLean's *American Pie*, David Bowie's *The Rise and Fall of Ziggy Stardust* or Stevie Wonder's *Music of My Mind*: 'Never Been Alone' could easily have slotted onto 1968's *Idea*; 'Sea of Smiling Faces', likewise, had the open-air feel and medium-wave catchiness of Barry's *Odessa* songs; 'We Lost the Road' was self-explanatory and autobiographical, with some fierce Barry soulification on the fade; while Mo's 'You Know It's for You' featured Mellotron and casual whistling, his jacket slung over his shoulder, winking to the camera. 'Please Don't Turn Out the Lights', at just under two minutes, was a perfect interlude of mournful Gibb harmony – don't forget us, they hummed; don't turn us away.

It was easy for critics to knock the album and say that it showed how out of touch the Gibbs were with the white heat of pop. This assumes they should have been competing with Bowie, Bolan and Alice Cooper – but that was never going to happen. Their balladry had a little more musically in common with contemporaneous Elton John songs like 'Slave', or 'Mona Lisas and Mad Hatters', but his 1972 album *Honky Château* would leaven its slowies with spritely things like 'Honky Cat' and the lyrically *moderne* 'Rocket Man'.

The Bee Gees shared orchestration but little else with the nascent Philly Soul of the Stylistics and the Gamble–Huff-led O'Jays. As these groups forged to the fore in 1972 with 'Betcha by Golly, Wow' and 'Back Stabbers' respectively, it would have taken remarkable prescience to recognise this was the direction in which the brothers would soon be heading. Mind you, 1972 hits by

Chicago sweet soul act the Chi-Lites – 'Have You Seen Her' and 'Oh Girl' – were very much in the same universe as 'Run to Me' and 'My World'; what's more, you could barely slide a cigarette paper between the Chi-Lites' orchestrated epic 'Coldest Days of My Life' and the darker corners of *Trafalgar*. Meanwhile, down in Memphis, Al Green had no doubts about the innate soulfulness of the Bee Gees' work. His 1972 *Let's Stay Together* album included a six-minute meditation on 'How Can You Mend a Broken Heart' that located its spirit of quiet but intense sadness: 'I can think of younger days, when living for my life / Was everything a man could want to do.' Producer Willie Mitchell stripped this back to skeletal deep soul, with help from a low churchy Hammond organ hum and a constant, cyclical guitar riff. The strings were high and haunted; there was just enough colouring for the restrained but irreverent Green to let fly. Al Green understood.

Soon enough the Bee Gees would be reconnected with R&B. For now, they waved goodbye to their London years with *To Whom It May Concern*'s oddest and arguably best song, the Moog-folk drone 'Sweet Song of Summer', which felt like 'Every Christian Lion Hearted Man' had been co-produced by Brian Eno and Joe Boyd. 'Your music comforts my lonely reign / I can hear you in evil darkness.' Behind the brothers, there was little more than funereal tom-toms and Barry's anaesthetised acoustic guitar. The melody tipped over from the melancholy into the eerie. As the last track on the album, 'Sweet Song of Summer' couldn't have found them more in flux. It had a twin in the title track of the equally unstable Pink Floyd's *Obscured by Clouds*. Floyd's career was about to turn a dramatic corner, but what about the Bee Gees? 'Yesterday is history,' went the brothers' sweet song, in perfect Ellan Vannin harmony. 'Who knows what there is gonna be?'

10

LOS ANGELES

Record Mirror UK top ten, 16 February 1973

1. Mud – 'Tiger Feet'
2. Suzi Quatro – 'Devilgate Drive'
3. Lulu – 'The Man Who Sold the World'
4. The Sweet – 'Teenage Rampage'
5. Andy Williams – 'Solitaire'
6. Cozy Powell – 'Dance with the Devil'
7. The Wombles – 'Wombling Song'
8. The Stylistics – 'Rockin' Roll Baby'
9. Diana Ross – 'All of My Life'
10. Leo Sayer – 'The Show Must Go On'

The conundrum at the heart of the Bee Gees was that they were huge pop fans; they fed off pop; they needed to know what was going on. Yet at the same time, they didn't need anyone; they were entirely self-sufficient; they could write, sing and play together and they very much had their own thing going.

So they left IBC, Bill Shepherd, everything record-wise which had been there since they first arrived in the UK, and they decided to set sail and try something new just as they had in 1967. It was all alright, the brothers told themselves. Everything was going to be okay. It was fine.

Robin was confident enough to give this as his parting shot in 1973: 'England is now far behind the rest of the world's music scene.' Take that, Aladdin Sane.

On 19 February, the Bee Gees had played at London's Festival Hall. It was their first UK show since 1968. A clue as to where the Gibbs saw themselves in the scene that year lay in their choice of support act. Colin Blunstone had been the singer with the Zombies in the '60s. He was blessed with a precise voice, creamy and choirboy-like but with a calm, cool sensuality. It was like brandy in a Hertfordshire pub, like the Chilterns made into music. It was very English. Blunstone released a brace of albums – *One Year* and *Ennismore* – which were entirely made up of ballads, with the slightest of *du jour* West Coast leanings. His cover of Denny Laine's 'Say You Don't Mind' had been a top-twenty hit the year before and it was made up of nothing but Blunstone's vocal and a string quartet – there were no drums, just tasteful cello and a dab of classy piano. 'Simple melodic ballads put over with a lot of feeling,' as Barry had put it.

The brothers had finally healed themselves. It had taken three albums since the reunion, but they were back in sync as a group and as a family. They also looked more like a group than they had in years – Robin had ditched his full Victorian garb of waistcoat and pocket watch and got on board with scoop-neck T-shirts. It suited his ever-longer wavy hair, and sat nicely alongside his brothers' more laidback look. Getting a new wardrobe was a start. Their real problem was that familial insularity had completely cut them adrift. By 1973 they didn't really have a clue what their place in the pop pantheon was beyond orchestrated ballads, and it wasn't 1971 anymore. Even Bee Gees fans needed a little grit with their oysters.

'We're a very closed-up group. To us, our music is the ulti-mate thing,' said Robin. 'We don't like outside influences and we don't believe we need them.' They were back home, they bedded in, they drew the curtains. And with no particular place to go, without really noticing, they drifted into irrelevance.

On tour and in the studio, the Gibbs remained less than totally harmonious. They were also unreliable narrators. Their former drummer Geoff Bridgford was not circumspect: 'There was an extreme amount of substance abuse, which was taking its toll on everyone in its own way.' Barry later shrugged and said, 'There wasn't anybody you knew that wasn't on some form of drugs.' Robin explained it away by saying he 'took the pills to stay up all night and make records. You had to work through the night because studio time was expensive. I never took serious drugs like LSD or cocaine – I was scared stiff of them. And I never stayed up all night for reasons of fun, it was always for work.'

In the 1920s, Hollywood scriptwriter and bon vivant Anita Loos had claimed that she never drank. Yet on every other page of her memoirs she's downing champagne like the prohibition cops were outside her door – so we can assume that champagne didn't count as drinking for her. Somehow the Bee Gees would still claim, individually, that they were clean. Many years later, contradicting drummer Dennis Bryon's stories about Linda's delicious hash brownies ('cosmic cookies' as he recalled them),

Barry would tell Alexis Petridis, 'I was married to a lady who wasn't going to have it. I could bring drugs into the house but they would end up down the toilet. She never allowed me to go in that direction. I had to deal with my brothers being pretty much out there, but I was lucky.'

They had sampled New World seduction as innocent teenagers and not been eaten alive; they had survived. They would revisit the US – to record there, to plot their future – on their own terms. On arrival, it soon turned out they didn't have a clue.

In the city of angels, the world's largest sound stage, the Bee Gees had their first musical screen test. Their Hollywood dreaming would become a 1973 concept album about a man on the run, travelling across America, by the name of Johnny Bridie. For no apparent reason the album would be called *Life in a Tin Can*. Of its mere eight songs, four were written by Barry and two by Robin, while 'Saw a New Morning' and 'My Life Has Been a Song' were joint efforts. The man-on-the-run theme may have had something to do with yet another TV series in which the brothers were meant to star – a western series, according to *NME*, based on the 1971 movie *Zachariah*. Alternatively, *Life in a Tin Can* could have been Barry retreating into a fantasy world while he watched one of his brothers sat in the corner, holding tight to a bottle, incapable of playing more than the odd piano part.

What had happened to Maurice? We know that one night before they left for the States he was dining at the Montcalm Hotel on Great Cumberland Place in London's West End. He ordered corned beef hash, off menu, which the hotel cooked especially for him. An American at a neighbouring table took offence at this for some reason, and punched Mo in the face.

We also know his marriage to Lulu was breaking down; returning from an American tour of her own, she told him that she'd had enough. Going out clubbing every night in their first year of their relationship had been fun (though Maurice could drink a whole bottle of whisky in the daytime before they set out) but it wasn't what she wanted from a marriage. And with Lulu gone, her brother Billy could no longer work with Mo as a writing partner. They'd come up with some beautiful stuff together, giving Mo his songwriting confidence back, whether it was as the Bloomfields, singing the butterflies-in-flight film theme 'The Loner', or on the tubthumping, would-be anthem 'Back to the People', cut by Australian singer Bev Harrell in 1972. But that comforting rug was suddenly pulled.

The arranger on *Life in a Tin Can* would be Johnny Pate, a veteran who had worked on Chicago soul group the Impressions' run of '60s hits. Pate was concurrently working on Isaac Hayes' soundtrack to *Shaft in Africa*; he was well connected. *Life in a Tin Can* was cut at the Record Plant in LA and Pate brought in Sneaky Pete Kleinow on pedal steel and Tommy Morgan on harmonica. The producer gave lead single 'Saw a New Morning' a full, widescreen, Hollywood production. Barry talked it up and made the album sound very much like a new morning for the Bee Gees' career: 'We've been experimenting with lots of new sounds, we've tried an entirely different approach. The best thing we've ever done, we think, and everyone who has heard it agrees.' Everyone in Los Angeles, of course, will tell you exactly what you want to hear. They lie. Barry hadn't sussed this out yet.

'Saw a New Morning' was certainly a promising opening. The Johnny Bridie character, unsurprisingly voiced by alpha male

Barry, claimed that 'sixteen people are waiting to get me'. Away from Bill Shepherd, away from London, it sounded a lot like the vision of America that the Bee Gees had expected – Hollywood, cowboys, big open spaces, lonesome lullabies with mournful harmonica accompaniment, just as they'd imagined it as kids in Chorlton and Douglas: 'I must run till my back it is breaking / Desperately I must keep on.' 'Saw a New Morning' was quite literal – Barry's bad back was giving him gyp while they made the album – but the lyric worked as a metaphor for their career trajectory as well. At the end of the song, it goes BOOM! and ominous filmic string stabs lead into the next stage of the Johnny Bridie saga. After such a technicolour opening, 'I Don't Wanna Be the One' surprisingly slowed the pace down – it was sung by Robin, and he'd gotta get a message to his girl: 'You know as well as I know, that you're my only friend.' Lyrically it didn't sound much like Robin was on board with the Johnny Bridie story-line, but it fitted. You'd have expected the feel of the album to pick up speed at this point but instead it only got slower: 'South Dakota Morning', 'Living in Chicago' ('In my life I'm together on my own / With my own private eggshell, and my phone') and 'While I Play' ('I cry tears of emotion / To spread across the USA') all meandered and sounded undercooked, in spite of the slightly demonic fiddle line on 'While I Play''s chorus. Mostly there were no harmonies, just Barry on his own.

Robin put in a travelling minstrel turn on 'My Life Has Been a Song', the album's only other truly memorable song. It sounded quite final; like Barry's 'Swan Song' from *Idea*, it came across as a rehearsal for retirement. 'My Life Has Been a Song' would be the first of a handful of Bee Gees songs that sound like weird Gibb World time travel, different sections strung together as if from different decades, some yet to come. Barry's lovely bridge part, warm and enveloping, anticipated their late '70s sound – it was as though 1966's 'Jingle Jangle' and 1979's 'Spirits (Having Flown)' had conjoined in 1973. The song's only weakness was that the same lyric is repeated in its entirety. Not twice, but three times, word for word. If you let yourself surrender to this, it becomes hypnotic, almost hymnal, with Johnny Pate's arrangement gently, very gently, building behind the vocals, until just as you expect Robin to come back in for a fourth time the whole thing drops down to Tommy Morgan's lonesome harmonica line. It wasn't remotely commercial, but it was another soft Gibb experiment.

The whole of *Life in a Tin Can* felt like an experiment, as if they were trying to create the slowest album imaginable. Beyond the spirited 'Saw a New Morning', the pace never rose above a plod. Lyrically, it possibly evoked a film too literally, based around picaresque characters, frequently set against a rainy backdrop. But as a character 'Johnny Bridie' needed to be either fleshed out, or sunk further into the canvas. Besides which, Robin seemed just to ignore him, and the script, and go his own way. The closing 'Method to My Madness' saw Robin head back to the tortured vocalising he had featured on *Trafalgar*: 'There isn't time to count the shoulders I have cried on.' Incredibly, this was released as a single in some countries.

'People in England don't value their art,' Robin told the press from the safety of Los Angeles. 'I mean, there's no other group like us. We are always original and never use other people's material.' He sounded both rude and clueless, a terrible combination. Presumably, 'other people's material' was a reference to the number of Nicky Chinn and Mike Chapman productions hogging the UK charts, giving a string of hits to the Sweet, Suzi Quatro, Mud and others. As if they could smell the air of the near future, the Gibbs were quite prepared to cut themselves adrift of Britain, with the

165

States as their new home, a country that apparently understood them far better. But now wasn't the time. America didn't get *Life in a Tin Can* any more than Britain or Germany or Australia did. It simply wasn't a commercial prospect. 'Saw a New Morning' was a fair single but even that could have benefited from a little more zip, while the rest of the album ached to be played at 45 rpm. A roughly sketched storyline had taken the place of their trademark harmonic richness, and they were yet to discover the rhythmic impetus that would transform their lives.

Life in a Tin Can would be the first album released on the RSO label. It may have only been a vanity label for Stigwood, but its strike rate during its ten-year existence would be remarkable. The company chairman was one David English, who it's fair to say had stumbled into the Gibbs' path one afternoon in 1971. 'There was a bit of a commotion in the street below,' he later told biographer David Leaf. 'I nipped downstairs to find Barry and his wife Linda standing next to a Rover saloon. "What happened here?" I enquired. "I'm not sure. It could be the battery," said Barry. "Let me see what I can do. By the way, my name is David English." Hands were shaken, laughter ensued, the battery was forgotten.' Two years later, Stigwood told English: 'You're the one. I've decided to start my own record company and you are going to make it the greatest in the world. What logo would you suggest?' English suggested the Japanese *akabeko*, a traditional wooden toy that was meant to bring good luck; the *akabeko* was a red cow, and its cartoon likeness soon featured on the beige label of *Life in a Tin Can*.

Rolling Stone noted that 'Robin's throbbing histrionics now seem at odds with the group's currently trivial and simplistic repertoire'. They found the album 'vaguely pleasant and certainly innocuous enough to fit right in with the prevalent '70s soft-rock ambience . . . But the group itself can be considered artistically moribund for the present. There's really nothing to get excited about.' And so the harmony they had worked so hard to rebuild, the lush style that had put them back at number one in the States with 'How Can You Mend a Broken Heart' and in the UK top ten with 'Run to Me', just crumbled. Artistically moribund! What an indictment.

A few short weeks after completing the recording of *Life in a Tin Can*, the Bee Gees were back in an LA studio, this time with arranger Jimmie Haskell, a man who could wrap songs in a cashmere blanket of violins or heighten a song's eeriness with a well-placed string. He had taken Bobbie Gentry's 'Ode to Billie Joe', a minimal swamp-country death ballad, and helped to make it an American number one in 1967 with a few murderous cellos and the odd swooping string line.

The Gibbs didn't ease up. Incredibly, they had recorded another entire album before *Life in a Tin Can* was even mastered – the idea seemed to be that they could release another album a matter of months later. What was this, 1964? What on earth were they thinking? Possibly the plan was to get the new RSO label off the ground with a couple of big sellers, but when the sluggish and/or meditational *Life in a Tin Can* bombed in January 1973, it suddenly seemed like a very bad idea. And not even a Japanese wooden cow could bring any luck to this lame duck.

In November 1971, Hugh and Barbara had moved from an England obsessed with hot pants and 'Hot Love' to Ibiza, which, despite being part of Franco's Spain, had become a haven for beatniks, homosexuals, artists and other outsiders unwelcome in a fascist state. Andy, aged thirteen, went with them – and this effectively meant he was out of education. 'I never got around to going back to school because I knew I wanted to be a singer,' he said in 1977 – after all, he reasoned, leaving school at thirteen hadn't done Robin or Maurice any harm. Andy began singing, 'playing the hits of the day for the tourists', at a place called Debbie's Bar. As he was underage, he was paid in beer. The brothers would fly out to Hughie and Barbara's place on holiday with their wives, and it would be the first place Maurice headed when Lulu told him their marriage was over. They would turn up and surprise punters at Debbie's Bar, harmonising, with kid brother Andy taking Robin's place. Andy was enjoying life. He was even allowed to drive around the island by his carefree parents, who after a while had the notion to set up a bar of their own.

By 1973, though, Hugh, Barbara and Andy were back on the Isle of Man, living on Alexander Drive in Douglas – Franco's bureaucracy had foiled their Ibiza beach bar plans, and scuppered their possible part in a future musical revolution. Douglas was not Ibiza. Hugh and Barbara were now running the Union Mills post office rather than a beach bar. One night, Barbara found Andy crying in his room. His long-held hope had been to prove himself as a musician and to join his brothers in the Bee Gees; he tearfully blurted out his ambition. Barbara nodded, bought him some gear of his own, and helped him to set up a band. His parents also bought him a motorbike and his own car, even though he had yet to turn sixteen. The house on Alexander Drive, which Hugh decked out with an impressive array of musical instruments and electronic gadgets, including one of the earliest video cameras, would now become a welcoming place for local musicians to drop by. Meanwhile, over in Los Angeles, Andy's older brothers kept their heads down, avoided outside influence, and ploughed their way through *A Kick in the Head Is Worth Eight in the Pants* without pause.

The first single from the new album, in June 1973, was a straightforward enough Barry ballad called 'Wouldn't I Be Someone', no better or worse than anything on *Life in a Tin Can*.[18] Again its pace was super-sluggish, but it was lifted up by Robin's cameo on the second verse: 'Midnight stars are shining on my shoeshine,' he sang abstractly, and all seemed Gibb-like once more. On the B-side was an astonishing piece called 'Elisa', which built and built, never delineating verse from chorus, climaxing with Robin in full wordless soulful wail, underpinned by nothing but baroque and beautiful strings.

Some tracks on *A Kick in the Head* were a clear continuation from *Life in a Tin Can*'s short-story Americana: Robin's 'Home Again Rivers' saw Johnny Bridie mooch to Virginia, while 'Harry's Gate', set 'somewhere on 5th Avenue', had the clock moving gradually forward – 'back in 1958', 'back in 1964' – but still sounded some way short of 1973. 'I hear some music,' sang Robin to a solo violin, 'some old-fashioned music / It's played so often in my head.' They were lost boys, trying to find somewhere to call home. There was a suggestion of modernity as a keyboard arpeggio led from 'Harry's Gate' into the chugging 'Rocky LA', one song that allowed guitarist Alan Kendall to let rip. But elsewhere dolefulness ruled. 'Castles in the Air' featured Robin's chorus yet it was notable for Barry's lost, lonely vocal above Jimmie Haskell's big arrangement and one of Mo's more minimal, affecting piano lines: 'One o'clock in the morning, I was in between the shadows . . . We're all living together and no one's going to win.'

---

[18] According to Bee Gee lore, both 'Saw a New Morning' and 'Wouldn't I Be Someone' were number-one hits in Hong Kong, but it is quite likely this was hard-to-disprove misinformation from the RSO press office.

Poor Gibbs. Outside the studio door, Los Angeles was electing its first – and, so far, only – black mayor, Tom Bradley. He defeated Sam Yorty, the incumbent, who had been in position since 1961. This was a big deal. Yorty was a Democrat, but his proper villain's pencil moustache betrayed an anti-feminist, pro-segregation stance. Yorty had hung the black district of Watts out to dry after the 1965 riots. He thought Nixon was soft on Vietnam. He thought Sunset Strip was full of commies. But now Yorty was gone, having campaigned on a portrayal of Tom Bradley as a dangerous black radical. The kids of Sunset Strip and Watts were all old enough to vote now, and were delighted to deselect him. Four hundred miles up the California coast, the openly gay Harvey Milk was running for city supervisor of San Francisco. California was now a long way from Surf City, let alone the cocooned Hollywood dreams of three strange brothers from an island with a three-legged flag. California in 1973, frankly, was not in the mood for *A Kick in the Head Is Worth Eight in the Pants*.

Nor were Atlantic Records. The album was rejected.

In the age of YouTube, we can listen to and assess this cancelled work, and we can discover with our own ears why Atlantic turned it down. It isn't as if there weren't some good songs on it. There were some real standouts, things head and shoulders above any of *Life in a Tin Can*. 'Losers and Lovers' had a strong French feel, reminiscent of singer Julien Clerc, who – coincidentally or not – was by now working with Bill Shepherd. 'It Doesn't Matter Much to Me' began with a similar plangent chord to Bowie's 'Starman', but soon revealed itself as a classic Barry–Robin dual vocal ballad. The playing is terrific; presumably it's the great LA session man Jim Keltner on drums. The song builds towards Robin's extended soulful improv, breaking into a long falsetto wail at the end.

In June 1973, topping the American chart the week 'Wouldn't I Be Someone' came out was Paul McCartney and Wings' 'My Love'; nuzzling behind it at number two was Elton John's 'Daniel'. There was nothing too cosmically different about *A Kick in the Head*'s ballads, just something intangible – a sense of purpose, maybe. Both Macca's and Elton's songs had a very '70s sensuality. The rest of the top ten dropped clues in the Gibbs' direction, like little R&B bombs – Stevie Wonder's electric piano on 'You Are the Sunshine of My Life' mirrored that on 'Daniel'; Barry White's 'I'm Gonna Love You Just a Little More' had a slo-mo drum track that wouldn't quit. Elsewhere, the Americans had succumbed to be the beautifully basic bar-chord charms of the Sweet's 'Little Willy'; a record Robin would have considered thoroughly out of touch, embarrassingly primitive, which went all the way to number five on *Billboard*. Midnight stars weren't shining on the Sweet's shoeshine, or Elton John's, or Stevie Wonder's. Nothing as muted as that. These acts wore electric boots and mohair suits.

'Wouldn't I Be Someone' died without even troubling *Billboard*'s Hot 100. There was nowhere to hide. This was a low.

In other corners of the world, Gibb siblings were just beginning to find their way around a studio. Sister Lesley in Sydney was finally captured on record – for the first and only time – duetting on an album by local club singer Ian B. MacLeod, which included a version of the *Odessa* album track 'Give Your Best'. In London, brother Andy had a few days booked at Nova Sound Studios. Maurice flew over to produce a brace of songs they had co-written: already, Andy sounded uncannily like his oldest brother. 'Windows of My World' could have easily sat on *A Kick in the Head*, and similarly would remain unreleased: 'When I woke this morning, didn't know the time of day . . . / I try to forget the fun.' Mo was kicking his heels without Lulu or her brother Billy to hang with. The other song he cut with Andy, 'My Father Is a Rebel', was a blues-rock affair and as unconvincing as the Bee Gees' forays into similar territory.

The other brothers quietly abandoned Los Angeles and slunk back to Europe after *A Kick in the Head* was rejected. Barry and Linda followed Hugh and Barbara back to the Isle of Man, where their first child, Stephen, was born in December. The family rented a semi on Bray Hill in Douglas, waiting for their new house on Princes Road to be renovated. Many of Barry's melodies apparently came to him while he was in the bath, so – possibly taking his cue from Norman Wisdom in *Follow a Star* – he had a battery-operated tape recorder fitted in his new bathroom. He would be unguarded about the couple's reasons for moving back to the tax haven island: 'The government in England raised taxes to something like 83 per cent in the pound, which was terrifying to anyone who was actually making good money.' The tax threshold only kicked in once you were already making vast sums – Barry might conceivably not have been told that by his accountant. Robin stayed on the mainland at his home in Berkshire, near Virginia Water. Newly single Maurice moved into a house that he self-deprecatingly described as a flat above a chip shop in Douglas, though, to be fair, it was decidedly modest compared to the lifestyle to which he had become accustomed. He no longer claimed to own several Rolls-Royces.

'It took five years for us to get to know one another again,' sighed Barry. 'We shut the door on everybody and said, "We like what we're doing, go away!" That did us a lot of damage.'

11

BATLEY

Billboard top ten, 5 January 1974

1. Jim Croce – 'Time in a Bottle'
2. Steve Miller Band – 'The Joker'
3. Helen Reddy – 'Leave Me Alone (Ruby Red Dress)'
4. Charlie Rich – 'The Most Beautiful Girl in the World'
5. Al Wilson – 'Show and Tell'
6. Brownsville Station – 'Smokin' in the Boys' Room'
7. Elton John – 'Goodbye Yellow Brick Road'
8. Barry White – 'Never Never Gonna Give You Up'
9. Stevie Wonder – 'Living for the City'
10. Gladys Knight and the Pips – 'I've Got to Use My Imagination'

Flash-forward now to late May 1974: Arif Mardin is sitting in his New York office, after hours, playing Duke Ellington's *Such Sweet Thunder*. The Duke is dead. His last words had been: 'Music is how I live, why I live and how I will be remembered.' Arif is looking around at the office walls – there was a signed photo of him and the Duke sat under the gold disc for Aretha Franklin's 'Respect', maybe the record Mardin was proudest of working on. 'It was like making a soup,' he would tell people. 'You know, the guitar player plays a lick and we all say, "Keep that, but do this." Aretha would go next door and rehearse the background parts with her sisters. I would write down chord changes and be the liaison between the control room and the musicians. It was incredible. The atmosphere in the studio at Atlantic on 60th Street was electric.'

Mardin, born in Istanbul in 1932 into a family of Ottoman nobles, had grown up in the Western jazz and pop tradition. He had bought his first Duke Ellington record when he was just ten years old. Even at that age, he looked for something different: 'I rejected everything old and wanted only the new.' He had initially worked on the fringes at Atlantic, mostly as an arranger. On 'Respect', in 1967, he had still only been an assistant, to Jerry Wexler, the man who had coined the phrase 'rhythm and blues'. Everywhere you looked at Atlantic, there was heavy studio talent, lots of competition. But right now, in May 1974, Mardin was considering two things: the majesty of Ellington's *Such Sweet Thunder*, and his day job. The other album sat on his desk – fresh off the press, the last one Mardin had produced – was the Bee Gees' *Mr Natural*. He sighed. Already, it was looking like a flop; the title track had gone nowhere as a single, stalling at a miserable number ninety-three. *Phonograph* magazine had called it 'spirited' and that was the extent of rock critics' interest. Mardin had to make up his mind whether to go again, try another album with these strange blue-eyed soul brothers, or write *Mr Natural* off as a failed experiment and move on. What would the Duke have done?

In April 1974 and into May, the Bee Gees had taken on a season at Batley Variety Club. The name alone was surely enough to make a sensitive soul like Robin Gibb wince: a small, nondescript industrial northern town, and a venue that, from the outside, looked more like a builders' merchants than a theatre. In reality, the club had modelled itself on Las Vegas – and why shouldn't it? It was no more far-fetched a setting than casinos in the desert. At least Batley had a railway station. The club had also recently hosted superstars from Louis Armstrong and Roy Orbison to Eartha Kitt and Shirley Bassey. Perhaps playing Batley wasn't a hip move, but when had that ever bothered the Bee Gees? The money was good, and their records weren't selling. It made sound commercial sense. Hugh Gibb and Robert Stigwood would have looked at the fees and told the boys they couldn't really say no.

When he made it back home to Berkshire that summer, Robin told his wife Molly that being on stage in Batley had made him feel physically sick. It wasn't the Yorkshire hospitality – club owner James Corrigan was so legendarily generous that the place would go bust a few years later – but the realisation that they were back where they started, playing social clubs to disinterested drinkers. Worse, the place was half full. This hadn't concerned them back in Australia, where twelve-year-old Maurice had gleefully shared dressing rooms with strippers, but by 1974 they were grown-ups, Barry and Robin with infant boys. And here they were, all these years later, once again walking across a sticky pub carpet. Just two years earlier they had sold out the Festival Hall. 'Robin always hated night-clubs because of Australia,' said Barry. 'It was like a nightmare to him . . . but there was not much else happening.' Robin had stood outside the single-storey building, with slag heaps behind it, mill chimneys belching beyond them, and announced he'd rather the Bee Gees split up than set foot inside. The major upside of the Bee Gees' dispiriting week in Batley had been that Maurice was introduced backstage to the manager of the club's steak restaurant, Yvonne Spencely. She wasn't a Bee Gees fan. She even told Maurice that she thought the show was 'disap-pointing'. She also assumed he was gay. You had to admire his persistence – by the end of their week at Batley, he had asked her to move in with him. Yvonne handed in her notice, and stayed with the group for the rest of the tour.[19]

The Bee Gees had started out as children on the stage of a cin-ema in Chorlton, south Manchester. The week in Batley would be followed by one at the Golden Garter, Wythenshawe, a vast post-war housing estate 5 miles south of Chorlton, on the outer reaches of suburban Manchester – and it must have felt to all three brothers that a fifteen-year cycle had been completed. It was both the beginning and the end. At least Batley had the beautiful moors beyond; Wythenshawe housed 70,000 people, was cut off from the city, and the most fun to be had there was going to the nearby airport to watch the planes flying away to anywhere but Manchester. At the Bee Gees' Golden Garter shows, there were sometimes as few as thirty people dotted around a room that held over a thousand. Finally, in this sad, early summer season, there was a week at the 1,300-seat Fiesta Club in Sheffield, where they

---

[19] It seemed an unlikely romantic setting, yet Roy Orbison also met his second wife while he was performing at Batley Variety Club.

followed in the footsteps of Robin's early heroes the Shadows as well as those of Glen Campbell, Lynsey de Paul, Tommy Cooper and Les Dawson. And, with the Fiesta shows out of the way, the Bee Gees abandoned the club circuit for good – a further week at a venue called Bailey's in Liverpool was cancelled.

In Wythenshawe, they played a ballad-heavy set each night, starting with 'My World' and 'Run to Me', climaxing with non-UK hit 'Lonely Days'; the closest it got to uptempo was 'Spicks and Specks' ('It is dead! It is dead!'). They played nothing from *Mr Natural*, which was new in the shops that very week. Strangely, between the doom-storm likes of 'I've Gotta Get a Message to You' and 'I Started a Joke', they had reverted to the comedy routines they had premiered in Brisbane, back when they were children. Songs about loneliness and death, plus 'Puff, the Magic Dragon' and jokes about Al Jolson – it must have come across like a high art project. Reviewing it for the *NME*, Chris Salewicz was generous, saying Robin was 'definitely the one to watch under the spotlights,' but he described the comedy as 'so super-kitsch that the audience was baffled rather than amused'.

Robert Stigwood had been nearby to give Maurice a helping hand in 1970 when he found him a role in *Sing a Rude Song*. But in 1974 Stigwood was too busy to travel to Batley, Wythenshawe or Sheffield. He suddenly had a surprise hit album on his hands with Eric Clapton's *461 Ocean Boulevard*, and he was deep into the production on *Tommy*, a filmed version of the Who's concept album – exactly the kind of enduring record that Stigwood had hoped *Odessa* would become. He was too involved in other projects to nursemaid the Bee Gees right now.

'Mr Natural' was released as a single in the UK on 29 March 1974; other new releases that week included three from fellow '60s survivors: as glam entered its terminal phase the latest monument to '50s teen dreams from Roy Wood's Wizzard was 'Rock 'n' Roll Winter'; Procol Harum's 'Nothing but the Truth' was a tremendous steam-powered thing that could have come out in 1969; while 'Side Show', a solo single by the Hollies' Allan Clarke, had a certain dark bubblegum soul energy. For the first time in years, though, the Bee Gees' single sounded well ahead of the competition. It had a groove, for starters, thanks to Dennis Bryon and Alan Kendall's interplay with Arif Mardin at the controls. 'Mr Natural' was closer to contemporary American releases picking up plays in the burgeoning San Francisco, Chicago and Brooklyn discotheques, such as the Love Unlimited Orchestra's flowery, chucka-chucka 'Love's Theme'; or the Sons of Robin Stone's 'Got to Get You Back', a dramatic Philly production. The easy shuffle of 'Mr Natural' was definitive blue-eyed soul, and it had a lyric that was hard to read as anything other than autobiographical: 'I don't feel it so much 'cause I am so out of touch / With my heart and it won't sing.'

The single came and went, only making any kind of real dent in Australia, where it peaked at number eleven. The *Mr Natural* album would follow a few weeks later. Stuck in Batley watching their tentative steps into modernity go almost entirely unnoticed, the brothers bickered and became more withdrawn.

If they felt they had lost their live audience in 1974, downgraded from playing to 60,000 in Jakarta a year earlier to the Lancs/ Yorks chicken-in-a-basket circuit, it must have been an even bigger blow in late 1973 when Atlantic told the Gibbs they could no longer be trusted to produce their own records. Having thrown *A Kick in the Head* in the bin, label boss Ahmet Ertegun had told

Robert Stigwood that he was going to impose an outside producer on them or else seriously consider dropping the Bee Gees from Atlantic's roster.

Since 1968, Arif Mardin had made a point of taking British acts and unlocking their most intimate performances: Dusty Springfield's 'Just a Little Lovin'', in fact pretty much the entirety of the *Dusty in Memphis* album; Petula Clark's atmospheric and sensuous 'Loss of Love' from 1971's *Warm and Tender*; and Lulu's intense, sobbing US hit 'Oh Me Oh My (I'm a Fool for You)', her best ever single, even though (to the shame of the United Kingdom) it had stalled on the charts at number forty-seven. Wonderful, wonderful records. Mardin had taken these singers and explored their minds. Maurice nodded and smiled ruefully when Ertegun suggested that Mardin might be able to revive and rebuild the Bee Gees' career, just as he had for Lulu after 1969's wretched 'Boom Bang-a-Bang' had threatened to send her career to Prestatyn. Or Batley.

Most significantly, an Arif Mardin-produced album called *Abandoned Luncheonette* had just come out on Atlantic. It was by Daryl Hall and John Oates, a Philadelphia pair who had worked in blue-eyed soul outfits for a few years and never got very far, leaving some great obscurities in their wake. Oates had been in a group called the Moods, whose 1970 single 'Rainmaker' had a falsetto chorus, sweeping strings, and a floor-friendly beat; Hall meanwhile had been signed to Elektra as a member of Gulliver, whose sole album skipped between doo wop revivalism and the odd lovely McCartney-esque ballad. Their debut as a duo, 1972's *Whole Oats*, had seen Mardin emphasising their soulful vocals on songs like 'Lily (Are You Happy)', but the combination still sounded like a work in progress. With *Abandoned Luncheonette* they delivered a stone classic: soft rock, folk and soul in perfect harmony with their storytelling lyrics – it was ahead of its time enough that its first single, the urban heartbreaker 'She's Gone', wouldn't become a US top-ten hit for another three years.

In time it would become apparent that at least some of the Bee Gees had no idea Mardin had even worked on *Abandoned Luncheonette*, or 'She's Gone', but collectively they certainly liked its blend of singer-songwriter moves with emergent Philly soul. The Bee Gees asked Hall and Oates to support them on their next US tour.

Initially, though, they were loudly pissed off that not only had Atlantic rejected their last album, but had also foisted this producer on them. Hadn't they shown that they could produce themselves for the past few years? Heck, hadn't 'How Can You Mend a Broken Heart' been a number one? Yes, it had, said Atlantic gently – but that was more than two years ago. Now, work with this producer or the Bee Gees will no longer have a record deal with Atlantic. What do you say now, boys?

'They were very grumpy with Arif,' according to engineer Damon Lyon-Shaw. 'He was fantastic, trying to keep them together. He was a real gentleman.' Mardin had the evidence of 'I Can't See Nobody' and 'Don't Forget to Remember', proof of their clear, long-held love of American country and soul. He knew that Etta James had covered 'Sound of Love' from *Odessa*, he was well aware of Al Green's 'How Can You Mend a Broken Heart' and Nina Simone's 'To Love Somebody'. Arif wasn't having to push them in a new direction that was alien to them. 'In fact, he did very little,' said Lyon-Shaw. 'He very tactfully guided them into this American sound, which I thought was amazing.' What Mardin suggested, kindly, politely, was that they simply listen to the radio.

They had initially gone back to their favoured IBC Studios with him in November 1973, licking their wounds after their failed studio experiments in Los Angeles. Taking on board his advice, to listen more to the sounds emerging from the States, Barry wrote

'I Can't Let You Go', whose intro bore a slight resemblance to that of Seals and Crofts' 'Summer Breeze'; beyond this, though, Barry used the song to channel one of his old-school heroes, Burt Bacharach. Straight off, 'I Can't Let You Go' was a stronger and more commercial song than anything on *Life in a Tin Can* or *A Kick in the Head*. Mardin's production and Alan Kendall's mournful guitar gave it propulsion, while Barry threw in odd changes and jumps, foreshadowing much of his work in the '80s. It's a great song. The same session also produced the try-hard 'Heavy Breathing' – maybe Arif had suggested the brothers' lyrics steer away from romance and rainfall and get a little hotter and heavier? Again this prefigured later and more overtly sexual Bee Gees lyrics – which would almost always sound slightly uncomfortable. Still, whatever the reservations Maurice and Robin had about an outside producer, something had clearly changed for the better.

Something else, though, had changed for the worse. Maurice's drinking had become so bad that he was no longer entrusted with playing keyboards. Those lovely rich piano chords which graced everything from 'Words' to 'My Life Has Been a Song' were gone, and substitute Geoff Westley came in to help out. At least Mo was still on bass. There was another new player on all these recordings: former Amen Corner drummer Dennis Bryon had been a flatmate of Alan Kendall's, and he would remain with the Bee Gees until 1980.

Bryon's memoir, *You Should Be Dancing*, reveals what a warm place the Bee Gees' extended family was, even at this tense time. His audition took place at Barry's new home in Berkshire. Alan Kendall met him and led him into the kitchen where Linda was cooking bacon and eggs as her parents offered Dennis tea and biscuits. 'The vibe in the kitchen was beautiful; fun and affection were everywhere.' Linda's dad George seemed to be on permanent tea-making duty. 'I immediately noticed how close the brothers were. They seemed to read each other's minds, finishing off each other's sentences. All they had to do was look at each other and they knew exactly what the others were thinking . . . We walked past a full-size snooker table and I noticed all the walls were blanketed with gold discs and awards. Every flat surface had a prize or trophy on it.' When they began to play together, Maurice cheekily suggested they do Amen Corner's 1968 hit 'Bend Me Shape Me'. 'Maurice, *please* be serious,' Barry sighed. He then politely asked Dennis if he was familiar with any of their songs: 'How about "I've Gotta Get a Message to You". Do you know that one? Have you heard it?' Dennis Bryon said yes, trying not to sound facetious. And so it went on. 'Do you know a song called "Words"?' They played for no more than fifteen minutes, then Barry said, 'Right, let's go and have a cuppa tea.' The next day, Dennis called Dick Ashby at RSO. Yes, he'd got the job. The audition had been as much about his sense of humour as his drumming, but he would play a crucial part in the band over the next few years. Maurice called him Den Den.

As the Bee Gees recorded at IBC that December, Britain was about to enter the 'three-day week', when an energy crisis and ongoing industrial disputes forced the government to restrict the opening of factories and other workplaces: it would be Britain's greatest modern domestic crisis until the 2010s. Television broadcasting restrictions were introduced on 17 December 1973, with all channels closing down at 10.30. Three days later, the Bee Gees recorded 'Charade'.

The absolute bleakness of life outside the studio doors, with the threat of the power being cut at any moment, fed into the total dreamstate of 'Charade'. At Arif Mardin's instigation, there was a clarinet solo from jazz player Phil Bodner, a veteran of outfits led by Miles Davis and Gil Evans, and more recently Hugo Montenegro. The intrusion was as surprising as the saxophone punctuating *Idea*'s 'Down to Earth' had been back in 1968. The Fender Rhodes electric piano shimmer of 'Charade''s intro says 'welcome to our world'. The production is entirely aqueous. Barry gives one of his most seductive performances, embracing the 'music the ocean was playing', before Robin comes in on the chorus and suddenly the meaning of the lyric is revealed: 'And this feeling, knowing you've left me forever.' The whole situation, the whole song is revealed as an illusion. Possibly the line is 'blessed me forever' – but what is a charade, after all? Who is falling for it? The setting is almost comically idyllic, highlighted by the clarinet solo, like a Jazz Age scene in the Hamptons. We picture Barry sat on the beach with a Manhattan in his hand, watching the girl remove her top and walk into the ocean for a moonlight swim. Much of the song's atmosphere would be retained four years later, for possibly their best-loved single, 'How Deep Is Your Love'. Barry Manilow would later claim 'Charade' as one of the Gibbs' very best. But for now, it would miss out on every chart on earth except *Billboard*'s Easy Listening chart – where, thanks to radio play on the more undemanding stations, it reached number thirty-one.

Commercially, *Mr Natural* would be the Bee Gees' worst international seller to date, and the biggest flop of their career, peaking at number 178 on the *Billboard* album chart. If it hadn't been for Arif Mardin's faith in their talent, then it's very likely they'd have been let go by Ahmet Ertegun and Atlantic. But artistically it's one of their key records, the connection between their early success and their supernova phase.

'Throw a Penny' in particular blended the now (Fender Rhodes piano, whispered Barry verse, full-blooded catchy chorus) with the ghost of Bee Gees past. Robin's spectral voice broke the song down into a ballad form halfway through, as if he was heard at the end of some Victorian telephone line, a very real bridge between what they were leaving behind and where they were going. Released as the album's second single, 'Throw a Penny' would be their absolute commercial nadir. It made no charts at all, anywhere in the world, except Canada, where it squeaked in at number ninety-one (granted, many countries didn't even bother releasing it, including Britain).

'Voices' was another song that showed the brothers in fascinating flux. After the first minute, it audibly broke out of its early '70s straitjacket (and curious finger-in-the-ear folk 'doo dah day' backing vocals) as mysterious voices called the Gibbs, beckoning, luring Robin into a rather frightening-sounding, unknown future: 'But in my bed again last night, those voices spoke of wrong and right / They spoke of fire and falling rain, of health and wealth and death and pain.' The song built into a full-on singalong, with wordless harmonies tumbling over themselves.

Not every track was a winner: 'Give a Hand, Take a Hand' sounded like a well-meaning message song from *Sesame Street*; 'Lost in Your Love', with Barry in boss brother mode, was a manly soul ballad without much depth; 'Heavy Breathing' pointed another way forward with its wah-wah guitar and brassy funk undertow, but it lacked charm and somehow its groove was a little lumpy.[20] Dennis

---

[20] It is rumoured on some fan sites that they played 'Heavy Breathing' live in Batley, but given the ballad-heavy Wythenshawe set we know about a week later, this seems like wishful thinking.

Bryon would soon get that side of the group together. Though it had another suggestive title, 'Had a Lot of Love Last Night' was sung by someone who had frittered it away by the following day. The harmonies were exquisite, and Arif Mardin's spare strings added just the right amount of pathos: 'I always used to think that I was better than my kind . . . / Who will cry this time?'

'Dogs', meanwhile, was classic Gibb weirdness and another album highlight. The lyric appears to be about, well, dogs. Beyond that, it seemed to be a plea for togetherness, though with hard-to-read lines like 'I was hungry and I was cold, had a father far too old' and 'It was a quarter to three in the summer of '73'. The tune, though, was a real killer, brimming with confidence and riding its powerful, filmic string arrangement. The lyric also spookily pre-empted their miserable Yorkshire spring of '74, with a line about going to a nightclub in the town to get some bread. And there's a very significant Bee Gees moment at the bridge. As Barry sings, 'Well, the days get shorter', he does so in an octave above his usual range. It may be a little way down in the mix, but that is Barry Gibb's falsetto, and we'd soon be hearing quite a lot more of it.

The Bee Gees were not pictured anywhere on the album cover. The front and back showed an old guy sat in a bar, carefree and presumably half-cut on the front, and being booted out of the establishment on the back. The brothers actually looked pretty good, and pretty together, at this point – Robin had given up on both his high-Victorian and scoop-neck looks, and was now going through a roll-neck phase, while Mo had a sleepy look, as if he was Mr Natural himself. Some have proposed that Atlantic wanted to hide the fact that they were white Englishmen, though the name was probably a strong enough clue. More likely, their faces just didn't sell records anymore and anonymity was a safer bet.

In the outside world of May 1974, Paul McCartney and Wings were in both the UK and US top tens with 'Jet', a joyous rocker with nods to reggae, fizzing synth lines, a daffy, impenetrable lyric and energy to spare. This was McCartney's belated response to terrace-chant glam; it was also a ten out of ten. Maybe if they'd kept Vince and Colin on board, the Bee Gees could have pulled off something similar, but by now they had drifted a long way from rock. The soundtracks to nostalgic hit movies *American Graffiti* and *That'll Be the Day* leaked into contemporary pop: in France, singer-songwriter Michel Polnareff embraced bubblegum doo wop novelty with 'Tibili'; in the UK, the Rubettes scored a monumental hit with '50s throwback 'Sugar Baby Love', an exercise in pure pop to rival the Archies' 'Sugar Sugar'; and internationally Ringo Starr had a huge hit covering Johnny Burnette's 1960 teen jiver 'You're Sixteen', all ribbons and curls. Elsewhere, the American top ten featured such aerated delights as Joni Mitchell's 'Help Me' and Maria Muldaur's 'Midnight at the Oasis'. The top three was made up of Scott Joplin's 'The Entertainer', the theme from *The Sting*, at three; the Jackson 5's ahead-of-the-disco-game 'Dancing Machine' at two; and Ray Stevens' 'The Streak' at number one ('Don't look, Ethel!'). The Bee Gees may have been cocking an ear to the radio, but they weren't yet listening closely enough. Everywhere, there was lightness.

But Mardin believed in the brothers. He knew that he could take them a significant step further, and told Atlantic that he wanted to work with them some more. Robert Stigwood pencilled in sessions early in 1975. The brothers decided they were gelling as a group on stage and wanted to bring that sound and feeling into the studio. Dennis Bryon suggested adding keyboard player Blue Weaver, who had played with him in Amen Corner;

he could replace their reliance on string players, and modernise their sound into the bargain. Blue Weaver would be the final piece in the jigsaw, though no one knew it – no one had a clue what was coming next.

★

At the start of 1975, the Bee Gees flew to Miami Beach to work with Mardin at Criteria Studios, which had been nicknamed 'Atlantic South'. The timing couldn't have been better. Musically, Miami was having a moment. A few months earlier, soul singer Gwen 'Rockin' Chair' McCrae had been recording at the city's TK Studios. When her husband George came to pick her up, writer-producers Harry 'KC' Casey and Rick Finch played him an instrumental which was pitched a little too high for Casey's voice – did George fancy giving it a try? Happily for everyone, George McCrae had a spare hour or two. Within days, the reaction to 'Rock Your Baby' from Miami DJs meant that it felt like the roof of TK Studios had blown clean off; within weeks the whole of America was demanding to hear it; and by late summer 1974 it was an international number one. 'Rock Your Baby' would be followed by KC and the Sunshine Band's string of top-ten hits – 'Queen of Clubs', 'Sound Your Funky Horn', 'Get Down Tonight', 'That's the Way (I Like It)' – and by 1975 the Miami Sound was everywhere.

Criteria had been built in 1958, and until Atlantic started to book it regularly in the late '60s it had been mostly used for TV and film work. A host of modern classics were recorded there: Brook Benton's 'Rainy Night in Georgia', Aretha Franklin's 'Day Dreaming', Stephen Stills' 'Love the One You're With'. The Allman Brothers cut *Eat a Peach* there, which led to their pal, the Robert Stigwood-managed Eric Clapton, recording there and staying in a deco house at 461 Ocean Boulevard. Which led in turn to Stigwood's other charges taking up residence in the same rented house. Fans would knock on the door, Maurice remembered, asking, 'Can Eric come out to play?'

If Batley and Wythenshawe had reminded them of the grittier, grimmer, beer-drenched aspects of life in Australia, not to mention their hand-to-mouth childhood in Manchester, then Criteria's beachside location reminded them of their late '50s relocation to Surfers Paradise. It was as if someone had opened a window – of *course* this was where they should be recording. They loved Miami so much that Barry, Robin and Maurice all bought houses there in 1976 and would go on to build their own recording studio, Middle Ear, in Miami Beach in 1980.

The team that went on to make the enduring late '70s Bee Gees records would solidify as soon as they arrived at Criteria: the brothers, Blue Weaver, Alan Kendall and Dennis Bryon. Along with Arif Mardin, there was Criteria's engineer Karl Richardson. In some respects, the slimmed-down line-up – no string section – was a cost-cutting exercise, but Bryon and Clapton had both separately suggested to Barry that a tauter band was the way forward. For a solid six years this line-up would be subtracted from, but never added to. Blue Weaver, in particular, was a strong new influence on the group, even earning himself rare non-Gibb writing credits on a handful of Bee Gees songs.

Still, old habits were hard to break. On 6 January 1975, the Bee Gees recorded the first song for the Miami sessions, a slowie called 'Was It All in Vain', which Blue recalled as having the dummy lyric 'as I gaze into my can of beer'. He also remembered them having a crack at the Marbles' 1968 hit 'Only One Woman', with Barry singing his own song for the first time. On day two, they wrote 'Country Lanes', a very early '70s-sounding Robin ballad. On day three came 'Wind of Change'. And on day four, 'Your Love Will Save the World', one of the earliest tracks they recorded for what would become the *Main Course* album.

There was a theory for a while that the Beach Boys' critical re-evaluation in the 1970s was entirely built on music that almost no one (at the time) had ever heard. The Bee Gees have put out enough classic music over the years that their reputation doesn't simply rest on unheard archive material – but there is nevertheless a whole hidden parallel career in there. 'Your Love Will Save the World' is just such a lost gem. The story is that Robert Stigwood heard the songs from this session and urged them to start again, concentrating on the R&B direction that had been artistically (if not commercially) fruitful on *Mr Natural*. But 'Your Love Will Save the World' is beautiful, heartfelt R&B – okay, it's not uptempo, but it's definitely R&B – with fabulous interplay between Robin and Barry, giving it their all. The lyric is one to hold onto in the darkness. Alan Kendall's single-note hook at the end of each chorus lifts it further heavenwards. It's a tearfully good song, and performance, and the fact they got talked out of releasing it is a great sadness.

Stigwood, though, didn't just want something tearfully good – he wanted a guaranteed hit. You couldn't blame him. Robin remembered how 'Ahmet [Ertegun] was so quick to turn off to us, to say "This is it?" We thought they weren't even going to give us a chance. They were burying us. Only Arif kept faith in us . . . He said, "Don't hide what you love, don't try to do things you think people will love, do what you love . . . stay true to yourself, and the rest will take care of itself." And he was right.' Maurice described him as 'a producer and a referee', who persuaded Atlantic to be patient. As it turned out, Mardin's faith was thoroughly justified – they wouldn't be short of inspiration.

These same initial sessions had also provided a rough draft of 'Wind of Change'. This was a robust enough song for Dennis Bryon to add a drum pattern that drew on Barry White's 'Never Never Gonna Give You Up' – those years he'd spent marinating in Amen Corner's white Welsh soul were being put to good use: 'The first one where we all realised that we'd hit on something that was going to develop was "Wind of Change". I knew that we were going to come away with a hit album no matter what – I mean, we all did . . . As soon as the new thing started to happen, the pressure was off.'

Ertegun and Stigwood remained unimpressed, but Arif Mardin's faith was unshakeable. He continually reminded the brothers: '"Look at what's happening now, rather than what's happening to you. Your minds seem to be stuck in one place" . . . We decided to change a little bit. I suggested they listen to current R&B artists who had hit records, like Stevie Wonder.' They were fans, first and foremost, and – like all the greats – magpies of the first order; it made no sense for them to exist in splendid isolation, no matter how cosy it had made them feel. They now listened to the local Miami radio station solidly. They were in the right place at the right time, and once they heard contemporary records that struck a chord, they were inspired just as they had been in Manchester, Brisbane and London. Mardin hadn't imagined his covert wizardry would ever work quite this well: 'It became like something out of a movie, with everybody being incredibly creative and dynamic.'

Ten days after the session that Stigwood rejected, they were back in the studio recording 'Nights on Broadway'. Originally it was called 'Lights on Broadway'. Mardin suggested the subtle but significant lyrical change, which moved the scenario deeper into the evening: 'Here we are in a room full of strangers / Standing in the dark where your eyes couldn't see me.' A bleak tale of being an eternal plus-one, tagged onto someone else's dream, lost and lonely in New York, it was a terrific song and their confidence was running high when Arif said, 'I think we need more energy.' He then asked Barry: 'Can you scream? Can you scream in tune?'

Mardin doesn't remember saying that, but the Gibbs did. He was shy of taking any credit for this dramatic shift in their vocal style. 'I didn't say, "Hey, sing falsetto, I'd like to invent this sound for you,"' he told writer Tom Cox in 2004. 'But there was a melody in one of the songs and I said, "Can you take it up an octave, please?" And Barry said, "If I take it up an octave and shout like an opera singer, I'll sound like a fool." He sang it in that voice and the brothers and everyone were saying, "That's great, that's great, keep that." So that's how it came about. I just said, "Kick it up an octave."'

In truth, all three had been experimenting with falsettos way before 'Nights on Broadway': Robin had added a falsetto ending to 'It Doesn't Matter Much to Me' on the unreleased *A Kick in the Head*; Barry had given us a smidgen on *Mr Natural*'s 'Had a Lot of Love Last Night'. There was also a story that Arif had heard them messing about in the studio doing impressions of the Stylistics' singer Russell Thompkins Jr, and that this inspired him to add a touch of primary colour and energy. However it came about, it worked.

Falsetto singing in pop had always meant heightened excitement. In the Gibbs' childhood there had been Del Shannon's 'Runaway', an international number one in 1961, built around the twin hooks of Shannon's otherworldly 'Wah-wah-wah-wah-wonder' and the space-age, proto-synth Musitron solo played by Max Crook. Jan and Dean's 'Surf City', written by Beach Boy Brian Wilson, screamed 'two girls for every boy' to horny teenagers in 1963, and that promise helped it to number one in America and Australia. Also in 1963, Frankie Valli and the Four Seasons scored a third US number one with the extraordinary 'Walk Like a Man', with a lyric that would seep into Barry Gibb's subconscious. Valli's voice was so otherworldly that from 1964 onwards the Four Seasons' record labels, on hits like 'Rag Doll' and 'Let's Hang On', were credited to the Four Seasons featuring the 'sound' of Frankie Valli. Not the voice, the *sound*. And those quote marks aren't mine – they're on the label. Valli's fire siren falsetto sounded almost inhuman. These were not songs you would try to sing in the shower. But if one record bottled the essence of falsetto power, it was 'Lightning Strikes' by Pittsburgh singer Lou Christie, a US number one in 1966, the year the Bee Gees had cut 'Spicks and Specks' – the anticipation, the release, the sheer simple joy of pop noise is defined by Christie on that chorus.

'I've never had reservations about using it,' said Barry in 1998. 'When I look back, it's something I ought to be proud of. Brian Wilson, Frankie Valli and even Prince – they don't make any bones about doing that. The first rock 'n' roll record I ever heard was "Little Darlin'" by the Diamonds, and that was falsetto. I think falsetto has been an integral part of rock 'n' roll. I think it's nice to be one of those falsetto voices that's quite well known.'

It wasn't just the range of his voice that now surprised Barry. His new-found power really shook him. When he had gone for power before he had always switched to his 'soul' voice, a chest voice rather than a head voice, and one clearly borrowed from his heroes, with the twitches and signifiers, the 'got-ta got-ta' vision of soul exemplified by Otis Redding in the mid-'60s. Barry would employ this style on his most leonine songs; *Idea*'s 'When the Swallows Fly', or *Mr Natural*'s 'Give a Hand, Take a Hand'. It signified old-school, alpha-male masculinity.

But now he discovered he had a way more powerful voice, right up there, that signified something much more ambiguous. Though he would continue to write lyrics that suited his old soul voice, he would now be singing lines like 'You can tell by the way I use my walk I'm a woman's man, no time to talk' in falsetto. His voice sounded fluid, more effortless, and he seemed capable of holding notes longer (try singing the long, descending, final syllable on the chorus of 'Stayin' Alive': it is nigh on impossible). His voice was now *louder*. It cut like a laser through any obstacle in its way. Of the new 1975 songs, it was the midtempo 'Fanny (Be Tender with My Love)' that contained all the proof Barry, or anyone else, needed. It was a sound that stopped you in your tracks.

The most commercially significant song on *Main Course* had no falsetto. Alan Kendall started 'Jive Talkin'' with a precisely clipped rhythm guitar, based on the sound car wheels made driving over a nearby road bridge; the song simply wouldn't have existed had they recorded *Main Course* anywhere else. Next, Blue Weaver played a way-down-there ARP bassline. It sounded intriguing – so Mo doubled it up on bass guitar and it sounded better still. The lyric was also an accident. Barry's initial lyric was about dancing; Arif gently explained that jive talking had nothing to do with jiving. It was slang for 'bullshitting', and so the song took a new direction. On such happenstance, some of the greatest pop records are built. 'Jive Talkin'' was a pure groove. The (mostly Welsh) rhythm section had done them proud – and when Barry's understated, feathery vocal was added, they knew they had something special. 'Our dream is not to be the best group of the '60s, but the best group of tomorrow,' said Robin. With Arif, Dennis and Blue in the extended family, they'd given themselves a real chance.

There would be fibs about the single – or at least myths that built around it, some of which still get repeated. First, the brothers claimed the label didn't want to release 'Jive Talkin'' as a single, but once Stigwood had sent promos out and the response was so strong they had no choice. It's a most peculiar fib, as Stigwood was clearly the head of RSO Records, so it's unclear who the 'they' in this story is meant to be. Second, all of the promo singles contain complete artist and title information – no copies of 'Jive Talkin'' were sent to radio stations with a blank artist credit to fool prejudiced DJs. If such a single exists, no copy has yet to surface. A similar tale had been spun in 1967 about 'New York Mining Disaster 1941', and no blank-label 45s of that have ever shown up either. It's quite likely that the brothers are repeating these tales in good faith – they are great Robert Stigwood stories, the tallest tales for the biggest impact, but there is no documentary evidence to back them up. Still, the Bee Gees were nothing if not pop conscious – you can understand why everyone prefers the myth.

The usually supportive *Billboard* was not taken with 'Jive Talkin''. It appeared on a list of 'recommended singles' in its 10 May 1975 issue, which suggested it thought the record would end up shy of the top twenty. It didn't even bother with a review.

On 31 May, 'Jive Talkin'' entered the *Billboard* Hot 100 at number eighty-seven. If that had been it, even if it had dropped off after one solitary week on the chart, then it would already have been the Bee Gees' biggest US hit in two and a half years. But instead it kept climbing; by August it was number one.

★

'Working with Arif was like a dream come true,' said Dennis Bryon. 'He had the ability to bring out the best in everybody. Not once did he ever tell me, or even try to tell me, what to play. He wanted to know what I thought the drum part should be.' It might not have felt like Arif was suggesting what anyone should play, but with the band tied down in Miami, away from one-night stands or other distractions, he only needed them to concentrate and he could subtly nudge them, moulding the sound without them even noticing. Maurice, like Dennis, would play Arif his basslines which then got gently squeezed into a *Main Course* shape.

Released in the States in June 1975, *Main Course* was, according to *Rolling Stone*, 'genuinely exciting' and 'the best-sounding Bee Gees album ever ... due to Arif Mardin's spectacular production.' The review suggested it also represented 'a last-ditch effort to reestablish the group's mass popularity' and they weren't wrong on any of those counts. 'Edge of the Universe' was dismissed as 'dumb psychedelia' and 'Come On Over' as 'characteristically sugary' – but neither was a single and, frankly, the brothers were wise to concentrate on positivity at this juncture.

Then there was 'Fanny (Be Tender with My Love)' and its 'spacious arrangement'. In a 2001 *Billboard* magazine interview, Barry remembered: 'We had a lovely housecleaner named Fanny when we stayed at 461 Ocean Boulevard during the making of *Main Course*. We were sitting in the lounge at Criteria writing the song with the lyric idea, "be tender with my love". Maurice turned around and saw Fanny and said, "Wouldn't it be a better song if it was a woman's name in there, and you're asking her to be tender? Fanny!" So full credit to Maurice.' In the same interview, Maurice Gibb added, 'We all love that one, but it's just a bitch to sing.' The interweaving falsetto and natural harmonies of 'Fanny' would become the Bee Gees' trademark sound for the next few years, culminating with 1979's *Spirits Having Flown*. It was also notable for Mo's melodic bassline – what a bassline! – and the double key change towards the end, suggested by Blue. 'The key change in "Fanny (Be Tender)" was a complete rip-off from *Abandoned Luncheonette*,' he later admitted, rather red-faced. 'From "She's Gone". I only had it on tape, and I didn't know that Arif had produced it.' After 'Jive Talkin'' and 'Nights on Broadway', 'Fanny' gave them a third US top-twenty hit as 1975 turned into the bicentennial year of 1976. In Britain it bombed as a single, presumably because many potential customers were too embarrassed to say the word 'fanny' out loud, let alone 'fanny, be tender'. If they'd called it 'Annie (Be Tender with My Love)', it would probably have been top ten.

One of the standout tracks was 'Wind of Change'; it was decidedly urban, an acknowledgment of life going wrong, of people losing hope, of broken dreams. It was also an acknowledgement that the Bee Gees had needed outside help. Heck, the whole world needed some good advice in power-cut-riddled, last-flight-out-of-Saigon 1974: 'Do you understand what I'm sayin'? / We need a god down here / A man to lead us children, take us from the valley of fear.' Arif Mardin may have been the 'god' in this instance – they had admired him, no question – but while recording *Mr Natural* they had also still felt that they needed no one else, that the Gibb brothers alone should be the architects of their own destiny. But Batley had beaten them. They had accepted they were onto a good thing with Arif, even if *Mr Natural*'s sales had been negligible. By the time *Main Course* was released, they couldn't operate without him.

Main Course was a front-loaded album, with Side One including all three singles, plus 'Wind of Change' and 'Songbird', a ballad co-written by Blue, with Barry's topline and lyric ('You'll never really know how beautiful you are') and a melodic suggestion of the Osmonds' recent hit 'Love Me for a Reason'. Arif Mardin took the early '70s Bee Gees ballad style and gave it some solidity, some relevance. Dennis Bryon's in-the-pocket timekeeping also lifted the brothers' songs, pushed them onto the dancefloor. The soulfulness had always been there – in Robin's voice, as well as in their taste for R&B – but now it sounded confident, and it was striving for classic status.

Side Two provided very little of the R&B that people remember *Main Course* for, but that doesn't mean there aren't delights to be found. There were Robin's piano-led pair 'Country Lanes' and 'Come On Over', the latter quickly covered by Olivia Newton-John; 'Edge of the Universe' took Blue's synth lines and weaved an FM yacht rocker around them; and 'Baby As You Turn Away' once again anticipated their 1980s sound, with its skipping metre and Barry's falsetto, while the chorus was more like a mid-'70s Denmark Street concoction. It could have been written for Dana or David Soul, and, if they'd stayed at IBC producing their own records, maybe it would have been. Instead, the Miami effect made it sound like a soundtrack to sundown in the Keys.

The second side opened with a true curveball, the album's most peculiar track. 'All This Making Love' was thoroughly Beatles-esque, creating an imagined '70s Beatle world where Lennon tore chunks from Paul McCartney's 'Monkberry Moon Delight', with lyrical cues taken from Eddie Cochran's 'Twenty Flight Rock'. The unlikely problem here was too much sex: 'And I can't keep still, gonna make a will, 'cause

I'm losing all my hair . . . / But I'm all right, I'm really fine.' It suited the brothers – in a *Confessions* or *Carry On* way – to make comical sex songs.[21]

Many of the tracks on *Main Course* – notably 'Songbird', 'Country Lanes' and 'All This Making Love' – could have featured on earlier albums. The real difference was the tangible positivity, the sense of a future for the Bee Gees, and that was down to Arif Mardin. Maurice must have been thrilled that his long-time love of synthesisers now made him seem ahead of the game – they were all over *Main Course* – and the brothers realised they could move on from their full orchestral sound without necessarily losing the lushness of their ballads.

The thoroughly modest Mardin was clearly proud of *Main Course*.[22] 'You know, I was blessed to have worked with incredible artists,' he told Tom Cox. 'Sound is not that important if you work with Donny Hathaway or the Bee Gees. They're just incredible singers and they inspire you. With the Bee Gees, when we were doing the *Main Course* album in the mid-'70s, there was a total stream of creativity in the studio, everybody excited. We were using state-of-the-art machinery then, the ARP 2600 synthesizer – we created so much modern stuff at that time.'

With *Main Course*, the Bee Gees had rejoined the modern world.

---

[21] In 1975, they weren't the only group to borrow from the Beatles to move music forward – one of the biggest discotheque hits of the year was Roxy Music's 'Love Is the Drug', an aural rendition of pulling in a sweaty club that ended with a cascade of vocals directly taken from the Beatles' 'She Loves You'.

[22] Remarkably, Mardin had been multi-tasking. He was producing Scottish soul boys the Average White Band's *Cut the Cake* in one studio at Criteria as he mixed *Main Course* in another.

12

MIAMI

Billboard top ten, 4 September 1976

1. Bee Gees – 'You Should Be Dancing'
2. Lou Rawls – 'You'll Never Find Another Love Like Mine'
3. Wings – 'Let 'Em In'
4. England Dan and John Ford Coley – 'I'd Really Love to See You Tonight'
5. KC and the Sunshine Band – '(Shake, Shake, Shake) Shake Your Booty'
6. Wild Cherry – 'Play That Funky Music'
7. Walter Murphy and the Big Apple Band – 'A Fifth of Beethoven'
8. Elton John and Kiki Dee – 'Don't Go Breaking My Heart'
9. Boz Scaggs – 'Lowdown'
10. George Benson – 'This Masquerade'

'Every man's a boy deep down.'

– 'Children of the World'

All of a sudden, the lights went out.

At the end of 1975, RSO changed its North American partner from Atlantic, its home since 1967, to the European-based Polygram, which had long handled RSO products in most of the world. The Bee Gees had already been on Polydor since they took the *Fairsky* back to England, in the UK and many other countries. So what difference would it make to them?

Though it was just dry industry talk to most, this manufacturing and distribution deal meant that Arif Mardin could not continue as part of the Bee Gees' reinvention. Mardin had dragged them, often against their will, into a position where they were one of the hottest R&B acts in the States – but he was Atlantic's house producer, and Atlantic weren't about to let him work freelance for Polygram. Of course, Atlantic could have kept the deal going, if only they'd stumped a little more money. But Robert Stigwood went with the bigger financial offer and Atlantic were out in the cold. Arif Mardin could no longer work with the Bee Gees.

And this happened just as the rest of rock seemed to be catching up with *Main Course*.

A brace of huge American hits in 1976 detailed the desire of white rock musicians to move away from chugging blues rock and into something leaner and funkier, something with more cowbell. Something like 'Jive Talkin''. The Climax Blues Band, like the Bee Gees, had started out in northern England, though their single 'Couldn't Get It Right' didn't really suggest Staffordshire pottery. It was rubbery, with a lithe rhythm guitar line over little more than bass and insistent cowbell as seemingly half-asleep singer Colin Cooper sang about his restlessness, how time was drifting as rock began to roll, so he hit the road and made his getaway. What had happened to this bunch of bluff hairies to encourage them to get away from blues rock? Apparently, they'd heard the O'Jays, citing Philly Fever: 'I must admit it got the best of me / Gettin' down so deep I could've drowned / Now, I can't get back the way I used to be.' No return. Soul music had claimed them. They didn't seem sure or even happy about it, but R&B was now their calling, their future. The same reticence wasn't to be found in Wild Cherry, a band from the Ohio industrial towns of Mingo Junction and Steubenville, who had been 'burnin' up the one-night stands' from Pittsburgh to West Virginia for a few years playing unadventurous boogie rock. Wild Cherry's singer Rob Parissi knew that nobody would expect a white boy like him to play that funky music. In a voice somewhere between Disco Tex and Snagglepuss, he detailed how he had decided to 'disco down and check out the show'. He had a Damascene epiphany in a discotheque, and at that exact moment, somebody turned around and shouted, 'Play that funky music, white boy!' Rock 'n' roll was soon abandoned by Wild Cherry, and their single detailing this transformation went to number seven in the UK, and number one in the US.

Stigwood might have been instantly richer from the new distribution deal, but his prize assets were once more left to pick up the pieces. Barry called Arif on the phone – what should they do? You'll be fine, Arif told them.

They went back to Los Angeles, birthplace of the disastrous *Life in a Tin Can*, and spent three days in the studio with producer Richard Perry, the man responsible for mega-hits like Harry Nilsson's 'Without You' and Carly Simon's 'You're So Vain'. Lanky, with a look of horse-ish breeding, Perry listened to a new song Barry had written called 'You Should Be Dancing'. 'Nah,' he said. They buffed it up, made it more radio-friendly. Still Perry said no. In fact, he said 'You Should Be Dancing' wasn't even worth recording.

At this point, Perry had just taken on British singer-song-writer Leo Sayer, who was hoping to break America after a string of huge hits ('The Show Must Go On', 'Moonlighting', 'One Man Band') at home. Perry's great plan for Sayer, who considered himself a 'blues singer', was to ditch all of his own songs and ship in a load from other songwriters. In the short term this worked a treat – 'You Make Me Feel Like Dancing' and 'When I Need You' both went to number one in America – but his own songwriting credentials were demolished and in the medium term his career took five steps back, never to recover its momentum. This was the same Richard Perry who didn't con-sider 'You Should Be Dancing' was worth wasting a master tape on. It could stay on a quarter-inch tape and be discovered as an outtake twenty-five years hence, as far as he was concerned – that's how much Richard Perry thought of this song.

'We were in the studio in LA for three days with Richard,' laughed Barry. 'His constant position of sitting in the studio was this' (slouched, eyes half-closed). 'And he had a phone on his console that he always talked on. So things were either con-stantly out of it or constantly disturbing. What he does, I'm told, is that he's out of it most of the time, but when he comes to cut the tracks and actually function, he gets it done. And then he goes back to being out of it again.'

Arif got another late-night call from Barry Gibb. Richard Perry, he stammered. It hadn't worked out, and he's Richard Fucking Perry, apparently the best of the best. What on earth do we do now? Take it on yourselves, said Arif. 'Take it on ourselves?' 'Take it on yourselves. You are more than capable.' And then Arif Mardin hung up the phone.

Pissed off by Perry, and fired by that side of the Gibb mentality that wants to prove the world wrong, the Bee Gees went back to Miami, back to Criteria, and tried cutting 'You Should Be Dancing' again. There was no producer, but maybe Arif was right. Blue and Barry and engineer Karl Richardson knew how to press all the buttons and toy with the faders. Still, the intangibles weren't there, the clear positivity that Arif had magically brought to proceedings. Karl was technically a great engineer, but he lacked musicality and just couldn't suggest the subtle changes that Arif would have mentioned instinctively, almost without anyone noticing, the suggestions that had moved the group on from the failed *Mr Natural* to the best-selling *Main Course*. But Karl mentioned he had a friend called Albhy Galuten, a vibes man, who was often barefoot and carried his belongings onto flights in a cardboard box. He had just finished producing an album by Bees Make Honey, a London pub band who had kickstarted a roots rock scene with their shows at the Tally Ho in Kentish Town.

Galuten was twenty-eight years old. He had gone to the Berklee College of Music – he could play piano, he could play guitar, and he could write string lines. Barry, Robin and Maurice could only sing string lines to an arranger. Albhy's input was to become invaluable to Karl: 'He knew what would and wouldn't work. I, meanwhile, would take care of the engineering and I'd constantly be challenged by the guys to "Make it sound better, Karl". What's "better" mean? The console doesn't have a "better" knob. Still, the combination of Barry, Albhy and I worked in the control room, and the rest, as they say, is history.'

Pretty much the first thing Albhy Galuten did when he arrived at Criteria was to point out that Maurice was an alcoholic. So they needed to bring in another bassist like, say, Albhy's mate George 'Chocolate' Perry. Blue Weaver was a gentle soul, sparing with his negativity, and he considered new boy Albhy to be 'blunt'. He may well have used choicer words when, without consulting anyone else, the shoeless Galuten got himself an official co-producer credit alongside Barry and Karl on the new material. Albhy, it turned out, was a true hippy – he had his own agenda, and would soon be living in a solid gold house.

The Gibbs remained anxious without their mentor Arif. It may not have shown on the surface, of course, but the tell-tale signs were there. Maurice would drink bottles of Evian laced with vodka. Robin would have fewer lead vocals, and stewed in silence as Barry once again took control. Since the public spats of 1969, the appearance of being together and in control had been seen as paramount. But unlike Bill Gates or Ossie Byrne or Robert Stigwood, Arif Mardin clearly believed the boys were now men and could stand on their own two feet. Barry took this advice on board. He had always seen himself as *de facto* leader, as all big brothers tend to, but now he had the reserves and the will power to keep the group in the place Mardin and *Main Course* had put them. He understood pop music was 90 per cent perspiration, and that the 10 per cent inspiration would emerge from that. Robin may have liked to write his lyrics with a quill in a mid-Victorian garret. Mo may have liked joking over made-up song titles in the pub. But Barry just worked fucking hard, and he worked and he worked until choruses became verses, old choruses were replaced by better choruses, and over and over and so on and so on. Linda fed him hash brownies. Her dad poured him tea. He didn't stop. He became a machine.

'You Should Be Dancing' would be the first recording anyone heard from the new production team of Gibb, Richardson and Galuten. The bassline was a tremendous, solid, single-minded strut, and Richardson built the entire song around it. Stephen Stills, who happened to be in a neighbouring studio, and knew Barry from way back, added the layers of congas. Every new element that showed up on the song – the chk-a-chk guitars, the merciless congas, the horn stabs – obeyed and accentuated that bassline.[23]

The song soundtracked the late summer of 1976, hitting number five in the UK. It did better yet in America – after sticking at number two for three weeks behind Elton John and Kiki Dee's kissing budgie act 'Don't Go Breaking My Heart', it finally reached the *Billboard* summit in early September. And at that point the Bee Gees became the country's premier disco act, masters of the scene, its exemplars, displacing Miami forebears KC and the Sunshine Band.

Most of the Bee Gees' focus in 1976 had been on a single album; this didn't come naturally and was something they had learned from Arif Mardin. Take your time, don't push it, don't force it. First it was going to be called *Pacer*, which then became the more appropriate *Slipstream*. Then that had to change because the Sutherland Brothers had an album out called *Slipstream*. So

---

[23] A year or so later, Talking Heads would build their breakthrough song 'Psycho Killer' around a simplified version of the bassline played on 'You Should Be Dancing'.

it briefly became *Horizon* but – ah, wait – didn't that sound a lot like *Horizontal*? And so then it became *Response*, until after a while everyone agreed that was an absolutely rotten title. Eventually they named it after one of the album's standout songs, 'Children of the World'. It became their first truly 'disco' Bee Gees album, with Barry's falsetto, synthesisers and bare-naked funk entirely replacing the strings and acoustic guitars of just three years earlier.

'Stevie Wonder started everything for us, that era,' said Barry. 'Stevie Wonder started it. Nobody will say that, but it's the truth. Stevie Wonder was the maestro of disco music. "Living in the City", "Superstition". Nobody puts that down. That was the inspiration.'

'Disco music' was a new term for the mainstream. In Britain, 'discotheque' records had generally referred to 45s that were played by mobile disc jockeys: one of the biggest discotheque records of the early '70s had been Gary Glitter's 'Rock & Roll Part 2', which initially picked up zero radio play and only became a hit in 1972 after months of continuous build-up at youth clubs around the country; another had been R. Dean Taylor's 'There's a Ghost in My House', a Motown obscurity which earned plays from rare record connoisseurs on the northern soul circuit across the industrial belt of Lancashire and Yorkshire and was reissued to become a top-three hit in 1974. Pye Records started its 'Disco Demand' subsidiary label in 1974, which was purely for northern soul reissues, almost all of which had been recorded in the 1960s. The 'disco' for Pye, and pretty much everyone else, was a physical space rather than a musical genre.

K-Tel Records – the low-end, high street, TV-advertised compilation company – released soul and funk compilations in 1974–75 aimed at the discotheque market called *Super Bad*,

Soul Motion and *Souled Out,* with their *Disco Fever* not arriving until 1977. 'Boogie' was certainly a commonplace term for dancing in 1975 (see KC and the Sunshine Band's 'I'm Your Boogie Man' and 'Boogie Shoes') as was plain old 'rocking and rolling'. By 1975 'funky' had also become enough of an everyday term to be lampooned by both the Goodies ('Funky Gibbon') and Jasper Carrott ('Funky Moped').

It's difficult to pinpoint just when the 'theque' was chopped from the word 'discotheque'. It hadn't been when 'Rock Your Baby' had emerged as an important new soul sound in 1974, and perhaps not even when 'Jive Talkin'' borrowed McCrae's shuffle in 1975, knocking Van McCoy's similarly ground-zero 'The Hustle' from number one in the States. But 'disco' had become a sound rather than a geographical location by the time Donna Summer's 'Love to Love You Baby' moaned its way to the top in America and Tina Charles's 'I Love to Love' squeaked its way to number one in Britain at the start of 1976. By the time the Bee Gees were set to release the all-important follow-up to *Main Course,* 'disco' was definitely more than a buzzword. Novelty records are always a tell, a sign that a scene is over-ripe and heading for irrelevance – Rick Dees' 'Disco Duck', a huge hit in the summer of 1976, meant all bets were off. As northern club comedians did their Russell Thompkins and Tina Charles impressions in partially unbuttoned blousons, the genre seemed to have peaked and would now surely wither and die – or so you'd have expected.

Strange but true, *Children of the World* would be the Bee Gees' only disco album. But even then, it still featured soul ballads – 'Love Me' and 'Love So Right' becoming two of the album's most enduring tracks. The title song was barely danceable, with a cappella sections and chord changes suggesting a late

'60s Beach Boys record that had been given a Miami overhaul. 'Love So Right' was the only track that could feasibly have been included on an earlier Bee Gees album – the main difference now, of course, was Barry's falsetto: 'The perfect story ended at the start. I thought you came forever and you came to break my heart.' It went all the way to US number three in the autumn of 1976, held at bay by Rod Stewart's 'Tonight's the Night' and Gordon Lightfoot's 'The Wreck of the Edmund Fitzgerald'.

Every track on *Children of the World* sounded like a single. The confidence was flowing again. 'You Stepped into My Life' would become a hit for Melba Moore, 'Love Me' would be a (bigger) hit for Yvonne Elliman – they were, once again, having their albums picked over for potential hits, something that hadn't happened since they had re-formed back in 1970. 'Love Me', in particular, was a beautiful song full of subtle hooks, with an impassioned wail from Robin on the middle eight. The peculiar 'Lovers', with its growled chorus (possibly borrowed from the Miracles' recent hit 'Love Machine'), showed that they weren't only about falsetto; it had a structure that took several listens to get your head around, and gave the strange impression there were suddenly five or six different brothers. Barry, Robin, Mo, Zeppo and Gummo Gibb. 'Can't Keep a Good Man Down' had one of Maurice's brass hooks – he literally hummed the riff and the musicians worked it out. The weakest track, a Kool & the Gang knockoff with the generic title 'Boogie Child', was bizarrely chosen as the third single from the album, though it did at least have the usual peculiar Gibb mid-section that sounded like Benny Goodman had strolled in and screwed around with the time signature.

And still this wasn't *really* pure disco. There were no mechanised drum loops, basslines or synth parts, no tsss-tah! tsss-tah!

hi-hats. *Children of the World* is R&B. It was organically played, its prime influences were black radio stations and – as Barry had said out loud – Stevie Wonder. The closest comparison would be the *Young Americans* album. David Bowie had described his own sound as 'plastic soul', and a growing band of detractors would be happy to throw this line at the Gibbs over the next couple of years – though frankly the Gibbs sounded more at home in this setting than Bowie.

Outside the boundaries of Criteria Studios and the Hot 100, the Vietnam War had come to an embarrassing close for the American military, a moment which liberated America from a decade-long diet of daily death counts and horror stories. Gerald Ford, the short-lived president after Nixon's downfall, was soundly beaten in the 1976 election by Jimmy Carter, a liberal soul who scared Republicans and was later recalled as 'history's greatest monster' on *The Simpsons*.

And outside of politics, Barry, Robin and Maurice would have been proud of their kid brother, who had now written songs, rehearsed his band and played to tricky audiences. Just like his heroes, he had moved to Australia in 1975 to see if he could crack that market before trying his luck further afield. Andy's Melody Fayre bandmates John Alderson and John Stringer had followed after him from the Isle of Man. Melody Fayre's manager in Australia was original rocker Col Joye, a blast from the Bee Gees' past, and they got as far as a TV appearance on *The Ernie Sigley Show*. In a sign of things to come, though, Andy would slink off on his own for weeks on end, leaving Alderson and Stringer out of work and broke. Disheartened, they returned to Douglas in 1975, but Andy stayed in Australia, persevered, and put together a new band called Zenta who played essentially the same set. Col Joye found Zenta plum slots supporting both the Sweet and the Bay

City Rollers in Sydney. A solitary single, Andy's own 'Words and Music', became a top-thirty Australian hit under his own name. Still this all seemed very second-rate to the youngest Gibb, dancing in the shadows of his big brothers. By 1976, things were worse yet – Andy was playing Buttons in *Cinderella*. At least he had met and fallen in love with Kim Reeder. They married, and Robert Stigwood generously offered the couple his house in Bermuda as a honeymoon present.

Acts of generosity in Stigwood's world, as we know by now, usually came with strings attached. Not only was Stigwood at home in Bermuda when the newlyweds arrived, but so was Barry. By now, Andy looked very much like the late 1960s Barry, and sang a little like him too. He was eighteen, he was cute, and on his honeymoon Andy Gibb would be offered a deal with RSO Records. Kim sat outside Stigwood's holiday home, watching the waves crashing against the Bermuda beach. Her future suddenly seemed very different. At no point did anyone ask if this was what she wanted. Naturally, it was exactly what Andy had always wanted – he had never wanted to be anything other than a Bee Gee, and here he was, closer than ever, and getting to write songs with his hero, big brother Barry. He had recorded an album at Col Joye's studio – all originals, except for a cover of Don McLean's 'Winter Has Me in Its Grip' – which would now be shelved. Back in Sydney, the sidelined Col Joye sighed and shrugged. 'Obviously,' said Andy, 'I wasn't going to refuse an offer from RSO records.'

What happened next would set the tone for Andy's subsequent career. 'Me and Barry locked ourselves in a bedroom [in Stigwood's home], and Barry just started writing. When Barry writes, it's very hard to collaborate because he's so quick. And before I knew it he was starting to do the chorus and I thought,

"Wow, what a hook." Within twenty minutes he'd written a number-one record. And then we went right into another one. It's just unbelievable when you are working with him.'

The first song was 'I Just Want to Be Your Everything', and the second was '(Love Is) Thicker than Water'; both would become US number-one hits. Andy came up with the peculiar title for the latter but that was all he contributed – he just sat on the edge of the bed, marvelling at how Barry had just come up with not one but two golden tickets to fame and fortune in around forty minutes. Andy cut demos of both songs in Miami with Barry, Karl and Albhy, then went back to Australia with Kim. He wanted to take his Australian band to Miami but was talked out of it – with hits on tap from the best session players, why bother?

Released in the summer of 1977, 'I Just Want to Be Your Everything' was more teen-friendly than *Children of the World*, but its straight-up romance and puppy-eyed sparkle worked across all age groups. On the verse, lines like 'I would wait forever for those lips of wine' were delivered with similar softness and vulnerability to David Cassidy, or Rudy Vallee for that matter. The chorus was something else. The word 'I' is stretched over seven zig-zagging syllables to create a hook that's almost avant garde, as if Barry had done it for a bet. The chorus ended with a switch to a long, held minor chord, played on a string machine, which then jumped an octave – the effect was like an intensifying sunset on 1977 film stock. But it wasn't quite done yet – there was a sting that sounded like a cross between 'MacArthur Park' and the *Starsky & Hutch* theme followed by a pregnant pause that linked the mournful chords back to Andy's butterscotch vocals and the mooning verse. It was complex, easy on the ear, teen-dream-emotive and irresistible. The only wonder was that Andy didn't become an instant teen idol everywhere outside of

America. In 1977, Britain was oddly hung up on David Soul, the aforementioned TV star 'Hutch', who was already in his mid-thirties and confined to Denmark Street balladry. 'I Just Want to Be Your Everything' fell short of the UK top twenty despite heavy radio play.

What were Andy's goals in life? Did anyone ask him? His big brother was also his biggest hero. No one seemed to question how this set-up could easily damage his teenage confidence. When he mimed to '(Love Is) Thicker than Water' on German TV show *Top Pop* he stood alone with his guitar, but he didn't mime to Joe Walsh's lines, instead staying focused on the simpler rhythm guitar part that he had actually played on the record. He was very keen to point out that he was heavily dependent on family, and friends of family. He was a modest kid.

Recording his first album, Karl would keep Andy's vocals back in the mix. *Flowing Rivers* would be made up of songs Andy had written over the last couple of years, the cream of his work, now produced and recorded with the highest echelon of Miami musicians. It was fine. In particular, 'Dance to the Light of the Morning' was a terrific effort for a teenager, with a sunlit country touch allied to Miami's lite funk feel. 'Too Many Looks in Your Eyes' could have fitted onto *Mr Natural*. Andy shared Barry's affiliation with country; on 'Let It Be Me', he even had help from country rock superstars the Eagles, who happened to be at Criteria working on *Hotel California*. The lad had potential; it was unquestionable. The only problem was that the two strongest songs on the album were the ones his big brother had knocked together – with Andy perched, awestruck, on the side of the bed – in less than an hour. Was this success real? Did he have anything to do with it? He had written the title of 'Thicker than Water' – not even the bracketed part – and that was all. Albhy introduced Andy to John Oates as a possible co-writer, and someone with experience. Stigwood got wind of this. 'He called me up,' remembered Albhy with sadness. 'He said, "Don't let him do this, I don't want him writing with anyone but his brothers." To me that was a turning point in his life.'

Just two years after having a stand-up row in a Batley car park, the Bee Gees were now too big to record in either Britain or America. And so, like other tax avoiders before them, in 1977 they headed to the Château d'Hérouville in a village just north-west of Paris. The place had earned the nickname Honky Château after Elton John recorded his album of the same name there in 1971. Since then it had seen some scenes. Elton John had recorded not only *Honky Château* there but also huge hit singles like 'Goodbye Yellow Brick Road', 'Candle in the Wind' and 'Bennie and the Jets'; other Château-produced classics included T. Rex's 45-rpm commercial peak 'Metal Guru', and spooked album tracks like 'Spaceball Ricochet'; Jethro Tull started sessions for their *War Child* album there in 1974, before abandoning them; and Chris Bell, late of Big Star, would record his powerful and otherworldly 'I Am the Cosmos' at the Château in 1975 shortly before he was killed in a car crash.

Karl Richardson was amazed anyone had come away from the Château with anything that could be released to the public. 'It was in a funky state, with a 24-track Studer tape machine . . . the thing was barely on its last legs.' On the recording console, 'someone had coloured all the EQ knobs with nail polish, and the other fun thing about it was that the faders had worn contacts in them. There were holes where the audio would completely drop out, so I had to mark all the faders with tape: "Don't move across this line if there's any audio." Even the monitors were horrible. We used headphones and a little set of Auratone [speakers].'

Management had already committed the group to a few weeks there over the winter, so they had to make the most of it. Wives and girlfriends came too, which tested the facilities – there were only two bathrooms. 'The result', sighed Karl, 'was that we'd probably start recording at about two in the afternoon and stay up until about three or four in the morning. It was really stupid, but that was the only way we could get all of the showers done in the morning.'

There was no beach outside the window. Instead, the window in the control room was so icy that Karl recalled putting 'Heineken bottles there to keep them cold. It was great.'

The control room looked directly over a live area with wooden beams on the ceiling. Somehow Richardson recorded the four-piece set-up of Maurice on bass, Dennis on drums, Blue on keyboards and Barry on acoustic guitar. Alan Kendall would add electric guitar overdubs and Barry would double up his acoustic, but essentially this was the room, and the line-up, that recorded arguably their two best-loved songs – 'How Deep Is Your Love' and 'Stayin' Alive'. Richardson: 'I distinctly remember Barry saying, "Boy, Karl, have I got a song for you," and sitting down to play "Stayin' Alive" on an acoustic guitar. It was like a chant and it was unbelievable. I said, "Barry, don't forget that rhythm. That's a number-one record." I knew, five bars in, no questions asked. You couldn't get past the intro without knowing it was a smash.'

Inspiration was thick in the air at the Château. 'How Deep Is Your Love' came about from a rare shaft of sunshine, pouring through the window and coating Blue Weaver's electric piano in glorious light, inspiring the ethereal keyboard line. The brother's lyrics were similarly spiritual: 'You're the light in my deepest, darkest hour, you're my saviour when I fall.' In isolation, with only bottles of Heineken as an outside influence, they wrote some of the key Bee Gees lines: ''Cause we're livin' in a world of fools, breaking us down when they all should let us be.'

The significant thing about the Château songs was that there was no real pressure on the Bee Gees then. Though they'd had a career revival with *Main Course* and *Children of the World*, and a couple of American number-one singles which weren't to be sniffed at, they still weren't a huge group in 1977. They weren't the Eagles. They weren't ABBA. 'Jive Talkin'' and 'You Should Be Dancing' may have both peaked at number five in the UK but the other singles from those albums had barely registered in the top fifty. *Children of the World* had seen them finding their feet after Arif Mardin's departure, and the Château songs now found them in rather trying circumstances – which usually brought out the best in them. The new songs did so well purely because they were fantastic pop records. The Bee Gees were never 'cool', but that didn't matter – nor were ABBA, who they were about to dislodge as arguably the biggest pop group in the world.

The bare bones of Iggy Pop's crooked, metallic funk album *The Idiot* had been recorded at the Château a few months before the Bee Gees arrived. Iggy had turned up with producer Tony Visconti and mentor/saviour David Bowie; when they arrived they found the place gave them the creeps. Bowie took one look at the main bedroom and said, 'Well, I'm not sleeping in *there*!' Visconti remembered how one corner of the room was almost supernaturally dark and cold. Brian Eno came to visit, and said he had been woken one night by a cold hand touching his shoulder.

Iggy's gang would leave the echo of 'Nightclubbing, we're nightclubbing, we're what's happening' hanging in the air as they left. Robert Stigwood would catch the song's distant echo and place a phone call to his charges at the Château that would completely rearrange their lives. You are no longer recording a new album, he told them. Those songs you've recorded so far – 'How Deep Is Your Love', 'Stayin' Alive', 'Night Fever', 'More than a Woman' and 'If I Can't Have You' – are now going to be part of a film soundtrack. Stigwood had just signed the rights to a film called *Tribal Rites of the New Saturday Night.*

13

BROOKLYN

Billboard US top ten, 30 July 1977

1. Andy Gibb – 'I Just Want to Be Your Everything'
2. Peter Frampton – 'I'm in You'
3. Barry Manilow – 'Looks Like We Made It'
4. Barbra Streisand – 'My Heart Belongs to You'
5. Shaun Cassidy – 'Da Doo Ron Ron'
6. The Emotions – 'Best of My Love'
7. Peter McCann – 'Do You Wanna Make Love'
8. Jimmy Buffett – 'Margaritaville'
9. Rita Coolidge – 'Higher and Higher'
10. Pablo Cruise – 'Whatcha Gonna Do'

'Vincent was the very best dancer in Bay Ridge – the ultimate Face. He owned fourteen floral shirts, five suits, eight pairs of shoes, three overcoats, and had appeared on *American Bandstand*. Sometimes music people came out from

Manhattan to watch him, and one man who owned a club on the East Side had even offered him a contract. A hundred dollars a week. Just to dance.

Everybody knew him. When Saturday night came round and he walked into 2001 Odyssey, all the other Faces automatically fell back before him, cleared a space for him to float in, right at the very center of the dance floor. Gracious as a medieval seigneur accepting tributes, Vincent waved and nodded at random. Then his face grew stern, his body turned to the music. Solemn, he danced, and all the Faces followed.

In this sphere his rule was absolute. Only one thing bothered him, and that was the passing of time. Already he was eighteen, almost eighteen and a half. Soon enough he would be nineteen, twenty. Then this golden age would pass. By natural law someone new would arise to replace him. Then everything would be over.'

– Nik Cohn, *Tribal Rites of the New Saturday Night*, 1976

When the Gibbs got the call about Stigwood's new movie project, soon retitled *Saturday Night*, they had no idea whether it would be as big as *Melody*, or even *The Mini Mob*. Maybe it would join the list of abandoned Bee Gee movie projects, which stretched back to *Lord Kitchener's Little Drummer Boys* and would stretch on far into the cutting rooms of the future.

In the mid-'60s Andrew Loog Oldham, manager of the Rolling Stones and Marianne Faithfull, had shut Jackie DeShannon and her current beau Jimmy Page in a room together for several hours and demanded they stay in there until they had written a follow-up to Faithfull's first hit single, 'As Tears Go By'. By the time they came out, looking a little flushed, they had written

'Come and Stay with Me', her biggest ever hit. Sensory deprivation was also very conducive to the Gibbs – 'New York Mining Disaster' had been written during a power cut. Likewise,
the Gibbs sat on a staircase in the Château to finish writing
'Night Fever', imagining themselves in a neon city at night, all
electricity and anticipation, as far from dusty, rural France as
they could get.

They had 'How Deep Is Your Love' and 'Night Fever' done,
they had 'Stayin' Alive' on the boil, they were thrilled – they
were on the roll of their lives. And then Dennis Bryon had to fly
home to Cardiff as his mother was very sick. 'Stayin' Alive' was
a jam, they knew it, and they didn't have the drum track down
without Dennis – were they going to lose their momentum
again? No, not this time. Albhy Galuten and Karl Richardson
cut a piece of tape which featured four bars of Dennis's exemplary drumming from the already recorded 'Night Fever', and
spliced it into a loop. Galuten would recall how 'Karl spliced
the tape and rigged it so that it was going over a mic stand and
around a plastic reel. At first, we were doing it just as a temporary measure. As we started to lay tracks down to it, we found
that it felt really great – very insistent, but not machine-like. It
had a human feel. By the time we had overdubbed all the parts
to the songs and Dennis came back, there was no way we could
get rid of the loop.'

A literal tape loop – such an easy task in the digital twenty-first
century, but it was a rare and risky move back then, with little
room for error. Still, it wasn't as if they had anything better to do.
At the crumbling Honky Château, in rotten bad weather, without even a television set, maybe the only form of entertainment
was making tape loops. 'We were waiting for the Americans to
come and liberate us,' quipped Mo. Inside a month, with their

Heath Robinson studio setup, bound together by splicing tape and nail varnish, they had written and recorded their first UK number one in a decade, 'Night Fever', as well as 'How Deep Is Your Love', 'Stayin' Alive' (at this point entitled 'Saturday Night'), 'More than a Woman' and 'If I Can't Have You', all of which have since been UK top-ten hits at least twice over.

And now these pearls were going to be used in a movie based on a story printed in *New York Magazine*, written by an Ulster-born ex-mod turned country music enthusiast called Nik Cohn. Asked for a film title, Barry suggested *Night Fever*. 'No, that's too pornographic, too hot,' said Stigwood, who, like a child with no concept of numbers, had already been bragging about the possibilities of a 'hundred-million-dollar movie'. They merged two potential titles and came up with *Saturday Night Fever*.

To the pop world, 1977 had felt like a quiet Bee Gees year, with just the live *Here at Last* album and Andy's breakthrough hit – but it would end with the Bee Gees at number one again, over the entire holiday period. Only Debby Boone's 'You Light Up My Life', Meco's 'Star Wars Theme' and the ecstatic funk of the Emotions' 'Best of My Love' were at the top between 'I Just Want to Be Your Everything' and 'How Deep Is Your Love', two heart-meltingly romantic songs. In Britain, 'How Deep Is Your Love' couldn't dislodge Wings' 'Mull of Kintyre' and the Brighouse and Rastrick Brass Band's 'Floral Dance', and it stuck at number three behind these two for a solid month. Still, it became their biggest-selling single to date in Britain, and – in spite of the huge hits before and since – their best loved.

Robert Stigwood had the *Saturday Night Fever* double album soundtrack released in America just before Christmas, two months *before* the movie opened, which seemed a radical move to Hollywood but made sense with 'How Deep Is Your Love' already in the top five. The music would create interest in the film, Stigwood reasoned, and his instincts were spot on. The two LPs contained a total of five new Gibb-written songs. Just five, but they would be essential to the soundtrack's success.

In 1977, Robert Stigwood signed a three-picture deal with a young actor called John Travolta who had starred in a TV show called *Welcome Back Kotter*. Darkly charismatic, with a streak of dumb insolence, Travolta was perfect for *Saturday Night Fever* screenwriter Norman Wexler's anti-hero, Tony Manero. When the movie took $11 million in its first eleven days, John Travolta became a superstar.

Saturday Night Fever was clearly fictional, but relatable. *Tribal Rites of the New Saturday Night* had been presented as fact in *New York Magazine*, but also turned out to be fiction. In 1976, Nik Cohn had met disco dancer Tu Sweet, who took him to clubs in the borough of Brooklyn, which at that time was way off the hedonism map as far as most New Yorkers were concerned. Sandwiched between endless auto repair shops in the district of Bay Ridge, one of these clubs was called 2001 Odyssey. When the two arrived, they could see a drunken fight outside the venue. Cohn says that as soon as he opened the taxi door, someone threw up on his shoes. He closed the door and told the driver to head back to Manhattan.

From the taxi window, though, Cohn had spotted a kid in a tight black shirt and crimson flares, coolly observing the fight. Cohn recognised his type from London in the mid-'60s – the kid was a Face.

'I went back to Bay Ridge in daylight and noted the major landmarks,' Cohn recalled in the '90s. 'I walked some streets, went into a couple of stores. Studied the clothes, the gestures, the walks. Imagined how it would feel to burn up, all caged energies, with no outlet but the dancefloor and the rituals of Saturday night. Finally, I wrote it all up. And presented it as fact.' This barely mattered, unless you were *New York Magazine*'s commissioning editor, because Cohn's writing was spare and vicious and beautiful. Though Vincent's character was largely based on a mod he knew from the Goldhawk Road in the 1960s, Cohn made him real – his black shirt, his crimson pants, his stance and his cool. And then the movie made Vincent into Tony Manero, a double fiction, and a pop culture totem of the 1970s.

'It's already made [Travolta] a massive star in the States and will doubtless do the same here,' wrote the *NME*'s pleasantly shocked Nick Kent in March 1978. 'But that's only fair because he's absolutely as good as all the superlatives being currently tossed around by our national media. And the music? Well, the Bee Gees for one are a revelation with songs like "Stayin' Alive" sounding astounding within context . . . It's a bizarre chemistry all told, but it works – spectacularly so, most of the time. And if you dare to miss out on *Saturday Night Fever* due solely to your own dodgy preconceptions (as I almost did), then you'll be the loser.'

At one point, 'Stayin' Alive' was recut as an eight-minute epic, with a slow breakdown in the middle. Blue remembered how 'Stigwood came in and said, "Oh, they're on the dancefloor at this time and suddenly he sees her across the floor and it goes in slow motion and they walk toward each other" . . . so we wrote this whole section, but we threw it out in the end . . . I want to mix the long version. I think it would be very interesting for people to know that little story – I think it's a great version. And the end, as well, is different because it's got synthesiser bass.' Alan Kendall's opening guitar line was originally played by Blue on the Clavinet, aping Stevie Wonder's 'Superstition'. Does 'Stayin' Alive' sound darker than most Bee Gees songs of this period? That could be because the lyric had been started by Robin, who had first scrawled a few lines down on a Concorde ticket.

Andy had released '(Love Is) Thicker than Water', his second single, in September of 1977, and it began a sloth-like, six-month climb up the charts. But when *Saturday Night Fever* and 'Stayin' Alive' turned the Bee Gees into an unstoppable force, the song was ready to peak, ready to give Andy a second number one in March '78. In the adjoining studio at Criteria, the Eagles had been recording *Hotel California*, and their guitarist Joe Walsh, happy to help out the affable Gibbs, added some rays of tumbling California sunshine, and an almost aquatic feel to the Miami chicken-scratch guitars and tish-thack drums on 'Thicker than Water'. It was an oddly complex song, the slightly jagged Bacharach-esque chorus leading into floaty dream-pop verses and an extended wordless coda – it was far from immediate, and you certainly couldn't dance to it, but it was a slow-burning beauty. 'Thicker than Water' would be at number one for two weeks before it was displaced by Andy's big brothers.

That wasn't all. Samantha Sang, another old friend from Australia, had cut Barry's song 'Emotion' in April 1977 at Criteria, and it charted in early 1978. Stigwood had signed her up in 1969 to be his own Barbra Streisand, but nothing had materialised beyond a middling Gibb ballad called 'The Love of a Woman', which revealed her to have contrasting head and chest voices more reminiscent of Cilla Black than Streisand. On 'Emotion' only her head voice was utilised and it was very much in Barry's register. The breathiness and washiness of Sang's voice matched a promo clip in which her face was barely visible for the vaseline on the lens; it occupied an even more cushioned and weightless world than 'Charade', the song on *Mr Natural* that had signified a possible future back in 1974. It was exquisite. By the time Barry, Karl and Albhy had finished aerating the production, Sang sounded even more like a Bee Gee than Andy. 'Emotion' was originally intended for use in *Saturday Night Fever*, but instead ended up in the soft-blue Joan Collins movie *The Stud* a year later. That's a shame.

'Night Fever' was only ever going to be in *Saturday Night Fever*. Stigwood knew it was a hit title before he even heard the song, which was both nimble and portentous. It had come from an unlikely source – Blue Weaver had 'always wanted to do a disco version of "Theme from a Summer Place". I was playing that and Barry said, "What was that?", and I said it was "Theme from a Summer Place". Barry said, "No, it wasn't. It was new." I was playing it on a string synthesiser, and [Barry] sang the riff over it.'

Disco could be a heavy, unctuous perfume. There were reasons people hated it, and they weren't all homophobic or racist, they really weren't. On the chart in 1977 was La Belle Epoque's version of the German-Spanish '60s hit 'Black Is Black'. Originally it had been a hit for another act with a tempting European name: Los Bravos. This 1966 version had been a thing of slab density, a three-note organ riff with a Charlie Watts-alike's monotone drumming keeping it simple as can be, and an unreal human voice, half-crow, telling the world 'black is black, I want my baby back'. It sounded like the Stones fed through a telex precursor of Google Translate. It had been perfect in its monolithic simplicity. La Belle Epoque's version added every imaginable bauble; it went 'whooooo!!' on the beat. Musicians who longed to be in James Last's orchestra played with funkless fingers behind girls who cooed come-ons – but still you could tell they were the wrong side of thirty. This version of 'Black Is Black' was a fug, like the ground floor of a department store, a dozen different perfumes hitting you at the same time, far too busy, forced fun, nauseating.

But 'Night Fever' was not that dense, liquid perfume which makes you feel slightly sick. This was not the sound of too much air freshener. This was air itself. Night-time air. The city.

The song also transmits that feeling of nervousness. There is sweetness and there is fear. A club night can be a transcendent experience, one that can take you out of yourself, and it can also make you feel almost sick with anxiety and apprehension.

The lyric to 'Night Fever' isn't far behind the Kingsmen's 'Louie Louie' or the Skids' 'Into the Valley' in its murk and mystery – the odd line jumps out as a waymark, the rest lure you into the Gibbs' world; there is a reason they never printed lyric sheets with their albums. The emotion, as ever, is conveyed by the sound of the words, the feel of that sound. The Gibbs would always be first in line to say their lyrics were 'meaningless'. They really weren't doing themselves justice. 'Night Fever' is a great example of their abstract, almost outsider take on lyric-writing.

'Night Fever' is all love and abandon and desperation. The moment of surrender, the understanding that your time in the club can feel like the only time that counts. It's worth sweating through a forty-hour nine-to-five job just for those fleeting hours, precious hours when music and dancing were everything. You would share the feeling with every other boy and girl in the place. You let your inhibitions go. You were more alive than you'd ever been. This feeling is both exhilarating, and borderline terrifying. 'Here I am,' sang Barry at key moments, when the music swooped downwards, away from the light and air of the verse, and suddenly it was all self-awareness. 'I can't hide!'

Barry clearly understood this dynamic, and used classic Gibb linguistics to push the feeling on: as the song unexpectedly takes its dramatic turn, he sings 'Here I am, prayin' for this moment to last / Livin' on the music so fine.' That's it, the instant of delivery, the headrush, the euphoria, captured in a few words.

If you think of the classic disco sound – the generic, repetitive, hi-hat-from-an-aerosol version of disco – you might think of some tracks on *Saturday Night Fever*, but none of them would be the ones by the Bee Gees. In 1976 Walter Murphy's 'A Fifth of Beethoven' had taken a classical riff (the same four-note phrase used later the same year on the Damned's 'New Rose', the first British punk rock single) and turned it into suburban disco fodder. It was novelty pop, like 'Disco Duck', and both of those records became American number ones. The *Fever* soundtrack album skipped Rick Dees' quacking (though you could hear it in the movie) but did find room for Murphy, the Trammps' 'Disco Inferno' (infinitely better, but still the point where Philly soul was submerged by disco's repetitive beats) and Kool & the Gang's funky 'Open Sesame' ('Get on your camel and ride!').

'How Deep Is Your Love' had been the lead single from the soundtrack, and it could stand alone, but 'Stayin' Alive' and the movie – and the Travolta strut – lived off each other. They were inseparable. Barry's vocal echoed the blend of cocksure machismo ('No time to talk') and cyclical desperation ('Life goin' nowhere / Somebody help me') that mirrored Tony Manero's thin life. Its rhythm and dark mood, countering the irresistible looped rhythm track and the melodic, inviting bassline, were what producer Bob Ezrin had in mind when he mixed Pink Floyd's 'Another Brick in the Wall (Part II)' two years later.

It isn't too hard to imagine how a 1978 Bee Gees album might have turned out. There were a brace of Andy Gibb singles that year in 'Shadow Dancing' (which turned out to be an even bigger single than anything on *SNF*, spending seven weeks at number one in America) and 'An Everlasting Love' (his only top-ten hit in Britain), while former Marble Graham Bonnet was given the equally solid 'Warm Ride', whose thrusting lyric would have suited the movie's violent and emotionally illiterate Danny Zuko ('We must surrender to the powers that be – the angel in you and the devil in me'). Bonnet was just about to reinvent himself as a hard rocker by joining Ritchie Blackmore's Rainbow and cutting the deathless 'Since You've Been Gone'. The Gibbs' recording of 'Warm Ride' – 'a bit too sexual, a bit too hot under the collar,' reckoned Barry – was the only Château-written song left off *Saturday Night Fever*; it would turn up as a bonus track on a compilation many years later.

It seems a bit pointless to rail against an album that would be the best-selling movie soundtrack of all time until *The Bodyguard* was released in 1992. Still, it's galling that there is only half a Bee Gees album in there. Why didn't Stigwood give them another couple of weeks? Hell, even another couple of days? Their hot streak was unprecedented, and would never be beaten. In the knackered old Château, they had written 'Stayin' Alive', 'Night Fever', 'More than a Woman', 'If I Can't Have You' and 'How Deep Is Your Love' without pausing. Then came the phone call. Think of what more they might have achieved.

Billboard US top ten, 24 March 1978

1. Bee Gees – 'Night Fever'
2. Bee Gees – 'Stayin' Alive'
3. Samantha Sang – 'Emotion'
4. Eric Clapton – 'Lay Down Sally'
5. Barry Manilow – 'Can't Smile Without You'
6. Andy Gibb – '(Love Is) Thicker than Water'
7. Paul Davis – 'I Go Crazy'
8. Dan Hill – 'Sometimes When We Touch'
9. Yvonne Elliman – 'If I Can't Have You'
10. Jay Ferguson – 'Thunder Island'

For one week in April of 1964, the top five singles on the *Billboard* Hot 100 had all been by the Beatles. This remains the only time one single act has occupied the entire top five, and it will probably never happen again. In March 1978, the Bee Gees gave it their best shot.

The week that 'Night Fever' went to number one in the US, 'Stayin' Alive' was at number two and both singles would stay put for the next five weeks; the Bee Gees became the first group, post-Beatles, to hold down number one and number two at the same time. In that first week, the Bee Gees had written or produced four songs in the top five – the others were Andy Gibb's '(Love Is) Thicker than Water', on its way down from number one, and Samantha Sang's 'Emotion', which would peak at three.[24] A couple of weeks later they claimed

---

[24] The fifth record in the top five was 'Lay Down Sally' by Eric Clapton, another RSO act.

five records in the top ten as Yvonne Elliman's 'If I Can't Have You' climbed to number nine, also on its way to number one. The Beatles' achievement remains singular, but the Gibbs' moment was arguably more impressive in that none of the singles were cash-in reissues, as 'Twist and Shout' and 'Please Please Me' had been in 1964. What's more, the Gibbs wrote and produced the lot. They weren't just tapping into the zeitgeist as they had been with 'You Should Be Dancing' two years earlier. Now the zeitgeist emanated from Criteria Studios, and from the Gibb brothers themselves.

Was there a reason why brother Andy didn't get a song on the *Saturday Night Fever* soundtrack? He seemed an obvious candidate for one of the gentler romantic songs, like 'More than a Woman', which had inexplicably been given to Tavares, who weren't even part of the RSO family. 'I Just Want to Be Your Everything' – familiar, popular – could have slotted in as background music at any point. It was as if he was shut out of the party. Maybe his brothers wanted him to stand on his own two feet. If he felt at all isolated, he must have felt a little better when Barry gifted him another huge hit, his third straight US number one, with 'Shadow Dancing'. But by then Kim had gone, taken back to Australia after just a few months of marriage by her concerned parents. Stuck at number two behind 'Shadow Dancing' was Gerry Rafferty's 'Baker Street', another supernaturally powerful production buoying up a less than totally confident singer: Rafferty sang of a musician with a dream about buying some land, no more booze, no more one-night stands, just a plan to 'settle down in a quiet little town, and forget about everything'. Well, that scenario would have suited Andy down to the ground. He'd try hard enough to get there.

Robert Stigwood saw the Gibbs as a resource, a premium value asset that he owned, one that could improve the stock on any aspect of his entertainment empire. He rinsed them for material. While they could have been promoting 'Stayin' Alive' and *Fever* at the end of 1977, he had them in Hollywood working on his screwy idea to turn *Sgt Pepper's Lonely Hearts Club Band* into a musical. Blonde and curly Peter Frampton, an RSO act who had been hugely successful in 1976 with *Frampton Comes Alive*, and was still reasonably hot in 1977 with follow-up album *I'm in You*, was to be the star of the movie. It was apparent to all concerned while the movie was being edited that the Bee Gees – filmed essentially as Frampton's backing band – had become by far the bigger name. But that didn't help the movie, which, though it cost ten times the amount of Stigwood's other in-production musical *Grease*, was painfully bad.[25]

It was directed by Michael Schultz, who was working with the biggest budget ever given to an African American director. Schultz was hip. Having started with sarcastic political revues on Broadway, he had gone on to direct *Car Wash* (1976) and *Which Way Is Up* (1977), both of which featured soundtracks by psychedelic soul visionary Norman Whitfield. He could count Richard Pryor and Pam Grier among his close friends. All this and a bunch of Lennon–McCartney songs. What could go wrong?

The Gibbs had to record a bunch of Beatles songs for the soundtrack, handling impossible jobs like 'A Day in the Life'. Robin's crack at McCartney's raucous 'Oh Darling' – a throwback which could just as easily have fitted onto Stigwood's *Grease* score – gave the brothers yet another top-twenty hit. That would be as good as it got.

In the near half-century since it was made, cinema-goers' cultural literacy has shifted to accommodate an ironic way of

---

[25] Not even funny bad. Really, don't watch it.

watching bad movies, and a mainstreaming of what had previously been a niche camp aesthetic. Yet still *Sgt Pepper* evades all routes to rehabilitation. Susan Sontag said 'camp is a failed seriousness'. *Sgt Pepper* is possibly unique in that it manages to be failed camp. You can look at *Sgt Pepper* a hundred different ways on paper and it always looks, at the very least, intriguing. Other similar follies from the late '70s, like Olivia Newton-John's *Xanadu*, have charm and pathos as well as kitsch value. Until you see it, it's hard to believe *Sgt Pepper* has none of these. Somehow, in spite of the huge expense of the production, its scale looks embarrassingly small.

Among numerous star cameos, Steve Martin plays a cosmetic surgeon who sings 'Maxwell's Silver Hammer' as if it's 'The Monster Mash'; the skit sees him aimlessly running around an operating theatre, applying his stethoscope to women's chests – the song feels very long. Alice Cooper attacks *Abbey Road*'s 'Because' as if he hates it; Billy Preston sings 'Get Back' and appears to be God. The finale features everyone from Robert Palmer, Donovan and Dr John to Gwen Verdon, Keith Carradine and Dame Edna Everage. Congratulations if you make it that far.

'It's fun simply because it's so berserk,' claimed Michael Schultz. 'The idea is to take people on a trip, even those die-hard people who say, "Oh, Peter Frampton and the Bee Gees, they're not going to be the Beatles." Well, they're not the Beatles. They're goody-goody singers who have been entrusted with the magic music of *Sgt Pepper* to bring joy to the world. And if you accept that premise, you won't have any trouble with the picture.' Was this meant to put punters at ease? Schultz's unintentionally damning critique suggested that 'die-hard' Beatles fans – who included the Gibb brothers, as well as a large proportion of the music-loving world – were in for a rough ride.

If you're looking for highlights, there's a brief moment where Mo looks to the camera and wiggles his eyebrows as Stargard, fronted by Dianne Steinberg, magically lose half their clothes while singing 'Lucy in the Sky with Diamonds'. Now, if Stigwood and Schultz really had to redo the Beatles' catalogue for the late '70s, Elton John had left them a decent waymark with his extraordinarily odd and cinematic reimagination of 'Lucy in the Sky with Diamonds' in 1975. It trounces the lukewarm Stargard version. Indeed, all the music in the film is weirdly undercooked, though the soundtrack album somehow went platinum (again, the *Xanadu* album would become a bigger seller in spite of the movie, because songs like John Farrar's 'Magic' were simply terrific).

At the time, possibly in an attempt to define hubris, Robin proclaimed: 'Kids today don't know the Beatles' *Sgt Pepper*. When they see our film, that will be the version they relate to. The Beatles will be secondary. They don't exist as a band and never performed *Sgt Pepper*. When ours comes out, it will be as if theirs never existed.'

By the end of 1978, all of the Gibbs, including Andy, and even most of their in-laws, were living in Miami full-time. Well, nearly all: Robin and Molly, with kids Spencer and Melissa, stayed in England. Earlier in the year they had flown over to New York for a trip to the set of *Sesame Street* – Robin had recorded a song called 'Trash' for the *Sesame Street Fever* album with the stipulation that his kids got to meet Cookie Monster.

Released as a single in October 1978, it was lyrically more of a return to *Robin's Reign* than an exuberant anthem: 'When the great things that I've planned just get wrecked eventually / Trash, it's everything to me.' The album went gold, naturally, like everything else the Bee Gees touched in 1978. The family later flew back to New York to be presented with a gold disc by Big Bird.

The Gibbs were now a music mill, producing songs that were cut-to-fit Beatles tributes or '50s soda shop fantasies or kiddie disco albums or contemporary teen pin-up dreams. Stigwood saw them as his own diamond mine which miraculously produced stones that needed neither cutting nor polishing. The Gibbs had always been proud of the way they had written 'Lonely Days' and 'How Can You Mend a Broken Heart' in one 1970 session, having been apart for the best part of two years. In 1978, they wrote 'Too Much Heaven', 'Tragedy' and 'Shadow Dancing' during a day off on the set of *Sgt Pepper* – probably an afternoon off, in fact, as all three songs, all future number ones, were wrapped in about two hours.

'This is a life of illusion, wrapped up in trouble, laced with confusion. What are we doing here?' Barry's theme for *Grease* was an afterthought to the film's real soundtrack, requested as a favour by a nervous Stigwood – a title song written by the hottest songwriter in the world was a shoo-in to get the film some attention. It turned out *Grease* wouldn't need the helping hand, but Barry's song was startling, delivered by the never-gruffer, 44-year-old Frankie Valli, one of the Bee Gees' heroes when they had lived in Australia. Back then he had possessed the world's most famous falsetto, an unreal mix of androgyny and machismo. He holds the falsetto back for the entirety of 'Grease', maybe in deference to the bearded Mancunian who had just stolen his crown. Barry must have been humbled, see-ing a split screen: one screen showed him in 1978, next to Valli in the studio, coaching him through the song; the other showed boy Barry in Brisbane in 1963, holding his transistor radio to his ear listening to Valli siren-scream his way through 'Walk Like a Man', a direct New York forebear to the 'Stayin' Alive' strut.

'WHAT ARE WE DOING HERE?' Barry's 'Grease' also gave an edge to the soundtrack that songs like John Farrar's very pretty 'Hopelessly Devoted to You' or the yowling, cartoonish 'Summer Nights' didn't possess – 'only real is real'. *Grease* was no more an accurate depiction of the '50s than was mid-'70s TV show *Happy Days*, both being scrubbed whiter than white and exaggerating their source material until it became almost surreal. The transformation of Olivia Newton-John at the film's end into a late '70s pin-up suggested some off-camera *Back to the Future* time-travel sequence we hadn't noticed – 'conventional-ity', as Barry might say, didn't come into it. At the film's end, Olivia and John Travolta drove their car upwards, towards the sky, away from the Earth, waving goodbye to both their school days and the planet. Frankie Valli's theme was there to clear the air. This had all been a lurid dream of the past. From now on, let's look forward instead of backward, the song suggested; there's still work to do.

The original trailer for *Saturday Night Fever* had featured a long shot of Travolta's famous strut, followed by a few brief stills. It let 'Stayin' Alive' suggest the storyline. The trailer was wordless until an ominous voiceover: 'Where do you go when the record is over?'

'We're scared of the next album,' said Barry in 1978. 'We're the same desperate, worried, insecure songwriters we've ever been.' The bubble was yet to burst, but the Gibbs had been here before, more than once – it was only the scale that had changed. The year 1978, during which the Bee Gees had written and produced seven American number-one singles, ended with another one knocking on the door. 'Too Much Heaven' / 'Rest Your Love on Me', wasn't something you could dance to, but both sides were sweetly irresistible. 'Nobody gets too much heaven' – they already knew as much, so it was best to start diversifying. Black radio and country radio picked a side each. It looked like the Bee Gees would be able to move on from disco before the sound *du jour* inevitably began to fade.

14

CHICAGO

Record Mirror UK top ten, 3 March 1979

1. Bee Gees – 'Tragedy'
2. Blondie – 'Heart of Glass'
3. Elvis Costello and the Attractions – 'Oliver's Army'
4. Gloria Gaynor – 'I Will Survive'
5. ABBA – 'Chiquitita'
6. Edwin Starr – 'Contact'
7. Leif Garrett – 'I Was Made for Dancin''
8. Lene Lovich – 'Lucky Number'
9. Three Degrees – 'Woman in Love'
10. Darts – 'Get It'

'There are so many directions to take our music that we refuse to stay in one place. If you try to repeat, or hold onto a successful formula, you die. We are always changing.'

– Barry Gibb

'I received an invitation; "Come to the United Nations."
That was when I was somebody.'

— Bee Gees, 'In My Own Time', 1967

In 1971, David Bowie had appeared on the cover of his *The Man Who Sold the World* album in what he called a 'man dress'. In 1993, Suede's debut album featured a cover shot of two golden, androgynous beings, passionately kissing. Both album covers promised something new, a new way of being, something beyond gender. In both cases, they had male guitar rock, with riffs and lyrics about concrete and steel, slipped inside the promising packaging. Both Bowie and Suede may have aspired to androgyny in their music, but neither had the means (not yet, at least, in Bowie's case).

Androgyny is a British pop trait that dates back to music hall, with male impersonators like Vesta Tilley, and later pantomime dames like Danny La Rue. Falsetto singing in American rock 'n' roll had always signified sexual excitement, especially when a song started low and wound itself up for the tenor man to let fly, like Maurice Williams and the Zodiacs' 'Stay' or Lou Christie's 'Lightning Strikes'. By the '70s it had become the sound of the trustworthy lover man, defying macho norms and charming the birds down from the trees: songs like Eddie Holman's 'Hey There Lonely Girl', endlessly romantic to British kids in 1974. The emotion in the lyric was intensified by Holman's androgynous voice; likewise, the Stylistics' 'You Make Me Feel Brand New', another 1974 hit, used Russell Thompkins Jr's glass-shattering high notes to render Linda Creed's lyric wise and selfless. With the falsetto, the song's impact was heightened, time was suspended, and the boundaries between gender norms softened.

So the Bee Gees of the late '70s were in a grand tradition. When she was just five years old, a good friend of mine loved the Bee Gees cassettes her dad would play in the car and, with a child's simplified view of the world, she had assumed the Bee Gees were women. When her dad eventually showed her the cover of *Spirits Having Flown* – the beards, the hair, the metallic muskiness – she was so shocked she burst into tears.

Disco was music that impacted society, blurred lines, upset and excited people. It had helped to make 1978 a year of exciting flux, in London, in New York, around the world. But what about the Bee Gees and their insular world? What could they do after they had glimpsed, then helped to create, the future of pop music? This androgynous, machine-tooled, Gibb-coloured future they were now inhabiting? Where could they go next?

Not many groups play a farewell tour at the peak of their powers. Not many are so sure that things can't get any better, that it was better to get while the getting was good. The Bee Gees never announced their 1979 world tour would be their last, but the brothers knew it. They spent most of 1979 rehearsing and playing huge live shows in enormodome venues. They anticipated that their moment in the spotlight couldn't sustain; that their omnipresence was their weakness. Disco's fall from grace shouldn't have doomed an act as multi-faceted as the Bee Gees, but the public and the media tend to reduce things to a word, a catchphrase, and in the Bee Gees' case that word was 'disco'. The brothers had decided on a plan for the future by late 1978, before any backlash took hold – they would revert to being songwriters and producers.

Spirits Having Flown was their immediate answer to 'what next?'. Recording had begun as far back as March 1978; it finally emerged in January 1979. Barry, Karl and Albhy would be in the studio from three in the afternoon until midnight, every day. Occasionally stars like Glen Campbell and Willie Nelson came to Barry's house to jam. He was still smoking marijuana for England, but his kitchen cupboards showed how he hadn't completely adopted the Miami lifestyle – they were full of imported PG Tips, Bovril, Yorkshire pudding mix and tins of mushy peas. Still, the blend of Barry, Karl and Albhy made for quite the international grill.

A full-page ad in *Billboard* proclaimed *Spirits* to be 'the record the world's been waiting for'. It was the kind of Stigwood brag that rubbed many up the wrong way, but for now the public proved him right – it went straight to number one in Britain and America. *Rolling Stone* understood its intentions, calling it 'space-age pop . . . the Bee Gees, Galuten and Richardson offer a sugary, futuristic melange of ABBA-styled Europop, post-Motown R&B and Miami disco. The strongest songs outstrip ABBA in sophistication while maintaining the requisite Europop tone of brittle, ultra-accessible cordiality.'

The year 1979 would be the peak of high Bee Gees. They would crisscross America in a personalised jet plane. They were living in a Beatle-esque bubble of super-fame, which had been quite unimaginable five years earlier. They had gone from third-rate variety club act to multinational operatives. Barry had said out loud that he was aware the next album needed to prove the sensational success of *Saturday Night Fever* wasn't a fluke. This only heightened his tendencies towards furrow-browed studio perfectionism, and this in turn slowly began to rile the musicians around him, including his brothers.

To the public, the year had started with the Gibbs at pop's harmonious pinnacle. With 'Too Much Heaven' at number one in the States, the timing couldn't have been better for a huge charity concert Stigwood had organised for UNICEF to mark 1979 as the International Year of the Child. It took place in the United Nations' General Assembly Hall, David Frost compered, and the other acts included ABBA, Olivia Newton-John, Rod Stewart, Donna Summer and John Denver. It was shown on NBC in the US and on the BBC; 300 million people watched it worldwide. All these names, all this stardust, and the Bee Gees were the headliners. *Rolling Stone* noted how 'they were haloed in soft focus like blissed-out angels just back from a meeting with God'.

They donated all earnings from 'Too Much Heaven' to UNICEF in perpetuity, which would amount to more than $7 million over the years. It also earned them an invitation to the White House from President Carter. Andy Gibb appeared at the United Nations, too, singing 'Rest Your Love on Me', the B-side of 'Too Much Heaven', which can't have done his confidence much good. The rumour – direct from the desk of Robert Stigwood – was that Andy was stepping out with Olivia Newton-John; it at least served to keep his name in the headlines, ahead of recordings for his third album.

The songs on *Spirits Having Flown* are quite varied in style, but the sameness of the vocals – almost all Barry solos, almost all falsetto – can give the impression that they sound more alike than they really do. *Spirits Having Flown* is just as musically varied as any Bee Gees album, but Albhy Galuten's decision to use Barry's falsetto all over the album was probably a mistake. Years later, Albhy said that Barry felt more expressive in falsetto, and that it gave him greater range. Technically he may have been right. To the public, that voice reminded them of *Saturday Night Fever*, and that was all.

The album was their lushest to date, and it would produce two further US number ones, with 'Too Much Heaven' having already set the bar high. The next new song anyone heard from the album was 'Tragedy', with an opening guitar motif that would have felt at home on *Hotel California*, and anticipated ABBA's more aesthetically pleasing fusion of guitar and electronics on 'Gimme Gimme Gimme (A Man After Midnight)' a few months later. The ominous cello stabs then link this rather un-Bee Gees intro into more familiar territory – a never-higher Barry falsetto over restless bubbling sequenced percussion. The high anxiety of the verse sounds like a bridge, as if you're already mid-song, which gives the impression that the music is steadily, vertiginously climbing. All that tension breaks with a clap of thunder. It's all quite gaudy, the polar opposite of 'Too Much Heaven''s balm – but that also explains 'Tragedy''s huge success. It was also the only overtly disco song on the whole album.

Truthfully it did sound like Barry had been studio-bound, scared to leave the room, keeping the pro-disco and anti-disco agitators behind high metal fencing and security guards. In spite of its many high points, *Spirits Having Flown* felt more temperature-controlled and less naturalistic than the Château songs, or even Andy's solo records. If you listen closely to 'Search, Find' or the arid 'I'm Satisfied' ('making my love to you'), you can almost feel the chilled waft of the air conditioning.

There was a smidgen of Robin, and that's as much as you got – this was a Barry solo album in all but name. Still, *Spirits Having Flown* was a very good album, a solid eight out of ten, and only slipped in comparison to the absolute, objective greatness of the *Fever* songs. 'Stop (Think Again)' was a deep soul ballad, one of the few tracks where you could hear Dennis Bryon playing live drums. There are dark strings, and Chicago's horn section softens the distress; frustratingly it just starts to loosen up as the song fades. 'Living Together' began with a brass fanfare like a TV news bulletin, ready for action.

The strongest song was the one that landed furthest away from where they had been. This was the title track, sung in Barry's natural voice, one of only two tracks not sung in falsetto, which made it stand out immediately. It had a count-in from Barry, which again emphasised its organic nature. Floating on a bed of acoustic guitars, some kind of synthesised pipes and a cooling wave of vocal harmonies, it also had a chorus like a seafaring epic, Barry appearing as an elemental deity: 'I am your hurricane, your fire and your sun / How long must I live in the air.' And then he took the song back down again, into calmer waters – 'I'd like to take you where my spirit flies.' It ebbed and flowed exquisitely. It was worth the ten months it had taken to perfect.

The closing track, 'Until', was all Aero bubbles, Barry's voice ascending like the hot-air balloon he needed to take him away from New York's dark, dense dancehall dens and up into the clouds. Both the music and the narrative are left hanging suspended, glacial and heartbreaking. It was one of their more extraordinary songs, all atmosphere, no hook, because it didn't need a hook.

Mostly, the music press hated *Spirits Having Flown*. Less than a year earlier, Simon Frith had written about them glowingly, if tentatively, in a piece for *Creem* called 'Confessions of a Bee Gees Fan': 'I found that my most played record of 1977 wasn't the Sex Pistols' *Bollocks* but the Bee Gees' [*Here at Last*] – their double live album which not only has as clean a sound as any studio set, but also has a side with all their old hits . . . an instant synopsis of their career that proves that in all the moves, from psychedelia to ballad to disco, nothing has really changed.' He was right, of course. But six months later he was low on empathy. Reviewing *Spirits* for *Melody Maker*, Frith sighed: 'The Bee Gees have stuck to their disco formula: the tight falsettos and repeated phrases, the curiously mechanical rhythms. They make music for people who dance on tiptoe, and the album's only conceit is "Until", the last track, a quavery ballad with tragic pretensions.' He compared them to the Stylistics, soft soul kings of the mid-'70s, who, 'for all the sweetness of their work with Thom Bell, were a soul group – their art was the art of emotional expression. The Bee Gees aren't in the expressive business at all. Their sound might just as well be made by machines.'

So who needed the press? The brothers had already decided to spend most of 1979 on tour in the States, plugging the hell out of *Spirits*. They would milk the moment, take the applause and remuneration, then take a step backwards. Didn't they worry about being cooped up backstage, in limos, on planes, without a break for months on end? 'There was an adjustment period five years ago,' said Barry, ever the level-headed spokesman, 'but all the little hassles and hang-ups have disappeared.'

Back in 1977 the Bee Gees had been interviewed for *Circus* magazine. At that point, they were just about to head to the Honky Château for the writing session of their lives. Barry and Maurice were still living on the Isle of Man – they still had that connection to the old Bee Gees world, but were getting caught up in a new slipstream. 'Right now, it's a very vibrant band and the songs are pouring out,' gasped Barry. 'In the old days we took three or four weeks to cut an album, and now we're taking three months. It makes a hell of a difference, especially when you're in there with the right people. The band – Dennis Bryon, Alan Kendall and Blue Weaver – are more like Bee Gees than side musicians, these guys have been with us for years. On *Children of the World* everyone gets a cut, not just a wage.' The Bee Gees were delighted to be together, scoring hits, and writing great songs. What else could they possibly ask for? 'It must be a drag to be a solo artist,' mused Barry, 'because no one knows what it feels like except you. But the three of us can celebrate success together.'

Two years later, as the biggest band in the world, and despite Barry's assurances that all was well, the old doubts and jealousies had begun to creep back in. The private jet that would fly them around the States had an area sectioned off for the Gibbs and their family; Dennis Bryon felt less like a Bee Gee than a side musician, effectively sitting in economy class on the band's own luxury jet.

But things weren't much happier in first class. Robin and Maurice were barely present on *Spirits Having Flown* – the album was tied up by Barry and Albhy. Robin would come to the studio to give his judgement on what his big brother had done. If Mo wasn't capable of contributing, Robin sure as hell was, but he wasn't required by Barry, Karl or Albhy. Instead, the elder Gibb would add layers of his own harmonies to songs like 'Too Much Heaven' (which featured at least eight tracks of Barry) that his little brothers would then be expected to approximate on stage.

Linda and Yvonne would accompany their husbands on the tour. Molly, sanguine, stayed at home in Britain: 'There is no time for being helpless or jealous – that's what causes so many breakups. Of course, the children miss their father, but they have grown up with the situation. And there's always Concorde . . . You don't own your partner.' A family friend noticed that when Robin was home, his daughter Melissa would follow him around like a puppy. But Molly hated the regimented nature of a tour – the lobby calls, the soundchecks, the airlessness.

In May 1979, Robin left Molly and the kids in England for the 41-date American tour. Rehearsals had been intense – the group even skipped the 1979 *Billboard* awards which saw them scoop eleven trophies, with mum Barbara and thirteen-year-old niece Beri, Lesley's daughter, representing them instead. They booked just five hotels for the entire tour – after each show the band would fly back to the nearest one. It must have been exhausting. The first show was on 28 June in Fort Worth, Texas, and the first surprise the audience got was from Robin, who had dyed his long wavy hair red, apparently to match the coat of his Irish setter, Penny. In Houston, John Travolta jumped on stage with them to throw some shapes. And at LA's Dodger Stadium, fellow disco heroes Harry 'KC' Casey and Michael Jackson came backstage; also in attendance were Karen Carpenter, Olivia Newton-John – who had just recorded a brace of duets with Andy – and Barbra Streisand. Every night, there were fireworks and mirror balls. Every show sold out, including three nights at Madison Square Garden.

What was going on in the world outside? Well, *Spirits Having Flown* was on its way to selling 16 million copies, and spawning three US number-one singles in 1979. 'Tragedy' had made it there in March; the liquid 'Love You Inside Out' would be the third, just as the tour was starting up. This was their sixth number one on the bounce – only the Beatles had managed this feat before – and its lack of overfamiliarity has given the song longevity; Feist would cover it on her debut album, and its slow funk has dated very well.

Though they put on a brave face for an NBC special, hosted by David Frost, re-enacting the moment Barry made the thunderclap noise on 'Tragedy' for the cameras, the tour was a struggle. It generated $10 million in ticket sales alone, but the brothers were fraying at the edges. Barry later admitted he was often close to tears – 'I found myself either on top of the world or totally depressed . . . Being the Bee Gees is like three people being one person. It's impossible. We are each of us having an identity crisis.' Amphetamines kept him focused. Robin, meanwhile, said, 'To all intents and purposes this tour is like being in prison . . . to go out and buy a shirt would require two hours' planning for logistics and security.' Just after the tour started, catching him unawares, Molly asked Robin for a divorce. She had finally tired of his womanising, his continued heavy use of uppers and downers, and his near-permanent absence; the fallout from this split would be terrible. At the same time, both Barry and Robin were worried sick about Mo's drinking. More than once, he had to feel his way along the wall to the stage. It seems incredible he made it through the tour without them putting out another emergency call to Lesley. 'Every day, I didn't want to get up,' he said later. 'My biggest defect of character, if you like, is unworthiness. I just didn't feel worthy of what I was doing.'

He wasn't the only Gibb with huge insecurities. Andy had started his third album with Barry in late 1978 and attempted to complete it while his brothers were on tour – he wasn't capable, and tried to binge away his inadequacies. One listen to his 1980 songs 'Dreamin' On' and the tell-tale 'Someone I Ain't' showed he was a gentle soul, happier in softer waters where country meets AOR. He was not untalented by any means, but he was always going to try to measure himself up against Barry's talent and achievements, which could only end in misery. 'My brothers handed it down to me on a silver platter,' Andy would later say. 'I didn't have any confidence. I always thought that people were buying my records as an extension to the Bee Gees and I never thought there was an individual thing in there they liked.' Al Coury, RSO's president, said, 'He was treated like a superstar from day one, paid very well, lived like a king, private planes. You had to worry about him because you knew some day the hits were going to stop.'

What could help Andy to get over his inferiority complex? Well, it certainly shouldn't have been a screen test for *Grease II*, in which he was going for the role of Sandy's younger brother. He now lived on a giant houseboat called *Shadow Dancer* with a pet lion cub to keep him company; when it grew too big for the boat he gave it to Miami Zoo. Then he thought about getting a pet giraffe – he was talked out of that one. When he had first broken through in 1977, still a teenager, he had started hanging out with Susan George, who was some eight years older. But his party spirit was already too much for her: 'I would try my best and, to be fair, so would he. In the end, you feel helpless. He was such a natural boy. He had tremendous charisma and vitality,' she said. 'He was always very special to me.' Andy would lie on his vast bed – in the room where *Shadow Dancer*'s previous owner, a drug lord, had been shot dead – and stare at the mirrored ceiling, playing with guns, nothing to do and nowhere to go. Andy Gibb's childhood had basically been *Coronation Street* and this was, what? *Dynasty*? Not even that. Cocaine was a constant, and it fed his paranoia about Caribbean pirates. It was closer to a mafia movie, or something more surreal – maybe he was recreating the tail end of *The Man Who Fell to Earth*: 'I think Mr Gibb has had enough.'

When the Bee Gees tour ended in October 1979, Barry was straight back in the studio with Andy to try to finish recording *After Dark*, his third solo album. Andy had remained in the papers thanks to his love life. He had been dating Marie Osmond, the only sister of the singing Mormons. Andy told the press: 'I fancy her like mad!' How on earth could it have worked? 'He was doing tons of drugs and she didn't even drink Coca Cola,' laughed Albhy. The Mormon Osmond family turned him away; Marie took legal action to stop him calling. On the rebound, Olympic skater Tai Babilonia was Andy's squeeze for a while, and there were still RSO-instigated rumours about Olivia Newton-John. 'It takes two to tango,' said Andy, ruefully. At least Livvy would duet twice on the new album, including on a gorgeous new Barry ballad called 'I Can't Help It'; a sweet, floaty concoction that would become a US number-twelve hit in 1980. What the album lacked was much input from Andy. Cocaine and Quaaludes had wrecked his voice and often he just didn't turn up to the studio. Albhy Galuten remembered Andy being 'in such bad shape that we were just doing something to put on it'. What he meant was a lot of the tracks had entire vocals by Barry, doing his best impression of Andy. 'It wasn't an Andy album anymore,' says Galuten. 'It was a contractual obligation . . . It was Barry trying to rescue his brother. He was a basket case. His voice . . . was wispy, there was no character to it.' 'Desire' was the lead single, a song that had started out as a *Spirits Having Flown* track, which explains how all four Gibbs both wrote it and sang on it – Barry's lead vocal was simply replaced by Andy's. It was a terrific song, not unlike a midtempo 'Too Much Heaven', with a classic, unexpected Bee Gees lift onto the chorus. It outdid his last couple of singles and went to number four in 1980. It wasn't the intention, but 'Desire' was the closest we would ever get to hearing the Bee Gees with Andy as a fourth member.

By 1980, the world had moved on from disco. More than that, the world – at least the white American rock world – had decided to throw disco into a bin and set fire to it. That 'Desire' still charted as high as it did was surprising. Historical shorthand for 'disco backlash' had taken place on 12 July 1979, when Chicago WLUP DJ Steve Dahl organised a literal bonfire of disco records at the White Sox baseball game. He popularised the phrase 'Disco Sucks', and a campaign which quickly went viral. Guess who the chief victims would be?

Forty-five thousand were at Comiskey Park, Chicago, for the White Sox game on 14 July 1979, gaining admittance for just 98 cents as they had each brought along a disco record to burn. The Bee Gees had played the Oakland-Alameda County Coliseum the night before. They had a day's rest ahead of dates at the Center Coliseum, Seattle, WA; the PNE Coliseum, Vancouver, BC; the Veterans Memorial Coliseum, Portland, OR; the Civic Center Arena, St Paul, MN; the Hilton Coliseum, Ames, IA; the Dane County Coliseum, Madison, WI; the Market Square Arena, Indianapolis, IN; and the Silverdome in Pontiac, MI, before they saw July out with two nights at the Chicago Stadium, IL. Those shows must have felt quite strange.

Steve Dahl and his acolytes were straight white men who were threatened by disco's prevalence. They brought along Smokey Robinson records. They brought along Marvin Gaye records. They brought along Bee Gees records. They didn't like falsettos. They didn't like androgynous white satin shirts. It didn't accord with their idea of maleness. It was too gay and it was too black, and the records they brought along to Comiskey Park were either too gay or too black or both. So they built a funeral pyre. Dahl's stunt made the news and, very quickly, there were copycat DJs across America, whole chapters of anti-disco evangelicals.

When a one-shot garage rock band called the Knack released 'My Sharona' on 25 August 1979, it became the first number one of the year that wasn't R&B or disco. It was celebrated by Dahl's reactionary forces as if it was 'Blue Suede Shoes' liberating America from Eddie Fisher and Liberace.

History has recorded this moment as a seismic change, the death of disco and the return of rock; the reality was rather different. After 'My Sharona', there would be a sole week at the top for Robert John's milky mope 'Sad Eyes' before Michael Jackson's 'Don't Stop 'Til You Get Enough' took over, a recording very clearly influenced by the Bee Gees and one that upped the ante. Again, the anxiety. Again, the falsetto, the fever, only this time faster, more intense. It sounded very much like the future, and so did Herb Alpert's 'Rise', which replaced 'Don't Stop' after one week at the top. 'Rise' was jazz funk, pure and simple, played by the trumpet-playing smoothie who ran A&M Records in his spare time. Donna Summer and Barbra Streisand's diva face-off 'No More Tears (Enough Is Enough)' then spent a fortnight at number one in November 1979. 1980's number ones kicked off with KC and the Sunshine Band's 'Please Don't Go', which sounded like a farewell to a golden era from the original Miami hit machine, but would be followed in short order by Michael Jackson's 'Rock with You'; Lipps Inc's 'Funkytown'; Pink Floyd's 'Another Brick in the Wall' (with its drum track modelled on

'Stayin' Alive'); Blondie's Giorgio Moroder-produced 'Call Me'; Diana Ross's Chic-produced 'Upside Down'; and Queen's funk foray 'Another One Bites the Dust'. And following John Deacon's hip hop-fuelling bassline, the Bee Gees were back – at least Barry and Babs were, with Streisand's 'Woman in Love'. So did Steve Dahl and the Knack kill disco? Not really. The Travolta look was dead, of course, as the fashion wheel turned – Michael Jackson in his *Off the Wall* pomp was now a new and rather more radical role model for masculinity. Steve Dahl hadn't seen that coming.

But all the same, Dahl had helped turn the Bee Gees into an easy punchline. No question, they took the brunt of the public's change in taste. They were as passé as Bobby Vee, Helen Shapiro and Adam Faith after the Beatles arrived. R&B moved on but the Bee Gees were suddenly, and completely, out of fashion.

15

COVENTRY

'We went to pop heaven for about two years . . . we were suddenly living in a goldfish bowl and we couldn't perceive real life.'

– Barry Gibb

Record Mirror UK top ten, 8 November 1980

1. Barbra Streisand – 'Woman in Love'
2. Status Quo – 'What You're Proposing'
3. Bad Manners – 'Special Brew'
4. Adam and the Ants – 'Dog Eat Dog'
5. Blondie – 'The Tide Is High'
6. Matchbox – 'When You Ask About Love'
7. Odyssey – 'If You're Looking for a Way Out'
8. David Bowie – 'Fashion'
9. Orchestral Manoeuvres in the Dark – 'Enola Gay'
10. Ottawan – 'D.I.S.C.O.'

The year 1980 was that of seven minutes to midnight, the highest nuclear tension ever known: British number-one albums of 1980 included Gary Numan's *Telekon* and *Peter Gabriel* (known as *Melt*), two of the most emotionally desolate albums imaginable, full of paranoia and songs about mental illness. A wet, fearful summer was soundtracked by a reissued 'Theme from *M*A*S*H* (Suicide Is Painless)' at the top of the UK singles chart, and in the dark autumn UB40's 'The Earth Dies Screaming' became maybe the single most apocalyptic song to ever reach the top ten. On the album chart, that autumn saw Barry Gibb and Barbra Streisand standing on the cover of their *Guilty* album in white boiler suits, set against a brilliant white background. The feel was post-nuclear; Barry looked fierce and protective.

Once Andy's third album had been finally polished to the point where nobody could notice the principal actor's absence, Barry and Robin began to write the songs for Barbra Streisand's new album. She had been to see them at Dodger Stadium and decided she wanted them to work on her next record. And in 1979 Babs tended to get what she wanted. The initial idea was for the Gibb brothers to write and produce half of the album – but she got on so well with Barry they ended up doing the whole thing, without the need for either Robin or Maurice to be in the studio.

The first single from the album was 'Woman in Love', its cosmic isolation set up in the opening line: 'Life is a moment in space / When the dream has gone, it's a lonelier place.' Most people can relate to this, post-break up, or even in bereavement; it is one of the most exposed opening lines to any pop song. 'Woman in Love' is one of the ultimate Bee Gees songs, in that it defies conventional language but still burrows into your heart, carrying with it a depth charge of emotion. 'Woman in Love' wants to take you into the Gibbs' world, and hold you within: 'In love, there is no measure of time.' Bizarrely, Streisand had reservations about recording the song because of the line 'It's a right I defend', which she construed as rampantly feminist.

The album's production was as astral and gaseous as the lyrics. Those are recognisably guitars on the intro to 'Woman in Love', and on the chorus of 'Run Wild', but I have no idea how anyone could pick up a guitar and make it sound like that – I hear marbled floors, a sea breeze, the gentle ruffle of a canvas canopy on the balcony. *Guilty* was all warm, wide open Florida spaces; Fleetwood Mac's *Rumours* is often cited as the ultimate sunlit, open-highway, LA album, but it sounds boxy and wooded by comparison.

The cover saw Barry encasing lion cub Barbra with his giant paw pads. He earned himself a co-starring role. 'Make it a crime to be lonely or sad!' Babs implored on the title track. 'Make it a crime to be out in the cold!' roared Barry. And maybe the Bee Gees did feel it was their duty to bring their heroes back from pop's fringes – Robin and Maurice (once the latter was out of rehab) would team up with Blue Weaver to write and produce an album for former Motown singer Jimmy Ruffin in early 1980. He hadn't had a hit of any stripe since the darkly propulsive 'Tell Me What You Want' had been an early disco hit in 1974, and he hadn't troubled the *Billboard* top ten since 1966. The results were pleasant, but underwhelming – maybe Robin had been away from the mixing desk for too long. The *Sunrise* album is one of the more forgotten Gibb collaborations, possibly because it has never been on CD let alone streaming services (neither the Bee Gees nor RSO's legacy management has kept pace with changing technology), but also because it sounds a lot like half-thought-out demos. The tepid hi-hat, and weak one-note keyboard hook on 'Hold On (To My Love)', combined with its computer-generated lyrics – 'You're the light of my life / There's no living without your love' – make you pine for the abstractions of *To Whom It May Concern*. Still, 'Hold On (To My Love)' was enough of an earworm to reach the UK and US top tens in the spring of 1980, although it's largely forgotten today. Robin's idiosyncrasies appeared to be in abeyance. There were a few worthwhile songs on *Sunrise*: 'Changin' Me' was a Philly tribute that went on to become a staple on the Carolina Beach Music scene; 'Jealousy' had the urgency and intensity of 1967 Motown, while predating the high anxiety of Robin's solo '80s work; 'Searchin'' was a decent Gibb ballad with a sweet Blue Weaver piano melody, and Robin's lyric was the best (and most Robin-esque) on the whole album: 'Whenever I end up hurting someone, I always hurt myself / If only I could live my life over again, I'd like to be somebody else.'

Sunrise was cut quickly, and it showed. By contrast, the Streisand sessions would stretch on for months and they were all worthwhile. According to *Rolling Stone*'s Stephen Holden, *Guilty* was 'as beautifully crafted a piece of ear candy as I've heard in years.' Streisand slipped and slid around every melody, just as Barry intended, and she got to belt when she needed to. Her restraint on 'The Love Inside' was admirable; it had a neo-classical feel, but with Streisand holding back, immersed in white waves of strings and airy synths, the result was one of the greatest pieces of music Barry Gibb had ever been in involved in. It was womb-like, reminiscent of Phil Spector's early, insular productions from before the Wall of Sound, like the Teddy Bears' 'To Know Him Is to Love Him' had been updated for the nuclear boiler-suit age.

Aside from the title track, Barry and Barbra also duetted on 'What Kind of Fool', which featured some beautiful imagery

('We let the bough break, we let the heartache in') and vocal interplay on the second chorus which was a marvel. Babs, finally, got to cut loose and let her theatrical hair fly free – 'Was there a moment when I cut you down?', to which a chastised Barry sobs, 'No!' It was a third American top-ten single from *Guilty*, in every way a complete album.[26]

After finishing work on the Jimmy Ruffin album, Maurice started work on the soundtrack of a Stigwood-produced movie called *The Fan*. It starred Lauren Bacall as Sally Ross, an ageing actress on her way back with a musical called *Never Say Never*, who is stalked by a record company salesman played by Michael Biehn. Released in May 1981, its timing was unfortunate: this was just a few months after John Lennon's murder by an obsessive fan, and barely a month after John Hinkley attempted to assassinate Ronald Reagan, allegedly to impress his favourite actress, Jodie Foster. Mo's efforts would sadly be shunted aside for a new score by Marvin Hamlisch and Tim Rice. Still, it was a foot in the door – rather than having to compete with Barry and Robin, he started to work more on film scores. It was ironic, given the number of vaunted film projects that Robert Stigwood and the Bee Gees never saw through, that Mo would find a bit of peace and a sense of purpose in Hollywood.

Barbra Streisand's 'Woman in Love' was number one in America during the 1980 presidential election; winning forty-four states, gung-ho Ronald Reagan destroyed the relatively

---

[26] In South America, *Guilty* was released under the translated title *Culpable*.

peacenik incumbent Jimmy Carter. It was morning in America for some, but all those people were white and straight and none of them were teenagers. Forget Comiskey Park – this was the point at which American Rock reclaimed the high ground from the Vietnam surrender, the liberal consensus, the pervasiveness of disco and – most of all – the sound of the Bee Gees. REO Speedwagon, Journey and John Cougar made the new glossy, guitar-based records hogging the airwaves. Was it so far removed from what had gone before? Maybe the guitars were more centrally positioned, and records like REO Speedwagon's 'Keep On Lovin' You' may have seemed devoid of any black or gay influence, but their high-end productions owed more to the gloss of *Spirits Having Flown* than their listenership would care to admit.

An encapsulation of post-punk British pop in 1980 was knocking on the door behind 'Woman in Love' in October 1980: at number two, Status Quo's 'What You're Proposing' was their biggest hit since 1974's 'Down Down', inspired by the New Wave of British Heavy Metal (NWOBHM) scene's greasy embrace; at three was Bad Manners' 'Special Brew', a novelty hit that rang the death knell for the ska revival; and at four, outré double-drummer punk act Adam and the Ants had 'Dog Eat Dog', their first hit, and the single that opened the door for glamorous New Pop and a briefly glittering career for Adam. Had British youth culture ever been more splintered? 'Woman in Love' sounded aloof and adult in such company, middle-aged and quite separate, with the Gibbs' backing vocals swimming in these safer waters, away from laughing kids and disco deniers.

The Bee Gees were smart enough to know their hot streak couldn't keep going forever. In a year and a half, they had hit number one in America with six consecutive singles, something only the Beatles had done before. *Saturday Night Fever* and *Spirits Having Flown* had been blockbuster albums. Then they had tried working with someone else and – presto! – *Guilty* was another monster. But 1981 would provide nothing. Everything just stopped. With 1981's *Living Eyes*, the Bee Gees were to be made aware that they had no choice but to stay in the backroom, with Streisand and friends, and to keep their profile low.

Essentially, it was semantics. The scale of the backlash against them meant that it would become irrelevant how adept they were at writing hit songs in multiple genres – rhythm and blues, AOR, country, easy listening, rock or folk – because they were simply going to be tagged 'disco' no matter what they tried. That would be the public perception for an entire generation. '"How Deep" was an R&B ballad, but after the film [*Saturday Night Fever*] it was a disco ballad,' noted Maurice, sadly. Their fall had partly been their fault – by the time of *Spirits Having Flown*, their look (white suits, chest hair, medallions and teeth) was easily lampooned, and on 'Tragedy' (a transatlantic number one in '79) there had been none of 'Night Fever''s subtlety or 'Fanny (Be Tender)''s emotional glide. The Euro bombast of acts like Boney M. was sneaking in instead. Nevertheless, producers like Trevor Horn had been taking notes – a few months after 'Tragedy', Horn would score his first number one with the Buggles' 'Video Killed the Radio Star', before going on to be boss producer of the early '80s with ABC and Frankie Goes to Hollywood. But in fact it made no difference how influential the Bee Gees were. With the dawn of the '80s and a farewell to the disco era, it was also farewell to the Bee Gees. Those were the pop rules, and they had to abide.

The brothers understood this, to a degree. Things had to change. They never wanted to be stuck in a rut, though ruts were something they had only usually spotted just after they'd fallen into one (the aborted 1970 solo projects, or *Life in a Tin Can*). *Spirits Having Flown* was no different – again, they had crossed a line, broken unwritten pop rules, stayed on the same road just a little too long and got lost from the route of the pop mainstream. They had no way of knowing if they could get back onto it, or how much their fame had burned out, until they released another album. And so the sessions for 1981's *Living Eyes* started with disagreements, and then a massive alteration to the Bee Gees' line-up of the mid- to late '70s. Alan Kendall, Dennis Bryon and Blue Weaver were all fired, over the phone. Just like that.

It's often easy to forget that the Bee Gees had been child performers and that they had grown up in such an odd, isolated way. Foraging, they had always found things they liked on the radio and absorbed them – the Everly Brothers, the Goons, Stevie Wonder, Hall & Oates – with little regard for what anyone else might think of their taste. Old Super 8 footage from Australia showed them goofing around, but you never saw any other kids playing with them; it was just the three brothers. This airtight upbringing informed their insularity, their prickly, defensive behaviour, and their occasional lack of empathy. Barry, in particular, found it hard to be straight with his long-term friends and bandmates.

Dennis Bryon remembered the initial sessions for the new album as fraught and joyless: 'Blue and Albhy were at each other's throats all the time, disagreeing over everything. There was no flow or excitement about the music.' But what happened next still came as a shock. Dick Ashby called up one afternoon and said, 'I'm afraid I have some bad news – the boys want to use another band.'

The first thought that ran through Dennis's mind was: 'How could Barry do this to me? I thought we were best friends.' Blue Weaver was more angry than heartbroken and threatened legal action. They were a backing group, and of course the brothers had every right to move on and work with a fresh team, but Barry knew he had handled the situation badly. He tried to make amends by offering all three $150,000 from future earnings; meaning that a full eighteen years later, Blue Weaver, Alan Kendall and Dennis Bryon would receive a very welcome cheque. Within a few weeks everyone would be on speaking terms again, and the Bee Gees had moved on.

It was clear from a glance at the charts how different things were in 1981: Chic, Donna Summer, Giorgio Moroder – all were struggling: 'So unplug the jukebox and do us all a favour / That music's lost its taste, so try another flavour.' Adam and the Ants' hyperpop slogans were aimed squarely at the disco and punk age, the late '70s, as the dandy highwayman prepared us for an era of dressing up, when the bulk of new UK chart acts were not only British but from the provinces: Sheffield's Human League and ABC; Blackpool and Southport's Soft Cell; Birmingham's Duran Duran; the Wirral's Orchestral Manoeuvres in the Dark. Basildon new town, home to Depeche Mode and Yazoo, was as close to the bright lights of London as any of these acts came. This new wave was tagged New Pop, a literate and exciting reclamation of showbiz values wedded to both punk's rip-it-up philosophy and newly affordable synthesisers. Disco and punk were passé; small-town heroes with Korg MS20s were in. What could have seemed more gauche or unhip than a band originally from the fringes – Manchester, via Douglas – who had largely passed up the UK for life as tax exiles in Miami? US residents Rod Stewart and Elton John suffered similar career lulls in the early '80s, keeping the Gibbs company.

Living Eyes would be released in late 1981 to a world that simply didn't care. 'How could a band that produced three monumental albums in a row put out a set as pallid and bodiless as this?' groaned the usually supportive *Rolling Stone*. 'I wouldn't be surprised to learn from court depositions taken years from now that *Living Eyes* is indeed an LP of pre-"Jive Talkin'" outtakes the Bee Gees released to fulfil some crazy contractual obligation. If it's not, they're really in trouble.'

The cover of *Living Eyes* saw them on a dark Manhattan rooftop, the sun setting on them, far, far away from the brilliant white of *Guilty* and closer to the murk of *Horizontal* or *Trafalgar*. Only Barry was smiling.

What's so sad about the record's failure is that not only was it one of their very best, but the three brothers were all heavily involved. This should have been a cause of celebration for Mo in particular, who had barely been any help to the group – and more an existential worry – since *Main Course*. Side two of *Living Eyes* is almost faultless: 'Wildflower' marked Mo's first lead vocal since 1972's *To Whom It May Concern*, and it was a spring morning of a song, with the acoustic lightness of *Spirits*' title track merged with harmonies that channelled late '60s Beach Boys, the gorgeous cascading coda in particular sounding more Wilson than Gibb; 'I Still Love You' was a timeless, feathered Bee Gee ballad that could have fitted onto either *Trafalgar* or *Guilty*; 'Nothing Could Be Good' was R&B with odd folk-inflections, somehow reminiscent of mid-'70s Gordon Lightfoot;

'Cryin' Every Day' had a stripped-back electro backing and a classically maudlin Robin topline and lyric ('Well, your love is a cathedral / I came down here to pray') – you wouldn't be too surprised if a *Robin's Reign*-era demo turned up one day; finally, 'Be Who You Are''s lengthy orchestral intro was much closer to *Odessa* than *Spirits*. It was a quietly epic, orchestral closer, feeding on the same underdog strength and heart-on-sleeve emotion that had fed 'We Can Conquer the World' in 1970 and 'Your Love Will Save the World' in 1975: 'Be who you are / Seize life and find a way / And I will be that shadow loving who you are.'

Unreleased outtakes from the album show they had great songs to spare: 'The Heat of the Night' was all Barry, complete, a gem, and presumably held back to allow his brothers more space; 'The Promise You Made' was one of Barry's country numbers; the atmospheric 'Mind Over Matter' was from Robin's realm; and 'City of Angels' was Maurice and Barry's, with exceptional chords, not unlike a John Barry film score. What kept these songs in the vault? A lack of confidence, presumably.

With the exception of Barry's 'Be Who You Are', all of the songs were credited to B R & M Gibb, like it was 1967 all over again. There are good reasons why *Living Eyes* is a fans' favourite, like *Odessa* and *To Whom It May Concern*, why it's an underdog album awaiting rediscovery – and these are exactly the same reasons it sold around 5 per cent of the numbers *Spirits Having Flown* had done.

Barry, Albhy and Karl had built their own airtight production system for both the *Spirits Having Flown* and *Guilty* albums. With *Living Eyes*, Robin was working on songs with Barry, both moulding them in his vision and once again recording lead vocals.

What's more, Maurice was back in the studio again, hands on, sober, an equal member, and this was something neither Albhy or Karl were familiar with. Barry, understandably, saw himself, Albhy and Karl as a hit production team; at the same time, he must have been thrilled that the brothers were back together as singers, songwriters and producers, the original Chorlton dream reborn. Albhy wasn't so thrilled. Later he said that no one got what they wanted from *Living Eyes*. This was easy to say a few months down the line when the album had tanked, a commercial embarrassment. To anyone else, it sounded rather like *Mr Natural*, a post-trauma record, a healing album that was more about the brothers' wellbeing than the top forty. Whether it was down to the lack of sales or genuine rancour, the next few years saw the group split into two production teams, one of Barry, Albhy and Karl, and the other just Robin and Maurice. But the three brothers held it together to continue co-writing with some blindingly good results, artistically and commercially.

Management was where there was a genuine divide in the camp; a bitter split with Robert Stigwood had been inevitable once the money trail ran cold. It seems amazing, looking back, that it hadn't happened earlier. The Bee Gees announced that they were suing Stigwood and his companies, due to the conflict of interest that had been in plain sight since 1967. This was the same issue that cheeky young Colin Petersen had had the nerve to bring up in 1970, and he'd been sacked for his troubles. Stigwood was both their personal manager and their employer; no other record label could possibly get a look at the Bee Gees as long as this situation stood. The issue came to a head over the *Guilty* album – which Barry, quite rightly, had seen as something he was working on with Streisand, independently of RSO and the Bee Gees, give or take a few writing credits for Robin.

Stigwood did not see it that way. The Bee Gees sued for mis-management and withholding of royalties they were entitled to. Then they sent in the auditors. They decided to sue for $200 million. Stigwood counter-sued. Welcome to the 1980s.

This legal squabble was the backdrop to 'He's a Liar', their first brand-new single in two years. 'The Bee Gees were suing Robert at the time, and radio thought it was a personal vendetta,' reckoned Albhy. Maybe. More than two years on from *Spirits Having Flown*, any new single was going to be a statement. 'He's a Liar', released in June 1981, did not sound like anything else on *Living Eyes*. It was a clumsy, ugly noise – the instrumental hook is abstract, the vocal hook barked through gritted teeth: 'He's a *lye*-ah!' You could say the chords were interesting and jazz-based, the rhythm choppy, maybe, though it was also reminiscent of 10cc's less than modern 'Rubber Bullets'. You couldn't dance to it. You couldn't hum or whistle it (go on, give it a try).

In its way, 'He's a Liar' was ahead of its time, in that it anticipated the vacuous mid-'80s sound of bands with elec-tronic keyboards and jazz-prog upbringings like Go West and It Bites – 'He's a Liar' is deserving of a slow handclap for that alone. Either way, it did a great job of disguising a fine album.

1981 was a year of extraordinary new music in the UK, when synthpop and post-punk were merging in exciting, entryist ways, crossing over from the DIY underground and taking over the UK charts. *Living Eyes* emerged in November; the same month produced Orchestral Manoeuvres in the Dark's *Architecture and Morality*, Depeche Mode's *Speak and Spell*, Japan's *Tin Drum*, the

Teardrop Explodes' *Wilder*, Soft Cell's *Non-Stop Erotic Cabaret* and the Human League's *Dare* – from personal memory, the Bee Gees had as much relevance in 1981 as the New Seekers. The album would have had to be exceptionally prescient and close to synthpop's pulse to have made much headway, and it simply didn't come close. Their time had passed. No one, including radio stations, took a blind bit of notice of *Living Eyes*.

No one, that is, except the music industry. *Living Eyes* was the very first album to be produced in the 'compact disc' format and was demonstrated – jam-smearing and all – on BBC One's *Tomorrow's World*. In no other way was *Living Eyes* part of tomorrow's world. *Rolling Stone* described it as 'snoozy pop slush without a trace of the R&B urgency that propelled these three Australian siblings to the top of the charts in the '70s'.

The brothers would either dismiss *Living Eyes* or simply ignore it in later years. In the TV documentary *In My Own Time*, Maurice says: 'The whole "It's time to kill *Fever*, it's time to kill disco" period came in, so we just sort of took a back seat. The saturation point was ridiculous . . . we thought "The Bee Gees" better go on the back burner for a while until this dies down . . . So we couldn't do anything as "The Bee Gees" at all. We didn't make an album until '87.' He had erased *Living Eyes* from the group's history.

The commercially flunking Bee Gees also had to battle with the rise of the Hee Bee Gee Bees in 1981, an Oxford student act made up of Angus Deayton, Phil Pope and Richard Curtis, who all went on to fame and fortune of their own. 'Meaningless Songs (In Very High Voices)' became a radio hit, and took off the late '70s Gibb sound to a tee. The brothers were not amused: 'The world is very large / And butter is better than marge' was clearly too close to home. The lyrics were courtesy of Curtis, who claimed to be a big fan. It was a pastiche, but a good-hearted one, like *Austin Powers*. You could tell when Curtis, Deayton and Pope didn't like one of the acts they were mimicking; the Bee Gees fared a lot better in their take-offs than Prince (Ponce) or Queen (Queer) – proof that Oxford students could be just as bluntly homophobic as any northern club comedian.

The *Guilty* album had been a challenge for Barry, one he had worked hard on, and one that had paid off handsomely with rave write-ups, a number-one single, and a number-one album. In producing it, he realised the Bee Gees didn't need to be a band anymore, just the three brothers, and that they could work with whichever musicians felt right for individual projects. *Guilty* also allowed him to realise that he could pull off a massive success without having to worry about Robin's marital issues or Maurice's drinking. They were all grown-ups now, surely? He could work alone at the group's freshly opened Middle Ear Studios, bring in whoever he wanted, when he wanted, and please himself. The disastrous performance of *Living Eyes* was mere confirmation for Barry Gibb: the group should take a back seat.

The Bee Gees had been the biggest group in the world at the end of 1978. They went into enforced retirement at the end of 1981. Could they rise again? Of course they could.

16

THE BUNKER

Record Mirror UK top ten, 7 November 1982

1. Eddy Grant – 'I Don't Wanna Dance'
2. Dionne Warwick – 'Heartbreaker'
3. Tears for Fears – 'Mad World'
4. Culture Club – 'Do You Really Want to Hurt Me'
5. Marvin Gaye – 'Sexual Healing'
6. Kool & the Gang – 'Ooh La La La (Let's Go Dancin')'
7. Kids from Fame – 'Starmaker'
8. Barry Manilow – 'I Wanna Do It with You'
9. Michael Jackson and Paul McCartney – 'The Girl Is Mine'
10. Daryl Hall & John Oates – 'Maneater'

People often talked about the Bee Gees' lyrics in a derogatory way. The way they used words almost phonetically, to create a feel rather than creating poetry, was almost beyond language. Some people evidently preferred their pop to be more literal than lateral – 'Meaningless Songs' was an accusation that stuck. Let's turn this around: the Bee Gees understood pop music better than almost any other songwriters of the late twentieth century. Pop music isn't poetry. It's about conveying emotion in the most compact way possible. If we're talking about perfect pop singles, ones that get enormous emotion across in the most concise, impactful way, then one of the records we're talking about is 'Heartbreaker' by Dionne Warwick.

Unlike the year-zero aspirations of punk, the New Pop of the early '80s positively welcomed older acts, the ones who had trodden the boards, the ones who valued stagecraft, even if that stage had been in Wythenshawe or Batley. This meant Eurovision act Bucks Fizz were invited to the party where they gave us the shiny 'My Camera Never Lies', as were blonde cabaret duo Dollar, who were united with producer Trevor Horn to create seismic 45s like the fairground-on-ice 'Give Me Back My Heart' and 'Videotheque', possibly the most '80s song title ever. If these guys were invited, why not someone with real pipes? Why not Dionne Warwick?

We could ask why not the Bee Gees, but we already know the answer to that – nothing seems more distant and unappetising than the recently hip. The same wasn't true of their songwriting or their productions, which had plenty in common with currently cool UK, R&B-influenced acts like Culture Club and Imagination. And so Dionne – Burt Bacharach and Hal David's muse through the '60s – became the beneficiary of nine new Gibb songs for her *Heartbreaker* album in 1982, one that New Pop Britain embraced with open arms. 'Heartbreaker' the song, the first single from the album, and an international top-ten hit, deserves a book of its own. Almost every line, all of them with defiantly Bee Gees wording, is deeply sad: 'My love is stronger than the universe' sings Dionne, with the brothers giving spiritual support on the chorus to someone who has lost everything they ever wanted.

At heart, like 'Woman in Love', 'Heartbreaker' was aimed at mums and housewives, the same demographic 'Massachusetts' had sought out and won over in 1967, the one Robin claimed was owned back then by stereotypical beefcakes Tom Jones and Engelbert Humperdinck. Yet 'Heartbreaker' is defiant in its sadness, sophisticated in its misery, and it didn't need a man to sing it to strike at the female heart. In 1967, women weren't encouraged to think of themselves as sexual beings, but both the *Guilty* and *Heartbreaker* albums were indicative of how things had changed in fifteen years, and how the Bee Gees had – almost unwittingly – been a part of that change. 'I got to say it and it's hard for me,' sang Dionne; it may have been hard for a woman to say in 1982, but it would have been unsayable in 1967. The world-weariness in both 'Heartbreaker' and 'Woman in Love' was palpable, and hard-won. 'My love is stronger than the universe' works a lot better as a pop lyric, a representation of mental toughness, and probably as a state of mind, than something more obvious like 'I am woman, hear me roar'.

The lyric on 'Heartbreaker' also included cute nods to the early '60s, when Dionne first had hits: the line about crying in the rain was borrowed from the Gibbs' beloved Everly Brothers. Structurally, it seems a straightforward song, but the chorus has an unexpected extra line, additional to the sixteen-bar pattern, which catches you out, forcing you to pay closer attention to the words Dionne is singing: 'This world may end / Not you and I.' Oh my! It's a rarely deployed songwriting trick, one that Holland–Dozier–Holland used on the Four Tops' 'Baby, I Need Your Loving' (on the verse rather than the chorus) with similarly devastating effect.

None of this, of course, would have impressed the Steve Dahl school of rock fans, who continued to dismiss the Bee Gees as 'girly'. The Bee Gees continued to keep their heads down, below the parapet, sheltering in the bunker. Driving back from the recording sessions at Middle Ear, Maurice began to cry – he wanted to sing 'Heartbreaker', he wanted his brothers to sing it. It was their song. Instead, they remained in shadow, an unwelcome presence in the record stores of the 1980s.

The original plan had been to create an album with a bunch of the Gibbs' favourite female singers, including Gladys Knight. But when Clive Davis at Arista got wind of what was happening, he got on the phone to Barry and talked him into giving the lot to Dionne. Barry – put under pressure by industry big shots – invariably found it hard to say no.

Initially, Dionne didn't like 'Heartbreaker' that much: 'It didn't feel like me,' she told journalist Tom Cridland. 'Because of not only Barry's insistence, but also Maurice and Clive Davis, I thought, "Oh, maybe they know more than I do." By and large anybody knows more than I do. Don't ask me what's gonna be a hit!'

Looking back years later, she had become very fond of the album. 'It's wonderful. I had a wonderful time recording with them. They did not try to make me a Bee Gee. They respected that I was Dionne Warwick. They enhanced my sound.'

It lacked the theatricality of *Guilty*, but, then, Barry wasn't writing for Barbra Streisand – Dionne's voice was rich but altogether cooler. Occasionally the debt was plain – 'I Can't See

Anything (But You)' could easily have been a Bacharach and David song from 1964. But something like 'All the Love in the World' was just classic Gibb, a world of intense, understated emotion inside three minutes.

Somehow, Robert Stigwood talked the Gibbs into recording a few songs for *Staying Alive*, the 1983 sequel to *Saturday Night Fever*, which starred John Travolta but would this time be directed by Sylvester Stallone. Incidental music was provided by Stallone's kid brother Frank. Frank Stallone, to be blunt, was not in the same league as the Bee Gees. 'It was a dreadful movie,' said Robin. 'Sylvester Stallone should never direct a musical.' It was a contractual obligation to RSO, and in fact the soundtrack would be the last album the label ever released. How were the songs? 'The Woman in You' had falsetto vocals on its chorus, a sax break and a strange rock strut that would have placed it in the shadow of Michael Jackson's 'Beat It', were it not for the odd string flourish, a distant, rather sad echo of 1978 – just five years previously, but now so very far away. Against the odds, 'The Woman in You' reached the US top thirty; even more surprisingly, *Staying Alive* ended up in the top ten highest-grossing movies of 1983.

As with *Saturday Night Fever*, the Bee Gees' contributions took up one side of the soundtrack album – which is half an album, but for devotees of *Living Eyes* it was a thin selection. 'Life Goes On' was smooth and, like 'I Love You Too Much', had some neatly melancholy twisted chords, but neither had enough for radio to latch on to. 'Breakout' wore its shoulder pads proudly, the sound of the go-getting mid-'80s, smothered in widdly sax: 'And maybe you can be the thunder / If you follow your dream.' It was an unloveable sound, its only pleasures the brief coda of vocoder and Gibb vocal percussiveness. 'Someone Belonging to

Someone' was the ballad, the love song, which was a melodic standout even though you suspected it was a *Heartbreaker* outtake. And with *Staying Alive* in the shops and RSO Records a thing of the past, the Bee Gees lost the default sponsors of all their haps and mishaps. From this point on, for the very first time, they were running their own lives.

Robin had shelved his solo career for the good of the family some thirteen years earlier. Itching to get his songs and his voice back on tape, he released *How Old Are You* in 1983. It was a useful distraction from his personal life, now consumed by his divorce from Molly. Robin had broken a window to get into their Weybridge home in August 1980 and found what he claimed were 'incriminating papers'. It had been the final straw for Molly. Robin was 'very, very unhappy', said mum Barbara. 'You can't blame him, can you?' He wouldn't see his kids, or even hear from them, for six years.

He talked drily about the split on TV: 'I had been told to remove myself from the premises, as one does in a divorce, so I said, "Right, I'm off!" Anyway, I was in a hotel in London wondering what to do, because I'd never stayed in a hotel in England before, and suddenly there was a knock on the door, and there was Ken.'

Ken Graydon, who magically appeared at the door like the shopkeeper in *Mr Benn*, became the newly single Robin's personal assistant. It turned out Ken's cousin Dwina knew actress Sarah Miles, whom Robin had admired from afar, and Dwina helped to set up a date. Back at Sarah Miles's home, Robin was taken by a pen-and-ink drawing of her on top of the television. It had been drawn by Dwina, Miles explained. Robin was intrigued. He then commissioned Dwina to do some drawings, and that was that. Like Robin, Dwina had been born on 22 December, the winter solstice. They read the tea leaves, and would stay together for the rest of Robin's life.

Divorced from Molly in late 1982, he was interviewed by the *Scottish Daily Express* and blabbed details of Molly's alleged affair with a New York lawyer – he had become convinced the pair were cooking up a plan to take his money. Robin was duly issued with a writ from Molly, live on breakfast TV, during an interview – 'Rather unnecessary, I might add,' he said drolly to camera. In turn, he was sentenced to two weeks in prison. The Gibbs have said a lot of things over the years, but that was the only time their loose lips have resulted in a prison sentence. It would be overturned a few hours later, but even so.

Robin had started work on his solo LP in late 1982; he initially wanted to work with Arif Mardin, but he wasn't free, so instead he co-produced *How Old Are You* with Mo. The notion that Robin's distinctive voice wasn't suited to club material – something that was often mentioned when explaining his absence from *Fever* and *Spirits* – was now dashed to bits. The first single, 'Juliet', became a number one in Germany and a huge hit all over Europe (except the UK, to proud Englishman Robin's chagrin). Like the album, it was an extraordinarily upbeat and frictionless record – killer chorus, hook after hook, easily bound together by synths and solid grooves. It sounded modern and it sounded young, New Pop to a tee, just as the movement was becoming engulfed by pre-punk acts making a comeback with synths under their arms (Genesis' 'Mama', Rod Stewart's 'Baby Jane', Elton John's 'I'm Still Standing'). Robin did not sound like a square peg in a round hole, nor did he feel the need for a soprano sax or wailing guitar solo or the other signifiers of trad rock in New Pop clothes. 'I still like Smokey Robinson,' he said, 'and of the English new wave groups I like Culture Club and the Human League.' The album was simple, all clean Korg lines, and the melodies were irresistible. *How Old Are You* made the songs on *Staying Alive* sound try-hard.

Behind Robin was not only Maurice, but also – hatchets buried – Alan Kendall and Dennis Bryon. *How Old Are You* was a Bee Gees equivalent to the Ringo Starr solo albums that included every Beatle but Paul. It felt a little like a point was being made. But songs like 'Don't Stop the Night' and 'Danger' were just a breeze, embellished by electronic tinkles, the sound of late-night Munich. Robin brought back the anguished, emotive vocal sound that had been hidden for almost a decade. Unexpectedly, it was one of the best albums of 1983.

'Another Lonely Night in New York' would be the third single in January 1984, a ballad with a heavy debt to Foreigner's 'Waiting for a Girl Like You' (heck, if you're going to steal, you should steal from the best). Robin did plenty of promo for it on British TV. One show saw him alongside Russell Harty, blindfolded, and putting his hand into a bowl of cold porridge with lychees in it, trying to guess what they were. He also spent a day in Bristol with Leo Sayer, talking at length about Isambard Kingdom Brunel and the Clifton suspension bridge. It's a very sweet interview – Robin the history buff is clearly holding himself back from going into too much nerdy detail. 'My priority is still the Bee Gees,' he told Sayer, lest we imagined there might be a solo concept album about Victorian engineers coming next. On *The Rolf Harris Show*, he was filmed at home with a bunch of pet chinchillas. One, Robin revealed, was called Eric. He also appeared on shows hosted by Cannon & Ball and Rod Hull &

Emu, light entertainment veterans who had risen through working men's clubs, the showbiz lower rungs that made Robin feel
ill. Robin seemed pretty relaxed about the whole thing, but must
have been gutted when 'Another Lonely Night' only just crawled
into the UK top seventy-five. Germany gave it a hug and took it
to number sixteen.

★

In one of the busiest years of the Bee Gees' career, there was
also room in 1983 for a collaboration with Kenny Rogers,
which came about after Barry and Linda were in a pro-celebrity
tennis tournament. Rogers flew them back to Miami on his
private jet and, on white kid leather seats, asked Barry if he
fancied collaborating on a couple of songs. 'I said, "Kenny,
tell you the truth, I'd rather do an album." I don't know why
I was that crazy. Why not just do a couple of songs? And he
said, "Yeah, okay," and then I thought maybe I don't want to
do a whole album!'

Barry's odd mix of eagerness and reticence comes across on
Eyes That See in the Dark, a curious album in that, in spite of consistently first-rate material, doesn't cohere anywhere near as well
as *Guilty* or *Heartbreaker*. It might also be that Rogers wasn't that
engaged.

'We sent all the songs and when he came to start singing, he
didn't know the words,' said a shocked Maurice. 'The fact that
they have to have a piece of paper in front of them, and they've
been working on this album with you for three months . . .' continued Barry. 'If I was the artist and you were the producer, I'd
be at home memorising these words. It's a different thing when
you read and sing.'

The upside of the collaboration was that the brothers all worked on it together. Maurice played rhythm guitar throughout. 'Living with You' had all three Gibbs on backing vocals, and sounded strong enough, and complex enough, to have made it onto *Guilty*. Other highlights included 'Hold Me', a gorgeous, delicate ballad, no more than vocals and strings, hovering in the night air over Nashville. The ebullient and rhythmically tricksy 'Midsummer Nights' sounded like it could have been written for Cliff Richard. What *Eyes* doesn't sound like is a Kenny Rogers album – it's hard to hear how Barry had factored 'The Gambler', or 'Daytime Friends', or 'Ruby, Don't Take Your Love to Town' into any of the material. The disconnect isn't helped by Kenny copying the demos slavishly. After a few uninspired takes, Albhy Galuten had pointed this out to the singer – and as a result had to spend the rest of the sessions on gardening leave.

The title song was released as the first single and did nothing, failing to make the top forty anywhere. It didn't matter. The second single from *Eyes That See in the Dark* became the biggest-selling single in RCA's history. Named after an Ernest Hemingway novel, 'Islands in the Stream' had initially been written as an R&B song. 'It could easily have been done by Marvin Gaye,' said Robin, and he wasn't wrong. The chorus is yearning and uplifting, something beyond hope, sharing with 'How Deep Is Your Love' a lyric of splendid isolation. 'We were writing a song for Diana Ross', Barry recalled, 'but she never got round to hearing it.' Instead, Dolly Parton was brought in to make the song a duet. And what a song it was! Barry said that Dolly was '*the* pleasure to work with'. The sheer joy of her delivery on 'Islands in the Stream', combined with its multiple melodic and lyrical hooks, guaranteed another number-one *Billboard* hit.

This wasn't Barry's first brush with the world of country music. The Bee Gees' 1969 single 'Don't Forget to Remember' had been a hit everywhere but the US, and deserved to be cut by Faron Young or Waylon Jennings, but it wouldn't be discovered by America until Carrie Underwood recorded it in 2006. A decade later, 'Rest Your Love on Me' had briefly teased a new, post-*Fever* direction, and would be covered with success by Conway Twitty, reaching number one on *Billboard*'s country chart in 1981. But, given Barry's fondness for country that went right back to their debut single, it took a very long time for Gibbworld to collide with Nashville. When they entered the same orbit in 1983, 'Islands in the Stream' became the biggest-selling country single of all time. Dolly and Kenny sounded deliriously in love – seemingly a mismatched couple, their sweet-and-salty combination and the harmonies it produced were as powerful and as unusual as the Gibbs'. That it included one of Barry's most peculiar lines – 'I set out to get you with a fine-tooth comb' – didn't bother anyone. Everything about it worked, even the brass riff that seemed to quote ABBA's 'SOS'. 'Islands in the Stream' was just a timeless, wonderful record, both a perfect wedding song and a hymn of blissful independence: 'Sail away with me to another world.' Hitting number one in late October, it dislodged Jim Steinman and Bonnie Tyler's magnum opus 'Total Eclipse of the Heart', which had been gothically haunting America for a full four weeks. After a fortnight at the top, it would be replaced by Lionel Richie's oddly soothing party anthem 'All Night Long'. Though hidden from sight, the Bee Gees were still in good company at the year's end, still more than keeping pace.

So why not give solo records another go? After all, it was 'Bee Gee' rather than 'Gibb' that seemed to be box office poison. 1984 would see all three brothers throw their hats into the ring.

One-time manager of the Eagles, Dan Fogelberg and REO Speedwagon, Irving Azoff became chairman of MCA in 1983; he made it his business to sign Barry to a multi-million-dollar, multi-album deal, hoping that the energies of *Guilty*, *Heartbreaker* and 'Islands in the Stream' would convert into solo success. Meanwhile Robin signed for North America with Mirage, a small label distributed by Atlantic, after having focused on Britain and Germany with *How Old Are You*. Maurice would find work on a bunch of film scores.

A Breed Apart starred Kathleen Turner and Donald Pleasence as a widow and a conservationist who hire a mountain climber (Rutger Hauer) to steal bald-eagle eggs. Box office gold! 'I did the eagle sounds,' said an excited Maurice. 'You can make up any sounds if you have working knowledge of your synthesiser.' Mo was thrilled at the prospect of scoring a movie, and worked with Jimmie Haskell, the string arranger on 1973's unreleased *A Kick in the Head* album, who went to Miami to orchestrate Mo's synth demos. 'I've always wanted to write film scores,' he said – with evidence going all the way back to 1970's 'Journey to the Misty Mountains' – but his drinking and the group's fall and rise and fall had conspired against his ambitions. Now he was working on not only *A Breed Apart* (for which he played instantly recognisable piano parts), but also *Misunderstood*, again with Jimmie Haskell. *Misunderstood* was a touching if slightly sentimental film that starred Gene Hackman as a widower and Henry 'E.T.' Thomas as his young son.[27] Mo also scored *Ghost Soldiers*, starring *Star Trek* actress Nichelle Nicholls, in which he managed to make a cameo appearance as a Civil War soldier. His score

[27] *Misunderstood* also featured Rip Torn and June 'Dot Cotton' Brown in its cast. If nothing else, it was great source material for pub quiz questions.

was rejected, though, and the only record to emerge from any of these films, sadly, was a solitary single, the country-ish 'Hold Her in Your Hand', from *A Breed Apart*.

June 1984 saw Frankie Goes to Hollywood's 'Two Tribes' hog the top of the UK singles chart and Robin's *Secret Agent* dive just as deeply into the worlds of Roland, Korg and Fairlight. 'I don't like songs of the past. I like to get ahead,' said Robin. 'These songs are very 1984, maybe even more futuristic.' He described *Secret Agent* as 'very black and urban – it reflects street music'. The title track had a trademark Rob melancholy melody and a Latin freestyle production – that was about as of-the-moment as it was possible to be, with Shannon's 'Let the Music Play' still fresh in the clubs and Madonna's 'Into the Groove' a full year away. Neither of those records featured a fight scene mid-song, though. It was good to have Robin's oddness back. 'X-Ray Eyes', likewise, was as lyrically peculiar in its own way as anything on *Robin's Reign*: 'She comes to me with infra-red eyes and sees inside my head / I wish I was invisible.' Not all of it worked (the cod-reggae and vocoder blend of 'Robot' was more *Metal Mickey* than *Transformers*), but 'In Your Diary' was loaded with electronic fairy dust and another plum melody. Robin must have been disappointed when *Secret Agent* didn't match *How Old Are You*'s commercial success.

Songs about robots and X-ray eyes suggested a second childhood which, given Robin's new singleton lifestyle, might have been self-explanatory. But then he'd never really had a first childhood. He was making up for lost time, rifling through ads in the back of American comics and '50s sci-fi movies for lyrical inspiration.

A Barry solo record was never about to do anything like that. *Now Voyager* was named after an old Bette Davis movie, and – rather confusingly – was both a new album and a new movie, set in Britain. At last Barry could live out his actorly fantasies. Released in September 1984, the album-cum-movie's storyline was all over the place. Maybe as it was intended as a life story, or a 'visual album', which is what MCA had written into Barry's contract the year before. He argued with Albhy, who wanted to try something bigger, rehearsing the whole thing in a theatre, and to bring in Barry's favourite musicians – like the Sweet Inspirations – as guests. Barry got cold feet. Albhy gave up trying to convince him and went back to California.

The film would be directed by Peter 'Sleazy' Christopherson, formerly of avant garde experimentalists Throbbing Gristle. The storyline revolved around Barry and Michael Hordern – the TV voice of Paddington Bear – swapping inscrutable stories about the impossibilities of love; other actors included future Bond girl Maryam D'Abo, daughter of former Manfred Mann singer Mike D'Abo. It was an extraordinary meeting of minds.

Now Voyager opened with Barry driving a Mercedes around the Fens of eastern England, then veering off the road into a dyke (a scene which apparently almost killed the stunt driver) before entering a place between life and death which, for the sake of the film, was a swimming baths in Chorlton.[28] It's quite a shock to see a shaggy-haired but beardless Barry, looking like a scruffy Crouch End dad from the 2010s. In the clip for 'Fine Line,' he was even less characteristically leonine, wearing sideburns and a shell suit. Stranger yet, he played an unreliable cyborg on the Miami funk of 'I Am Your Driver'. It's a daft film, but considerably glossier and more enjoyable than either *Sgt Pepper's Lonely Hearts Club Band* or *Cucumber Castle*. Interviewed shortly after the

---

[28] Granada TV's late-'80s arts show *The Other Side of Midnight* would also be filmed in the baths.

movie, Barry said shaving off his beard had been 'absolute hell. I did it because I thought it was important to do it. I hate myself without my beard. We all have these little idiosyncrasies about ourselves, and I just don't like myself without my beard.'

He described *Now Voyager* as an 'adult rather than very young kind of video. I'm not a kid, y'know?' The album, meanwhile, seemed to abandon the unity and sense of purpose that had made *Spirits*, *Guilty* and *Heartbreaker* so successful. Barry clearly didn't apply these rules to his own recordings – instead he was trying to appease all his fans at once with 'something for everybody', he explained, as if he was still wooing the crowds on *Bandstand*. In this, he repeated the mistakes of 1970's abandoned *The Kid's No Good*, blending multiple styles in an unsatisfactory whole. It must have been galling that the Bee Gees' de facto leader couldn't score solo success while his brother had enjoyed brief but huge success, not once but twice.

Anybody who was anybody – Paul McCartney, Duran Duran, Queen, Bob Dylan – played at Live Aid in 1985. And if they didn't play, they at least had the chance to turn it down. The Bee Gees were not invited; they received no phone call from Bob Geldof or from Harry Belafonte. Barry Gibb watched Live Aid on TV, at home in his Biscayne Bay mansion, and wondered what the hell he had to do to get an invite. He saw the Beach Boys playing and thought . . . the Beach Boys? No hit in, what, ten years? Forget it. I don't care. He was surrounded by kin, that was what mattered. I know people don't like us anymore, he thought, and I just don't care. He was doing enough for charity anyway, wasn't he? 'Too Much Heaven' was still bringing in regular coin for UNICEF, and now he was hosting the regular Love and Hope Tennis Festivals to benefit Miami's Diabetes Research Institute every December. He looked at his TV and saw Phil Collins flying from Wembley to Philadelphia, strutting his poverty-smashing credentials, and thought . . . forget it.

Barry Gibb pondered his family's strange '80s existence – on the margins, in the charts, some sort of laughing stock, some kind of international hit machine. If Live Aid didn't want the Bee Gees, he'd create his own mini-superstar get-together. For fun, he had written a one-off country song for the Gatlin Brothers, called 'Indian Summer', which was recorded in the summer of Live Aid. Barry ended up singing backing vocals on the record alongside his hero Roy Orbison, who took the second verse. It sounded like an obvious hit, but it wasn't very 1985 at all; the Traveling Wilburys, who could have made it into a number one of 'Mull of Kintyre' proportions, were still three years away. 'Indian Summer' was effectively a dry run for that supergroup, with a dash of Jimmy Buffet's 'Margaritaville' thrown in for good measure. The video showed Barry and the Big O sharing a microphone, and Barry's delight at watching his hero singing his song – even if he was only lip-syncing – is something to see.

Forget Live Aid, thought Barry. He hunkered down at home in Miami until his beard had grown back. There must have been someone else who wanted a sprinkling of Gibb magic? The phone rang. And someone on the line mentioned Diana Ross.

Record Mirror UK top ten, 15 March 1986

1. Diana Ross – 'Chain Reaction'
2. David Bowie – 'Absolute Beginners'
3. The Bangles – 'Manic Monday'
4. Cliff Richard and the Young Ones – 'Living Doll'

5. Jim Diamond – 'Hi Ho Silver'
6. Prince and the Revolution – 'Kiss'
7. Culture Club – 'Move Away'
8. Whistle – 'Just Buggin''
9. Frank Sinatra – 'Theme from *New York, New York*'
10. Sigue Sigue Sputnik – 'Love Missile F1–11'

Barry's pop manifesto could have been 'walk like Travolta, sing like the Supremes'. He had loved Motown since 'Where Did Our Love Go' and 'Baby Love' had first taken the sound around the world in 1964. Sadly, it wouldn't be as much of a pleasure working with Miss Ross as it had been working with Barbra or Dionne. Barry tried to be diplomatic. 'It's only difficult because she's very much in control of her own destiny.' And, in a repeat of the Kenny Rogers recordings, he sighed, 'It's very frustrating to see that the artist doesn't always learn the songs.' Albhy was less coy about the recordings: 'Diana Ross is a woman of many parts and I think, it's not really a criticism, but I think she concentrates on about a dozen things at once. I'm not going to have the audacity to say that Diana Ross is unprofessional. All I'm saying was it wasn't comfortable.'

Barry was clearly proud that another one-time Motown legend, Michael Jackson, had co-produced 'Eaten Alive', which became the title song: 'Michael was lovely, he's a very shy person.' Apparently, he had taken Barry's demo, then sung a chorus onto a cassette, and sent it back. A very DIY working method. In the studio, Albhy described Michael as 'emotionally challenged'.

'Eaten Alive' sounded so much like a Michael Jackson recording it wasn't true – does anyone else even sing on the chorus? But it wasn't an especially strong song, and so even enlisting the help of the biggest pop star in the world couldn't turn it into a hit.

Besides, the disconcerting sound of bones being crunched and broken at the end was quite literal and rather unpleasant.

Barry and Michael got on way better than Barry and Diana. According to Frank Cascio's biography *My Friend Michael*, Barry talked about the creative powers of smoking weed, then lit a joint right there in the studio. It was Jackson's first experience with cannabis, but not his last – Cascio reckons that the pair would sometimes drive through the mountains around the Neverland Ranch getting high together. Michael would end up as godfather to Barry's son, Michael.

Eaten Alive would turn out to be a wildly diverse album. At the other end of the spectrum from the gory title song was the sweet, strings-and-piano-led 'More and More', which sounded for all the world like naïve jazz chanteuse Blossom Dearie, or Peggy Lee in a higher register; 'Experience' – a single in the UK – had a chorus like a rejigged 'Heartbreaker', with minor chords switched for major; while '(I Love) Being in Love with You' was classic Barry, a slow jam that could have slotted onto any album he had worked on since *Mr Natural*. The pleading 'Don't Give Up on Each Other' sounded as if it was pitched a little too high for Miss Ross, but was still maybe the strongest track on the album.

With 'Eaten Alive' coming and going and barely causing a ripple, the second single would be sink or swim. Like the title track, much of the album's lyrical content had a predatory edge, something slightly sinister. The main problem here was that Diana either wasn't fully committed or just couldn't live up to Barry's projected fantasy of 'Diana Ross'. There was 'Oh, Teacher', which came over as more than a little odd, with Diana playing a 41-year-old student (the lyric seems to change randomly from Diana being teacher to pupil, not that anyone ever looked for narrative logic in a Bee Gees lyric). It also had some uncharacteristically graphic lyrics: 'My lips are wetter, I do it better / And if you let me I will help you grow.' These images would be matched, at least, by those on 'Chain Reaction'.

Barry was initially nervous about running 'Chain Reaction' past Diana. 'We hadn't had the nerve to play it to her because it was so Tamla Motown-ish.' It became such a huge hit (only her second UK solo number one), and has since been such a radio staple, that it's hard to listen afresh to its featherweight, '60s-revisited charm. When you do, and listen closely, the lyric is a surprising mélange of military and orgasmic metaphors ('You get a medal when you're lost in action . . . / You let me hold you for the first explosion'). Here was an issue they shared with their West Coast brothers the Beach Boys – while they had an easy knack for deep sensuality on songs like 'Charade', 'Emotion' or 'Guilty', their attempts to write about sex directly almost always sounded uncomfortable.

Though Barry had enjoyed hearing Michael Jackson singing into a Walkman, he did not now turn to other contemporary superstars like Madonna or Prince for either collaborations or inspiration. Instead, in 1985, he was toying with the idea of writing albums for the edgeless Neil Diamond and for fellow Miami resident Julio Iglesias. He also decided to check in on his brothers; released in November 1985, Robin's third solo album of the '80s, *Walls Have Eyes*, would be co-produced with Mo, while eight of the ten songs would be co-written with Barry. Still the Gibbs shied away from a full Bee Gees reunion. They'd been sent to Coventry by the public and the media for four years now, but they sensed it still wasn't safe to poke their heads out of the door without someone cracking a joke about teeth, or chest hair, or very high voices.

A Swedish singer called Carola Häggkvist had visited Miami in September '85 and recorded some demos at Middle Ear.

The end result would be an album called *Runaway*, produced by Mo, co-written with Robin; Carola was 'the voice', and a rather strident one. The title track had one of Mo's nice Beatles-esque arpeggios; 'Spread Your Wings' and 'Nature of the Beast' both featured Mo on backing vocals; and 'Lost in the Crowd' was quite lovely, with an Olivia Newton-John-like, softer vocal. 'When Two Worlds Collide' sounded like a hit, maybe, but overall *Runaway* was quite flavourless. It could have been written and produced by anyone. It was a shame the brothers didn't at least add a few harmonies. Released in July 1986, *Runaway* sold a very respectable 200,000 copies in Scandinavia, but then Carola joined a religious sect called Livets Ord in Uppsala, Sweden, and that was that. The rest of the world barely knew the album existed.

While Mo and Rob were creating a sanitised mid-'80s sound with Carola and barely getting a murmur of appreciation, Barry decided to ignore the siren call of Julio Iglesias and record another solo album called *Moonlight Madness*. It was rejected by MCA. In September, Barry played a Democratic Party fundraiser with Barbra Streisand, the pair of them dressed in white and singing 'What Kind of Fool' together, recalling the glory days of just six years earlier.

What had happened since *Guilty*? They had lost their road, again. 'We'd lost our management and our record company,' Barry would recall. He had also lost Albhy Galuten and Karl Richardson, who in turn had lost Robin and Maurice some time before. Their foundations had crumbled beneath them, and now they just weren't sure which direction they were facing. Working with their niece – Beri Gibb, who recorded their song 'Girl Gang' in 1986 – or a Swedish singer from an obscure sect wasn't the right way to turn, that much they knew. Again, most songwriters would think they'd had a pretty good run. All pushing forty, here was an opportunity to step off the carousel with dignity. 'For those years we weren't a pop group and we enjoyed it,' said Barry. 'It was good for us.' At least it was good for them until the brothers 'got tired of listening to everything that was on the radio and knowing we could do just as well if not better'. Phil Pope, the upstart who had co-written 'Meaningless Songs (In Very High Voices)' wrote and produced a headache-inducing novelty called 'The Chicken Song', which became Britain's number-one single over Easter 1986 – it was stupid, childish. Of course the Bee Gees could make better music than 'The Chicken Song'. The Bee Gees wanted to hear the Bee Gees on the radio again.

17

OXFORDSHIRE

Record Mirror UK top ten, 17 October 1987

1. Bee Gees – 'You Win Again'
2. Abigail Mead and Nigel Goulding – 'Full Metal Jacket'
3. MARRS – 'Pump Up the Volume'
4. Jan Hammer – 'Crockett's Theme'
5. Kiss – 'Crazy Crazy Nights'
6. Michael Jackson – 'Bad'
7. Fatback Band – 'I Found Lovin''
8. LL Cool J – 'I Need Love'
9. Steve Walsh – 'I Found Lovin''
10. Rick Astley – 'Never Gonna Give You Up'

'We want to be the Bee Gees. We enjoy being the Bee Gees.'
– Barry Gibb, 1987

Imagine a rambling English country house, haunted by generations of ghosts, less *Scooby Doo*, more *Witchfinder General*. You are picturing the Prebendal. Robin and Dwina moved into the Prebendal, at the end of the main street in Thame, Oxfordshire, in 1984. Their lad Robin John was just a year old – home would now be a twelfth-century pile where for centuries priests had trained to be bishops. Celebrity visitors had included Elizabeth I and Henry VIII. It was very Robin. He would spend days scouring the country for period-correct doors, wood panelling and furniture. 'You don't really own a property like this,' said Robin. 'You're merely custodians for the next generation. But we love what we're doing – we even love the ghosts.' Dwina reckoned the house was rejecting the twentieth century: 'Washing machines would break down, televisions, video machines – they wouldn't function properly. An engineer from BT came out and said, "It's not us, it's the house."'

The atmosphere of the Prebendal had strangely been no influence at all on Robin's 1985 album, *Walls Have Eyes*. He may have been a history buff, but not when it came to music: 'I don't like songs of the past. I like to get ahead. You'd never associate [the songs on *Walls Have Eyes*] with the Bee Gees.' Given that Maurice co-produced and Barry co-wrote much of the album, that was a classic piece of Gibbspeak. Robin just couldn't stop himself.

It turned out to be a much less consistent album than *How Old Are You* or *Secret Agent*. Opening track 'You Don't Say Us Anymore' was strong, starting like Squeeze's squelchy 'Take Me I'm Yours', before settling into a classically sad Robin melody, albeit at a frantic speed and with typically child-like, English-as-second-language Gibb lines: 'And you don't fool me with your sexy innuendoes.' 'Like a Fool', the first single, was 'Another Lonely Night in New York' redux – 'So many lovers, too many nights,' moped Robin, '. . . standing alone in the rain.' 'Heartbeat in Exile' had a good title but sounded unfinished; 'Someone to Believe In' and 'Remedy' hedged their bets about where the mid-'80s might be heading (they guessed right, but that didn't make them good songs). Most of these tracks could have been written for anyone from Bonnie Tyler to Huey Lewis.

'Toys', though, was a genuine group effort and a terrific single. It had a super-minimal backing, and the kind of purple lyric you wanted from Robin: 'I would go anywhere with you / Into your private paradise . . . Into the depth of hell for you.' Barry was never breathier than when he contributed to the sinister, Lynchian chorus: 'I'd like to play with your toys.'

When *Walls Have Eyes* sold zip, the industry pretended it had known it was rubbish all along. Producer Tom Dowd talked about the malign influence of the album's UK-based A&R man who had kept asking for things to be tweaked and altered. Dowd's track record was second to none – Charlie Parker, Aretha Franklin, Otis Redding, Rod Stewart – though hindsight was a wonderful aid when he said, 'It wasn't really a worthy recording endeavour. I don't think it was the best Robin could do.' That may be true, not the very best, but there had been enough decent songs at the start of the sessions – what the middling results maybe suggested was that the brothers were sick of being dormant, lurking in the shadows. Another phase of their career had run its course. They were edging towards a fully fledged Bee Gees reunion. It wasn't a coincidence that 'Toys' was the best track on *Walls Have Eyes*. 'We're not used to working alone,' confessed Robin. 'We work better as a team. We don't work on our own very well.'

★

In October 1986, the Bee Gees were in New York to sign a long-term contract with Warner Brothers. The following October, *E.S.P.* became the first Bee Gees album in six years.

What's more, it reunited the brothers with Arif Mardin, their saviour in the mid-'70s, as Warner was under the same WEA umbrella as Atlantic. Yet anyone expecting the smoothness of *Mr Natural* or the blue-eyed soul of *Main Course* was in for a bit of a shock. The cover of *E.S.P.* had them standing next to the rocky outcrops of Castlerigg in Cumbria, a mystical setting which sadly wasn't echoed by most of the album – it sounded more like a cutlery battle at the bottom of a lift shaft. Having largely sat out the high '80s with its Fairlights, orchestral stabs and Phil Collins' angry-gorilla drum sound, the Bee Gees came back with maybe the most '80s-sounding record of the decade. By any-one. After *E.S.P.*, there was no louder, clankier place for the '80s drum sound to go. The entire pop world heard the album's lead single, 'You Win Again', and decided to reel it in a bit.

The Gibbs employed a new session band, only keeping on Rhett Lawrence (who had worked on Carola's *Runaway* album) and Greg Phillinganes (ditto Diana Ross's *Eaten Alive*). Karl and Albhy were gone. It was just the three brothers, once again, with hired hands. After an almost decade-long absence, 'You Win Again' put them back in the public eye and at the top of the charts with indecent haste. Barry and Maurice had programmed the drum patterns and bass lines, while newcomer Bobby Kondor played the sin-gle's other main attraction, the Christmassy, snow-globe keyboard sound. The reaction to the single was extraordinary – 'You Win Again' entered the UK charts on 3 October at number twenty-two, then jumped to six, and a week later it was number one.

'Strangely enough,' said long-time fan Brian May, 'one of my moments of "Gasp!" was when I first heard "You Win

Again". To me it's a modern masterpiece of production – devastating simplicity executed with devastating subtlety. What a wonderful wall of sound, yet what sensitivity!' Only someone responsible for such heavy-booted monsters as 'We Will Rock You' and 'I Want It All' could consider 'You Win Again' to be subtle or sensitive, but May's shock and pleasant surprise at the new Bee Gees sound was shared pretty much worldwide, with the notable exception of North America.

Once 'You Win Again' had put them back on top, Mo pulled the brothers' favourite 'The man tried to stop us!' line. 'Everybody said, "Take those stomps off,"' he commented, all peacock plumage. '"Take those banging stomps off. Can we lower them in the mix? Can we take them off the intro?" That was the whole signature of "You Win Again"! You hear those stomps on the radio and you know it's us! And everybody was really against it but we stuck to our guns.' It's hard to believe that after several hitless years they were in a position to argue with their new label, but there you go.

The title track – initially 'XTC' – was ushered in by a cappella harmonies. 'E.S.P.' would have suited Dionne Warwick's white witch energy. It featured neat interplay between Robin and Barry's leads and was built on synth pads and sequenced electro lines. Take away the excess and it could have fitted onto Roxy Music's *Avalon*, but *du jour* American rock guitar and dustbin lid drums rather got in the way – Alan Kendall and Dennis Bryon must have been listening to it, back home in the UK, with lightly furrowed brows. A remix would have been interesting (and still would). Released as a second single, it would reach the top ten in Switzerland but nowhere else.

'The Longest Night' was one of their most understated songs of the decade. Robin's restrained vocal – 'In your darkest hour, on your longest night / I'll be with you baby, make it right' – was underpinned by a processed acoustic guitar, gorgeous minor chord sequence and the clattering drums were replaced by the subtler, more programmed sound of *How Old Are You*. 'Angela' was similarly soft-hearted, bruised and beautiful, with a subtle melody and warm-windblown harmonies hovering and humming like drowsy bees over the percussion. Having bottled it up for three minutes, Barry finally let rip with his falsetto on the fade: 'I'm empty inside, I'm empty inside . . . I'm still alive!' A few territories bravely released it as a single, including Germany, where it swanned no higher than number fifty-two.

Barry's ongoing friendship with Michael Jackson might have influenced one of the oddest songs of their entire career. 'This Is Your Life' was a peculiar but intriguing misstep, included a semi-rapped mid-section – 'more rap less crap' – which felt like a strange exorcism, namechecking a bunch of songs from 'Lonely Days' to 'Tragedy' with a strong whiff of self-loathing: 'This is my world too, just run to me / If you ever want to mend that broken heart / I have seen those nights on Broadway too / Blaming it all / What about you?'

They seemed confused and conflicted by their own talent, their own success. At times 'This Is Your Life' sounded like a rapid-fire manifesto and a self-help aid. The first Bee Gees album in six years reached number five in Britain and number one in Germany. It barely touched the US chart, stopping at number ninety-five. They now had a platform, at least. 'The enemy is the mind / Don't let the future fall apart,' Barry had rapped, wracked. 1988 started with much promise, but there were black dogs at the door.

★

At the end of 1987, finally clean, Andy Gibb had recorded demos with his brothers in Miami. 'Man on Fire' was a decent song, proof on its own he had safely transitioned into the mid-'80s, but 'Arrow Through the Heart' was a melancholic Euroballad, a real gem with fine low-hanging harmonies and a gorgeous, unresolved chorus. He had filed for bankruptcy in September and was living on a weekly $200 allowance from his family. Still, another new dawn arrived with a deal from Island Records in London; Barry had arranged it by phone, and the two brothers flew over to England. 'The fact we'd done it together in the first place was what brought him back,' said Barry. 'Sometimes you have to hit rock bottom before you can lift your head up,' Andy told the press. 'I was very young when I was on top. I feel confident that I can make a significant contribution once again.' Andy Gibb was still just twenty-nine years old.

He had stayed in touch with ex-wife Kim and daughter Peta, though on his terms – management and family prevented her from actually contacting Andy. 'Peta and I were outcasts from the Gibbs,' said Kim. 'I once sent him pictures of Peta but I had to do it through the fan club.' Calling her on the phone after signing the deal, Andy sounded more rational and positive than he had in years. 'He wasn't raving on about dashing off to the Seychelles, or some exotic place. America was the ruin of him. I think that's why he finally returned to Britain. He thought he'd be safe there.'

Andy decided to stay with Robin and Dwina in Thame. He moved into the Chancery, a cottage in the grounds of the Prebendal; they spent evenings listening to cassettes of *The Goon Show* and *Hancock's Half Hour*, like it was still 1959. Before too long, Andy was hiding from the world again, skipping meetings, refusing to pick up the phone. He was meant to go to London to sign the deal – he never went. Island only wanted four more songs from him, but he couldn't write them. He stayed home, beating himself up, feeling like a failure. Robin recalled how he 'kept a watch at the window for hours because he was petrified of anyone coming to see him. When he spotted [my car] turning into the drive, he would start dashing around turning all the lights off.' Barbara flew over from Miami, and soon realised he had started drinking again. Robin reckoned Andy 'had developed a fear of life, almost driving himself to oblivion.' He was terrified that his comeback wouldn't work, but just as scared that he wasn't cut out for doing anything else. He told Barbara: 'I might as well be dead.' A few days after his thirtieth birthday, his mum took him to the John Radcliffe Hospital in Oxford as he was suffering from chest pains. They kept him in for tests. The following morning he slumped into unconsciousness as he was talking to the doctor; he was pronounced dead at 8.45 a.m. on 10 March 1988. Robin had to break the news to his brothers in Miami: 'That has to be the saddest, most desperate moment of my life.'

Really, what had it all been about? It was all about pop music, wasn't it? Making music together. Writing songs and singing them. That's what it was all about. Barry wanted to entertain people, keep them happy. Robin wanted to fray the edges, introduce his own fascinations and his own perspective, and sing in his unique voice. Maurice wanted to be a musician, to create soundscapes. These three approaches weren't incompatible, but somehow bringing Andy into the fold had been. He'd only wanted to join in the game, playing with his brothers, but somehow the timing had never been right: he'd been too young; he was doing his own thing; he was out of control; he was a recluse. It was too late now. 'What he really wanted to do was join the navy and be a pilot,' said Robin. 'But he had this feeling that he had to prove himself to us.' His ex-wife Kim agreed: 'He wanted to be a pilot, and he was bright. I just wish sometimes that he'd never had anything to do with the music industry.'

Did any of his brothers ever say as much to Andy? As a member of the extended family, Albhy Galuten got as close to the brothers' complex relationships as anyone. He had seen it with Maurice at the height of *Saturday Night Fever*. 'There was a lot of stuff around Maurice constructed so he could keep the façade going. Even in the social environment, when the family was sitting around, they'd all pretend . . . which for me never helps anyone solve their problem. You need to say, "Fine, we spoke to the press but you're fucking up, dude." There was a lot of . . . unclarity. A lot of going overboard to not hurt someone's feelings, to the point where you're really not telling the truth.' After Robin had been through the Hither Green train disaster, Barry had said: 'It seems to have marked his character somewhat. He's twice as serious about everything. And he's very quick to criticise everybody at the moment – he's usually right, but he's too fast to jump. He gets into terrible tempers and terrible moods . . . but that's Robin.' This was nothing more than dancing around someone's breakdown, but then families can be terrible at seeing what's right in front of them. Outsiders could see things much more clearly. Dennis Bryon recalled seeing a hopped-up Andy in his dressing room, sitting in silence, repeatedly kicking the TV set while his mum Barbara sat next to him, saying nothing, smiling beatifically.

Dennis had been the one to come to Andy's rescue back in 1985. His most recent record had been an anodyne cover of the Everly Brothers' 'All I Have to Do Is Dream', as a duet with his girlfriend, the actress Victoria Principal. She had literally been his dream girlfriend, he had admitted as much in public, and they were first introduced on a TV show. It was pure Hollywood. But even Pammy from *Dallas* couldn't keep Andy's habits in check. When she forced him on the spot to choose between staying together or leaving her for cocaine and alcohol, he told her he'd have to leave. He had a role in *Joseph and the Amazing Technicolor Dreamcoat*. He was the host on syndicated TV pop show *Solid Gold*. He was charming, charismatic and vulnerable. People kept giving him chances and, without fail, Andy blew them. As early as 1982 he had been selling his belongings to make ends meet, flogging his jewellery for cash on Sunset Boulevard. 'I think he was embarrassed by it,' said Barry. You bet he was embarrassed by it.

By 1985, after a stint at the Betty Ford Center in Rancho Mirage, Andy had been sober enough to start getting a new band together. He called Dennis and asked if he'd want to be the drummer. Not only that, he wanted Dennis and his wife Jenny to move into his house in the Los Angeles Hills. Jenny was a sobering presence; her and Andy were as fond of each other as siblings, with Jenny playing big sister, and so they readily agreed, leaving their house in Miami. The Andy Gibb Band played residencies in Las Vegas and Lake Tahoe. Andy was holding it together. He even got a role, as himself, in a sitcom called *Gimme a Break*. The Bryons stayed in his house for a full two years; Dennis and Andy were tight, playing tennis every day, keeping each other on the level. The pair had a daft, shared sense of humour. There was one running joke that went back to the mid-'70s when Andy, then about fifteen, had been sitting and strumming a guitar. Out of the blue, he had asked, 'Den, have you thought about it?' Bryon didn't have a clue what he was on about, so he answered: 'Of course I've thought about it. How about you, have you thought about it?'

'I've been thinking about it all day, but I just can't make up my mind.'

'Well, let me know when you've made up your mind. Think about it.'

'Okay,' said Andy, and walked away. It was a proper kid joke, and they would repeat it every time they met, while Jenny rolled her eyes.

By 1987, Andy was starting to spend more time alone in his room at home. Dennis and Jenny got worried as dubious characters they'd never met started hanging out in the house; after midnight, women were coming and going via the basement. They thought they should keep their thoughts to themselves. After all, they were only guests. Andy was hospitalised with chest pains more than once. Shows became less regular. At one point, Andy seemed to have been in his room for five days straight, and the only way the Bryons knew he was even in there was because of the milk that kept disappearing from the fridge. Eventually, Dennis decided he had to intervene, at least to have a talk with Andy. He knocked on the door. Andy shouted: 'Leave me alone!' Dennis kicked the door open to see Andy sitting on the bed in his dressing gown playing with an Uzi. There were days-worth of takeaway cartons on the floor, plates of mouldering food stacking up; an empty bottle of vodka was on the bedside table. Andy shouted, 'Get out of my room!' then ran out, jumped into his car and disappeared. The next day Andy's assistant told Dennis he was fired from the band, and that Andy wanted him and Jenny out of the house. The Bryons headed back to Miami.

A few months later, Andy ran into them at Barry's house. Everyone hugged, no hard feelings. 'I've missed you so much,' he told Jenny, sheepishly, all embarrassment. Then suddenly he broke away from her, with a serious look on his face. 'Den,' he asked. 'Have you thought about it?'

Andy Gibb was just a kid. They were all just kids. None of them had really grown up. The title track from Barry's unreleased album *Moonlight Madness* had a line that ran 'All my women cry and all my heroes die'. From the same album was a song called 'Childhood Days', an upbeat if gently wistful piece that would eventually become a solo single in 1988. It wouldn't have been especially memorable, if it hadn't been for the lyrics, 'Friendly faces will always be wrapped up in my childhood days / . . . oh lord, this is a lonely place.'

Solo projects, lonelier places for the Bee Gees than most groups, would be set aside after Andy's death. From this point on there were also to be no stylistic leaps forward. 'In many ways, I think we've all refused to accept he's gone for good,' said Maurice. 'His death has definitely brought the rest of the family closer together. We are united in our devastation.'

Initially the brothers tried to carry on like nothing had changed, but they knew that everything had changed. What the hell were they in this racket for anyway? This wasn't meant to happen. This just wasn't right. 'The week after,' said Maurice, 'we thought maybe if we get back to work we can get recentred . . . I was playing the strings [on keyboards] and it was very beautiful. Barry and Robin just started crying, and I just started crying. I said, "I can't play anymore." We went home.'

Barry, Robin and Maurice struggled greatly with the loss of their kid brother. They felt deep and real guilt. Barry tried to be philosophical: 'They say it causes soul growth when you lose somebody. Before, you don't look at the metaphysical side of life much at all. After, you start looking at everything like that.' They quickly recorded the excellent 'Shape of Things to Come', commissioned for the *1988 Summer Olympics Album*, then wrote 'Wish You Were Here' as a tribute to Andy. That really was too much.[29] They took six months off, and didn't finish what would become the *One* album until 1989. The remainder of 1988 saw the release of the soundtrack to a film called *Hawks*, credited to Barry, mostly made up of songs from the rejected *Moonlight Madness*. The film starred Timothy Dalton and Anthony Edwards as two terminally ill men making the most of their limited time on earth, cramming in as much as they could. They didn't script it, but the idea for the storyline had come from Barry and his mate David English. It must have rung a few bells. After Andy's death, the Bee Gees would never be workaholics again.

The brothers produced *One* themselves, working with engineer Brian Tench, who had co-produced *E.S.P. One* was a much gentler album than *E.S.P.*, the after-effects of Andy's death impacting its unfussy calm with sadness, most clearly on 'Wish You Were Here' and 'Tears'. The chorus of 'Flesh and Blood' melodically revisited 'Toys' from the *Walls Have Eyes* album, with an intro half-inched from the Pet Shop Boys' 'West End Girls' and an agitated middle eight from Robin. 'Tokyo Nights', also a working title for the album, had a Spector-esque feel and a straightforward

---

[29] Whitney Houston's ponderous 'One Moment in Time' would be taken from the album as a single, effectively becoming the theme for 1988's Seoul Olympics.

romanticism: 'I was lonely in western days, Tokyo nights / Well, she took me away by saving my life.' 'Bodyguard' was a highlight, a fine slow jam with a waterfall of harmonies which showed they could move into contemporary R&B with no trouble.

The title track was a soft and subtle earworm that went top ten when released as a single in America. The production was in the pocket, Barry's vocal rhythmically influenced by Michael Jackson; it sounded entirely in step without trying. Barry was now forty-two, the twins thirty-nine. 'If you're that age as a banker or account-ant,' said Barry, with the brothers' usual cock-eyed logic, 'you're coming into your prime.' But 'One' turned out to be no more than a gold watch from the US, a reward for longevity, a nod from the boomers that they'd been forgiven for their chest hair and medal-lions. They wouldn't score another top-forty American hit single.

The rest of the world remained unfazed by what the Gibbs continued to see as disco baggage. 1989 had seen club culture booming with rave in Britain, Balearic beats, Italian house, new beat in Belgium, and the metallic, mechanised futurism of Detroit techno. What's more, there was a gleeful disco edge to much of this new music – 'Theme from S-Express' had been a UK num-ber one in 1988 with a whacking great sample from Rose Royce's 1979 hit 'Is It Love You're After'. There were no raised eyebrows; house music came from the same hedonistic impetus to dance and have a good time that had fuelled disco the first time around.

In 1989, the American press suddenly saw the Bee Gees as underdogs. It was a re-run of the 'God Save the Kinks' campaign of the early '70s, or the Beach Boys' rehabilitation with *Surf's Up*. Paul McCartney, seen as a Pollyanna for much of the '80s, was given a similar reassessment with his Elvis Costello-produced 1989 album *Flowers in the Dirt*. 'Is it possible,' asked *Rolling Stone*, 'that we live in a country that can forgive Richard Nixon but not

his fellow '70s superstars the Bee Gees?' It reckoned that '*One* –
even more than the under-rated 1987 album *E.S.P.* – finds the
brothers back at the top of their game, meshing the sounds of
both of their past hitmaking eras into an impressive album that
still feels quite contemporary . . . If you think the Bee Gees' influence doesn't persist, listen one more time to your Fine Young
Cannibals records.'

The success of *One* in the States had fired them up to face the
public again.

On 15 May 1988, they had played a few songs – 'To Love
Somebody', 'Lonely Days', 'Jive Talkin'' – for Atlantic's fortieth
anniversary concert at Madison Square Garden. The following
month they had made their first live UK appearance in fourteen years at a Prince's Trust show at the Albert Hall, singing
'Jive Talkin'' and 'You Win Again'. And, a week after that, they
had appeared for Nelson Mandela's seventieth birthday show at
Wembley. Playing shows could be a way out of their funk. After
all, they'd been a live act years before they'd ever made a record
– they decided to tour the *One* album. 'We've got a lot of thanking
to do,' said Barry. 'There's a lot of people that have been really
good to us over so many years, and I think it would be nice to see
them sitting in front of us and be able to please them the same
way.' The tour started in Germany, with 50,000 watching them
in Hanover. The Germans had never lost faith in the Bee Gees'
music. 'For us it is the most fantastical place,' said a tearful Robin.

Playing Wembley Arena on the *One* tour in 1989, they
squeezed the *Saturday Night Fever* songs into an embarrassed
medley, and introduced them with some gag about falsettos,

one where Mo could pretend he had a vice squeezing his nuts. They were visibly taken aback by the reaction. The applause went on and on. People loved those songs. No one in Britain or Europe cared about the Hee Bee Gee Bees – if they even remembered 'Meaningless Songs (In Very High Voices)', they thought of it as vaguely amusing, a playful tribute, with less cultural heft than Peter Glaze's skits on *Crackerjack*. The Chicago disco demolition was barely known about in Europe. Living in the States, where rockism had ruled the '80s, where racism and homophobia stalked Reagan's land, the Gibbs were more than aware that disco was still thought of as a leftist aberration, never to return. They played 'One' on *Letterman*, and Barry said sadly, 'Hopefully the image of being disco wimps is now gone.' You just wish they'd all moved back to England, or Australia, for their sanity.

OCC UK top ten, 31 March 1991

1. Chesney Hawkes – 'The One and Only'
2. James – 'Sit Down'
3. Rod Stewart – 'Rhythm of My Heart'
4. Roxette – 'Joyride'
5. Bee Gees – 'Secret Love'
6. Pet Shop Boys – 'Where the Streets Have No Name (I Can't Take My Eyes Off You)'
7. Simple Minds – 'Let There Be Love'
8. Quartz featuring Dina Carroll – 'It's Too Late'
9. Hale and Pace – 'The Stonk'
10. Snap! – 'Snap Megamix'

While the *One* album had reined in the clattering percussion of *ESP*, allowing the melodies and harmonies on songs like 'Wish You Were Here' and 'Bodyguard' to shine through the *du jour* metallic techno production, 1991's *High Civilization* brought it back with a vengeance. It was recorded with Prince's sometime engineer Femi Jiya, whose preference for hard, loud percussion meant the Gibbs were pushed further back in the mix. What it lost in subtlety it more than made up for in high-concept lyrical weirdness. Gibb scholar Joseph Brennan discovered an early running order which tells 'a story of "secret love" that might be all in the singer's head and secret from the girl too. The contradictions give the story a dreamlike effect of details shifting.' Brennan reckons the group chose to undercut the concept by changing the running order on the album's eventual release. Either way, it was no *Odessa*. The single 'Secret Love' was another Motown tribute, and the catchiest thing on the album, charting across Europe where it reached number five in the UK, and number two in Germany and Austria. 'The Only Love' was Barry's big ballad, which foreshadowed boy band Westlife more than it recalled past glories.

After the nightcap of *One*, *High Civilization* was something of an over-egged cocktail. 'Who can stop your past from rushing by / Born to live one million storeys high?' asked 'Ghost Train', with a curious gravitas. It was a wild grab bag that summed up the album: there was the nervous energy of the song's intro, the fast phrasing of Barry's pre-chorus, the *woah-oh*s on the first part of the chorus, with Robin in his upper register for the middle chorus and the harmonies of all three brothers for the 'ghost train' refrain. Even by Gibb standards the song structure is complicated, and this is before we even get to the psychedelic outro, complete with sound effects of a children's playground, a military drum loop and then an abrupt end with a door slamming and Barry defiantly shouting, 'Right!'

A familiar face, guitarist Alan Kendall, was back but the electro-stabs of 'Party with No Name', 'Dimensions' and 'When He's Gone' weren't exactly helped by his wailing guitar interruptions – he was channelling late '80s hair metal just as grunge was set to sweep the genre out into the yard. Kendall's coiffed guitar workouts cancelled out the impact of the album's on-the-money 1991 drum programming. The album also felt overlong; only two of the songs came in at under five minutes. None of the Bee Gees' albums are without their charms, though, and the pop classicism of Barry's 'Happy Ever After' was the best track, with its multi-part melody, another struc-ture that took a few listens to fathom, and – for once – some neatly understated guitar (still, it had no real reason to clock in at six minutes fifteen). The pumped-up title track also stood out with its jerky chorus melody, rather like mid-'80s Level 42, and a peculiar dystopian lyric that traversed LA, Rome, Afghanistan, Cairo to Iran. 'No city can hold you, there's no one in Avalon to show you / Minutes into seconds, are you ready for the end?' 'Human Sacrifice' also featured a garish lyric, one that made 'Chain Reaction' seem sweetly romantic: 'It's you or me, gotta be a kill or cure / Maybe undergo a lover's operation / Nothing cuts like a knife can.' You had to admire the Gibbs' adventurousness, but *High Civilization* was a tough listen.

They toured the album, playing Wembley Arena again – this time, 'Night Fever' and 'Stayin' Alive' were played in full, with no apologies, no embarrassment. The balance of past, present and future seemed more closely aligned.

By Christmas, Barry – now in his mid-forties – was back in Miami, getting set to become a dad again. He confirmed the group's burgeoning national treasure status by making a cameo appearance on the *Only Fools and Horses* Christmas special, just as a tourist ship passed his Miami home. 'Look!' shouted Del Boy from the ship. 'It's a real-life Bee Gee! Alright, Bazza?'

The waters weren't calm for long; malign spirits waited on the shore. To Barry and Linda's horror, baby Alexandra was born four months premature on 29 December 1991, weighing less than two pounds, and her survival was touch and go for the best part of the next year. A few weeks later, while Barry was having back surgery, he had an allergic reaction to morphine and suffered a heart attack. Then, on 5 March 1992, Hugh, the Gibb patriarch who had been frowning his encouragement at them all for over thirty years, died, on what would have been Andy's birthday. 'I believe all this was meant to happen,' said Barry bravely. 'It was just a matter of time. He knew where Andy was, and he wanted to be with him.'

While Robin and Dwina were in Miami, Robin's assistant Ken Graydon opened up a wardrobe in the Prebendal one day in 1992 to discover an intruder armed with rubber gloves, a tape recorder and a Stanley knife. She had broken in and apparently just wanted to record her experience of being inside the house. Realising she was harmless, and horribly embarrassed at being caught, Robin urged the police to drop charges, but they wouldn't. The anonymous intruder's biggest concern was that she would be kicked out of the fan club – Robin ensured she wasn't.

That wasn't all. After touring the *High Civilization* album had finished, Mo had gone back to drinking: 'I was bored, absolutely bored stiff . . . My wife Yvonne was away for a weekend and I was like a kid in a toy shop.' He'd been sober for several years. His lost weekend apparently saw him polish off two bottles of brandy, four bottles of whisky and umpteen pints of Guinness. 'I was still sober. That's when the wife sussed that I was sick again.' At least he appeared to be sober. When Yvonne threatened that she'd move out and take the kids with her, Maurice pulled a gun on his family; his son Adam thought, 'Oh my God, he's going to shoot us.' But Maurice was too drunk to do anything. Yvonne and the kids moved in with Barry and Linda.

18

MANCHESTER REVISITED

OCC UK top ten, 26 December 1993

1. Mr Blobby – 'Mr Blobby'
2. Take That – 'Babe'
3. Chaka Demus & Pliers – 'Twist and Shout'
4. Bee Gees – 'For Whom the Bell Tolls'
5. East 17 – 'It's Alright'
6. Dina Carroll – 'The Perfect Year'
7. Meat Loaf – 'I'd Do Anything for Love (But I Won't Do That)'
8. Meat Loaf – 'Bat Out of Hell 1993'
9. Elton John and Kiki Dee – 'True Love'
10. K7 – 'Come Baby Come'

'A few years ago my kids would come home and say, "Why don't people like your group, Dad?" "All things pass," I'd say, but I'd be disturbed. Now they come home and say, "People think your group's really hip now, what's going on?"

We're enjoying a sudden resurgence – in five years' time we won't be.'

– Barry Gibb

One day in 1992, Maurice sat down in front of his dressing table mirror. He was alone in the house. The wife and kids were staying with Barry. His sad, handsome eyes looked rheumy and sore. He could smell his own breath and it was horrible. It was 1992 but it may as well have been 1972, with Lulu waking him up to tell him it was over. He'd been thinking about Lulu for the past couple of days, because his brothers were working with her on a song right now; it was called 'Let Me Wake Up in Your Arms' and it was going to be on her *Independence* album. Christ, Barry already saw more of his wife than he did, and now his ex-wife too? He'd had enough of independence. Maurice wanted his family back.

Desperate, he joined a course called New Life Transitions: 'I couldn't get back any trust from my wife and kids until I proved to them that I was an example, and that took a while.' Barry and Robin didn't write a note of music until Maurice was sober again. Finally, his treatment was complete. 'It's been beautiful,' he said. Mo and Yvonne renewed their wedding vows in 1992 on their boy Adam's sixteenth birthday – he was the best man and their daughter Samantha was maid of honour. 'It was to signify the start of a new lease on life,' said Maurice. The whole family felt much the same way. They were enjoying the third wave of their career, the autumn of the Bee Gees, and didn't need any more breakdowns. 'One more time on the merry go round,' smiled Barry.

★

Compared to many acts, the Bee Gees were opting out of the 1990s mainstream. They did not get a remix from K-Klass or Masters at Work (though they could have done, the material was there to be tailored). They did not angle for inclusion on blockbuster soundtracks, unlike Aerosmith or Whitney Houston or Bryan Adams. They did not cave in and record a Diane Warren power ballad.

It was quite astonishing, but they simply didn't need to. Instead they started to take stock, to enjoy themselves and their unique position. They allowed themselves to look backwards. Their insanely productive and varied career had been put into perspective by *Tales from the Brothers Gibb*, a four-disc retrospective. Other odd chunks of their history took on a new life. In 1991, the *Odessa* track 'Melody Fair' had been used in a Japanese Suzuki advert. It became a hit all over again, with the movie *Melody* getting screenings all over Japan, and its star, Tracy Hyde, now fully grown, flown over for a full promo tour.

Bee Gees albums would now become slower to emerge, while shows were fewer and further between. This was the kind of pace and productivity they weren't used to but, heck, they were all in their mid-forties. It wasn't as if the Beach Boys, or Donna Summer, or even Paul McCartney was bothering the charts in 1993 – none of the singles from McCartney's *Off the Ground* had made the US top forty. R&B was dominant in the States, where Mariah Carey was queen, while Robin's beloved Eurobeat bossed the UK; 2 Unlimited, Ace of Bass and Culture Beat all had UK number-one singles.

1993 was also the year that saw *Bat Out of Hell II* become a surprise success, ending up as the best-selling album of the year in Britain. The Bee Gees' *Size Isn't Everything*, released in late summer, stacked up very well compared to Meat and other veteran acts: Billy Joel's 1993 album *River of Dreams* was meditative and solemn, reflecting on middle-aged regrets, furrow-browed about fatherhood and relationships; Rod Stewart released *Unplugged and Seated*, which suggested he was ready to put his feet up and rest his eyes; while Elton John's *Duets* wore its elder statesman cloak heavily, roping in both Leonard Cohen and Chris Rea, daring you to spot the difference between them. In this company, *Size* had more in common with the sleek electro-romantic R&B of Toni Braxton's debut and Janet Jackson's third album, both best-sellers in 1993, or Gabrielle's 'Dreams', a new, laid-back strand of British R&B.

Size Isn't Everything turned out to be their best album in over a decade, one to file alongside *To Whom It May Concern* and *Living Eyes*. It sounded like fun. The Tony Manero of 1993, approaching forty, would have related to this side of the Bee Gees, as ageing, smooth R&B merchants who had too much pride to throw shapes on a dancefloor but still required a groove to their music.

In spite of its nudge-nudge title, the album was a return to more heartfelt work, with a softer, cosmopolitan production after the overthought techno apocalypse of *High Civilization*. 'Paying the Price of Love Part 1' (there never would be a part two) was one of the most minimal singles the Bee Gees ever released: it began with a drum machine's gentle pitter-patter, not unlike Marvin Gaye's 'Sexual Healing', before Barry's restrained, soulful vocal came in over Mo's swimming-pool keyboard pads, and finally the drums build and a nightclub sax seduces uptight, isolationist Barry: 'From a hard time, playtime, I took a trip around the world / I made myself invisible. The taste was in the wine.' The similarly pared-back 'Heart Like Mine' was outstanding – it would have been a highlight on any Bee Gees album, from any period: Robin sang the title with his full, quavering approach;

Alan Kendall added a woozy, atmospheric guitar part which only pushed the song further into gorgeousness. 'Blue Island' – dedicated to the victims of the ongoing Balkan wars – was reminiscent of 'In the Morning''s fragrance, while at the other extreme 'Fallen Angel' revisited Robin's chaka-chaka Eurobeat. It was terrific, all icy glissandos and driving Christmas drums. And if it leaned heavily on his own 'Juliet', who was going to complain about that?

'For Whom the Bell Tolls' looked back further still, with a busker's strum intro that evoked 'Black Diamond' from the troubled *Odessa* sessions. The production may have sounded closer to Air Supply than anything considered groundbreaking in 1993 – the debut albums by Björk and Suede, say, or Paul Weller's semi-acoustic, career-saving *Wild Wood* – but the brothers' harmonies and vocal interplay were spot on. *Size Isn't Everything* has aged very well. Lead single 'Paying the Price of Love' had been a UK top-twenty hit in August 1993, but 'For Whom the Bell Tolls' went all the way to number four at Christmas, sandwiched between Chaka Demus & Pliers' 'Twist and Shout' and East 17's 'It's Alright'. All this fine company was kept at bay by the Christmas number one, 'Mr Blobby'.

Suddenly they seemed spoilt for quality material. Some great songs didn't even make the cut. '855–7019' was a filmic adventure story about a private number, something that still made sense in the last days of landlines. The lyric, presumably Barry's, was darkly strange: 'There will never be a past or a future / If you kill my phone.' The joyous 'My Destiny', driven by Alan Kendall's T. Rex-borrowed riff, built up to a classically complex Gibb chorus, wrapped in riddles and convolution, and showing the full range of their vocal abilities; it would be tossed away on the B-side of 'Paying the Price of

Love', but was stronger than anything that had appeared on *High Civilization*.

Plugging *Size Isn't Everything* on Australian TV show *Bingo Wall of Death*, Mo laughed: 'It's our thirtieth album. We've been trying to get it right for years. We think we've done it this time.' *Bingo Wall of Death* was apparently a Gibb family favourite; it asked celebrities awkward questions. Would they pose naked for money. 'Yes,' said Robin quickly. 'For five quid, and all the tea I can drink.' What would he do if he wasn't a pop star? 'I'd open a small sewage farm on the other side of Oxford.'

They had relaxed, a little. They could have toured the album, but thought better of it. Mo may have been fighting fit again, but Barry's arthritis meant European shows in 1994 were cancelled. Ambitions were scaled back. They were then asked to write the theme for a remake of the Christmas classic *Miracle on 34th Street*, due in the cinemas at Christmas 1995, and wrote a song called 'Miracles Happen'. It was a great song, but the minor chords and sawing cellos had more in common with the book-burning *Fahrenheit 451* than a cosy fireside Christmas movie. It was dropped in favour of a more traditional festive soundtrack.

So maybe they hadn't ever got a call about a new Bond theme. Nor had they ever written a Eurovision entry (probably out of choice). But the Bee Gees joined the list of terrace chant immortals in 1995 when Ajax FC of Amsterdam decided it was time to pull the 25-year-old 'I.O.I.O.' from its *Cucumber Castle* home. Sometime actor and pastry chef Peter Beense made a single of 'Ay Ay Ay Ajax', which reached number thirty-four in the Dutch chart and sounded exactly as you'd imagine it might. On a similar working-class culture tip, BBC Radio 1 asked the brothers to turn on the Blackpool illuminations, the holiday lights on the mainland across the water from Ellan Vannin, in September 1995. As darkness fell they played 'For Whom the Bell Tolls' and 'You Win Again' to the tipsy crowds before throwing the switch at 9 p.m.; Barry said they were 'slightly overwhelmed' and Mo called it a 'huge honour'. Their bucket list was endearingly modest.

The Gibbs had always felt their influence affected younger generations of musicians, but holed up in Miami they must have sometimes wondered if this was wishful thinking; the mid-'90s would see an unavoidable tsunami of appreciation. A brace of tribute albums were released that dug into their extensive catalogue and pulled it in very different directions: 1994's *Melody Fair* saw American powerpop acts like the Sneetches, Baby Lemonade and Young Fresh Fellows unearthing obscurities like 'Mrs Gillespie's Refrigerator' and 'Kilburn Towers', with the album cover art borrowed from *Trafalgar*; a couple of years later, *The Soul of the Bee Gees* included Chaka Khan's 'Jive Talkin'', Jerry Butler and Thelma Houston's super-smooth 'Love So Right', and Mavis Staples' intense gospel reading of *Mr Natural* album track 'Give a Hand, Take a Hand'. A chance meeting with the Pet Shop Boys found the duo happy to admit to the Gibbs that their 1985 single 'Opportunities (Let's Make Lots of Money)' had owed a strong debt to 'Lonely Days' ('Where would I be without my woman?').

There was talk of a *Love Songs* compilation in 1995, part old songs and part new, but in the end the Gibbs just decided to slowly work towards their next full album. After going through the working titles *Crusader*, *Obsessions* and *Irresistible Force*, they settled on *Still Waters*, after one of the album tracks. Rumours had them working with heroic R&B producers Jimmy Jam and Terry Lewis. Daisy Age hip hoppers P.M. Dawn did get as far as recording a brace of songs (unreleased takes of 'Fire with Fire' and 'Still Waters'), but eventually the album was recorded with a solid crew of different producers – Arif Mardin, Hugh Padgham, Russ Titelman, Raphael Saadiq and uberfan David Foster. The first single, 'Alone', was apparently written with the Byrds in mind, only with their twelve-string drone replaced by some sort of synthesised bagpipe sound – it shouldn't have worked but it did, and sailed all the way to number five in the UK chart.

Still Waters was another excellent collection, even if it saw the brothers largely recording separately. 'Irresistible Force' had a rolling, minor-key feel and a fine, emotive Robin vocal. It could have been from the early '70s, though – intriguingly – not the Bee Gees' early '70s. Instead there were echoes of Barclay James Harvest and early ELO; the lyrics were a downbeat blur of 'fairweather friends' and 'all things must pass'. It was terrific. The *LA Times* described Barry's 'I Surrender' as 'an inviting slice of breathy, blue-eyed funk that reminds us whom George Michael learned some of his tricks from,' and wrote that 'Closer than Close' 'pulsates with a gently seductive energy'. The non-Christmassy Christmas song 'Miracles Happen' found itself a home, just ahead of closing track 'Smoke and Mirrors', which had melodic echoes of 'More than a Woman' and made merry with its overlapping harmonies. Its complex structure was hard to take in without a few listens. In the autumn of their years, the Bee Gees were not coasting.

Again, the outtakes were just as good, if not better than some of the album tracks. Robin's 'Rings Around the Moon', an unreleased song from the *Love Songs* project, ended up on the B-side of 'Alone' but was quite extraordinary – it had a circular melody, and a beautiful whirlpool of a chorus. Almost sung in the round, this was soothing, somnolent, modern folk music.

Still Waters was issued in Britain on 10 March 1997, and in America on 6 May, where it reached number eleven; their previous album *Size Isn't Everything* had peaked at number 153.

The album was a victory lap. They sounded comfortable in each other's company, comfortable – at last – as the Bee Gees, and the only album that stopped *Still Waters* from becoming a number one in the UK was the Spice Girls' all-conquering debut.

OCC UK top ten, 9 March 1997

1. Spice Girls – 'Mama' / 'Who Do You Think You Are'
2. No Doubt – 'Don't Speak'
3. Fugees – 'Rumble in the Jungle'
4. Sash! – 'Encore Une Fois'
5. Bee Gees – 'Alone'
6. Kula Shaker – 'Hush'
7. Mark Morrison – 'Moan and Groan'
8. Eternal – 'Don't You Love Me'
9. No Mercy – 'Where Do You Go'
10. Ant & Dec – 'Shout'

Manchester claimed them once again. *Still Waters* was complemented in March 1997 by a *South Bank Show* documentary called

'Keppel Road: The Life and Music of the Bee Gees'. They went back to their old Chorlton home with Melvyn Bragg, and were visibly excited and taken aback. For a group that always claimed to hate looking backwards, this was quite a big deal. They talked about taking the stage at the Gaumont, and they hinted at the cold, the damp, the fire-starting, the grinding poverty.

Liam and Noel Gallagher, a new generation of bickering Mancunian brothers, were happy to give props to the Bee Gees. Noel pulled out plums like 'Lemons Never Forget' from their back catalogue and talked about how special they were to him. His fascination had begun when one of the band's roadies 'played all their early '60s, mid-'60s stuff. I was knocked out cold. I couldn't believe it. It kickstarted a life-long obsession, and I've loved them ever since.

'I just love the story of that band. And I was lucky enough to meet them down the years, separately, and they were just a proper, proper songwriting machine. I'm even having *Saturday Night Fever* now. I love it! I've got the utmost respect for them . . . it's the melodies and the songwriting, but also the fact that they come from where I come from, and that they're brothers and all that. And it's great songs, great voices . . . they're just great.' The new-found optimism in Britain in the late '90s had impacted the Gibbs. The Bee Gees' greatest cheerleader from now on would be Noel Gallagher, writer and sometime singer with the biggest group in the country.

The Gibbs began to realise that their longevity meant new fans were happy to pick and choose from different periods of their career – and that this wasn't a bad thing. The fact they were still making contemporary hit records three decades on from 'New York Mining Disaster' was pretty much unique. Where were the Hollies or the Tremeloes on the charts of 1997, let alone the

Stones or the Who? 'Everything really started to change in 1997,' Maurice later told *Mojo*. 'We had four Lifetime Achievement Awards in three months, from the World Music Awards to our induction in the Rock and Roll Hall of Fame. I mean, that's quite weird. It just started turning around, and people started listening.'

In February, they were lined up to receive a Lifetime Achievement Award at the BRITs. Pulp's Jarvis Cocker was set to present them with the award, but Barry asked for someone else, since Jarvis had wiggled his bum for the cameras when Michael Jackson performed an overwrought 'Earth Song' at the BRITs two years earlier. BRITs organisers the BPI were doing some hand-wringing here – in 1995, they had kept silent as Cocker was arrested, spending the night in jail for having the temerity to suggest Jackson's saviour-like performance on a stage surrounded by children was rather dubious. Now all was forgiven. Still, Barry – half the world away – smelled a rat and had no reason to think Cocker wouldn't pull a similar stunt. 'Jarvis Cock-up,' he called him, sounding exactly like a teenager's dad – which, of course, he was. Tim Rice stepped in, a heartlands Tory who would never have dared to upset the establishment. Robert Stigwood, only sixty-two but looking older and frail, also joined them on stage. 'We love you,' said Barry, and suddenly a long-open wound was miraculously healed.

That was sort of sweet, but the world at large didn't really care about their management hassles. It was still waiting for them to step out of the kitchen and join the party. It wanted to celebrate the Bee Gees music in the same way it had embraced ABBA after their years in the wilderness, and had found a new way to love the Beatles harder, if this was even possible, after 1995's *Anthology* TV series. In April 1997, the World

Music Awards also honoured them with a Lifetime Contribution to Music award, this time presented by Princess Stephanie of Monaco. 'We feel we're into our third period of fame now,' said Barry. 'There was a huge backlash against us. Radio wouldn't touch us, we were censored. Now it appears we're fashionable again. It's quite confusing how suddenly you can be "in" again when no one wanted to know before.' Just nine days after *Still Waters*' US release, Barry, Maurice and Robin were inducted into the Rock and Roll Hall of Fame by Brian Wilson. Other entrants that year were Joni Mitchell, the Young Rascals, Parliament/Funkadelic, Buffalo Springfield, and Crosby, Stills & Nash.

They should have been happy, accepted their critical and public reappraisal, seen the awards on the mantlepiece and felt at peace with pop. They'd lost a battle but won the war.

Instead, they made fools of themselves by walking out of a live TV interview with former solicitor Clive Anderson, possibly the world's least likely chat show host. To be fair to the brothers, Anderson had shown an alarming lack of preparation ('I didn't know you were real brothers') before implying their music was 'shit' – which he would hardly have done if Paul McCartney or David Bowie had been his guests. The old defensiveness kicked in. The feeling of being ridiculed, that sense of underlying disrespect, had never really gone away, ever since the 'Bee-Gee-free weekends' on American radio in 1979. All the BRIT awards, Hall of Fame accolades, and generous words of Brian Wilson could never wash away the feeling that this was all temporary. One day, Barry thought, everyone would turn around and go, 'You know what? They were shit all along, weren't they?' Clive Anderson was massively out of touch with the public's love of the Bee Gees in 1997, but his low jibes – 'Sometimes you're fashionable, usually you're not' – were too much for Barry. 'You're the tosser, pal,' he audibly mumbled as he removed his microphone, walked off stage and back to the green room.

On a treadmill of interviews, they weren't always so tetchy, and were often still pretty funny. Filmed at Barry's Arts and Crafts pile in England for Dutch TV, the brothers were asked if they always dressed in black. 'We're going through our Beatle period,' said Mo. Asked what his epitaph would be, Robin said, 'I came and I went, and in-between was padding.'

If they were going to team up with any emerging pop act in 1997, you'd have expected them to emerge as godfathers of floor-friendly pop and teen heartthrob ballads. Instead, they made a big deal of writing 'Immortality' for French-Canadian chanteuse Celine Dion, the most mumsy big balladeer of her generation. Contrarian as ever, the Gibbs talked about 'Immortality' as if they'd had the chance to write 'Suspicious Minds' for Elvis. They flew to the studio in New York where Dion was recording, to see what she had done with their demo. 'They listened to the song and they were crying,' she remembered. 'I was very touched by it.' Barry has gone on to say it is their favourite Bee Gee cover of all time: 'To us, it is extremely special.'

This says much about how the Bee Gees see pop, and themselves within it. Celine Dion was hugely successful, as popular in Africa as she was America and Europe; Jamaica and Ireland alike bought her albums by the truckload. She followed in a tradition of dependable, relatable, solid singers with great pipes. She didn't seem showbiz at all. And in real life, she seemed even more maternally reassuring than her voice suggested.

The current crop of British stars were enjoying upsetting the establishment in the late '90s, whether it was Geri Halliwell attempting to resurrect the divisive Union Jack, Jarvis Cocker spoiling Michael Jackson's set-piece at the BRITs, or Liam Gallagher threatening to punch George Harrison, telling him to leave his Zimmer frame at home after the former Beatle had said the music of Oasis 'lacks depth, and the singer Liam is a pain'. Celine Dion, meanwhile, held nervous indie singer-songwriter Elliott Smith's hand at the Oscars and gave him the confidence to sing his fragile 'Miss Misery'. She sang duets with Streisand and Pavarotti. The Bee Gees were always going to take her mainstream sentimentality over Cocker's cynicism, whether or not they thought it was justified.

One of the few people to have earned a real insight into the brothers' writing process was engineer John Merchant. He had been working with the Bee Gees since *One* in 1989, after having started out as an intern at the Gibbs' Middle Ear Studios. He remembered Barry 'playing the intro for the song "Immortality". Maurice listened, and played the first chord, and then three and a half minutes later, they [had written] the song – in real time, in just one pass. I get goosebumps telling that story. It was unbelievable. Barry would change chords, and Maurice would be there immediately, like he knew where Barry was going. They locked in together in a way, both timing-wise and intonation-wise, that only someone who knows what the other person is thinking before they think it could do.'

The Bee Gees joined Celine Dion at her 1998 Fort Lauderdale show, on stage together in a hugging circle formation, to sing 'Immortality'. The song would end up in the score for Stigwood's new West End revival of *Saturday Night Fever*. It was included on Dion's *Let's Talk About Love*, a collection of ballads that also included the *Titanic* monster 'My Heart Will Go On' and went on to sell over 31 million copies. 'Immortality', soapy as it was, also gave the brothers another UK top-five hit single, credited to Celine Dion with the Bee Gees.

In December 1998, the UK singles chart saw boy band 911 at number two with 'More than a Woman', only held back from the top spot by Steps, who were at number one with 'Tragedy'. The '90s had already seen top-ten revivals for 'If I Can't Have You' (Kim Wilde, 1993), 'Stayin' Alive' (N-Trance, 1995) and 'Words', which Boyzone had taken all the way to number one in 1996. A solo Ronan Keating then recorded Barry's bespoke 'Lovers and Friends', while Pras's platinum-selling 'Ghetto Supastar (That Is What You Are)' interpolated 'Islands in the Stream' and went to number two in Britain in 1998. As song-writers, the Bee Gees were more bankable in the late '90s than the Beatles.

'We're durable, persistent little buggers,' said Robin.

19

WHERE WE CAME IN

OCC top ten UK albums, 14 April 2001

1. Hear'Say – *Popstars*
2. Eva Cassidy – *Songbird*
3. Gorillaz – *Gorillaz*
4. Dido – *No Angel*
5. Billy Joel – *The Ultimate Collection*
6. Bee Gees – *This Is Where I Came In*
7. LeAnn Rimes – *I Need You*
8. David Gray – *White Ladder*
9. Anastacia – *Not That Kind*
10. Rod Stewart – *Human*

This is the final chapter. You probably know what's coming next. The most peculiar thing is that the Bee Gees – who, throughout their lives, seemed to have telepathic sibling powers – seemed to share a feeling of endings and resolution. Loose ends needed to be tied, peace needed to be made with their past. Of course, it could also be that they were turning fifty and naturally becoming more conscious of mortality, but even so it was quite uncanny.

★

After the success of *Still Waters*, the Bee Gees and their legacy had finally been reunited with American pop culture. Part of this new acceptance came when the brothers played at a *Saturday Night Fever* reunion show at Madison Square Garden in January 1998 with Yvonne Elliman, the Trammps and KC and the Sunshine Band. Barry still sounded anxious: 'For about fifteen years we had some kind of leprosy, now it's okay to like us.' Talking about 'Stayin' Alive' in particular, he sounded almost angry about its resurrection: 'For a song that was so shunned, why is it that everybody wants it?' Robin, less hung up on what other people thought, had begun to wear a toupee in the late '90s, but only when he felt like it. Maurice just smiled, unfazed, the man in the middle.

So how did the brothers function as a group at the turn of the new century? New-found respectability brought with it a level of self-awareness. 'We're all boss of this band at one time or another,' said Barry in a *Mojo* interview. 'If I get really dogged about something and I don't want to do it and everyone else does, my wife Linda will turn around and say, "Get your pants on and go and bloody do it and shut up moaning." In fact, all the Bee Gee wives are good like that. They have no time for our egos. They'll say, "This is that showbiz ego thing – get rid of it, act your age." So we're like that with each other, as brothers. We drive each other.' The new century would be rung in with a sell-out show in front of 12,000 people in Sunrise, Florida. They played an acoustic version of 'Turn of the Century' from *Bee Gees' 1st*, left the stage just before the stroke of midnight to raise a toast with their now vast extended family, and returned to play an encore of 'You Should Be Dancing'. Some years earlier, Barry had said, 'We believe that on New Year's Eve 2000, people will still be dancing to *Saturday Night Fever*.' After all the aggro they had gone through in the intervening years, it must have been deeply satisfying to see that sea of smiling faces.

Nothing is forever. Back at home on Ellan Vannin, the singular island's cherished birching laws had been formally repealed in 1993, although actually no one had received a birching since January 1976, when a teenager from Northern Ireland had got six thwacks, the sixtieth on the island since 1960. George Waft, the politician who had steered the repeal bill through the island's House of Keys, reckoned the practice should be abandoned because it wasn't exactly a deterrent anymore: 'The individual and families of anyone birched', reckoned Mr Waft, 'would benefit considerably by selling their stories to the newspapers.'

On Christmas Day 1997, a radio special called *The Bee Gees Come Home to Ellan Vannin* had been broadcast on the island, with local DJ Bernie Quayle talking to all three brothers. To mark the occasion, the brothers had recorded the unofficial Manx national anthem, also called 'Ellan Vannin', and pressed a thousand CDs to raise money for Manx Children in Need. 'We've been very blessed with our kids,' said Maurice. 'We don't take it for granted.' The song was based on an 1854 poem by Eliza Craven Green, and given a full, windswept hilltop rendition from Robin on vocals and Maurice on synthesised pipes: 'It was such a proud moment for us. Believe you me, it was wonderful to do something for home.'[30] It was notable that Mo called it home.

First Manchester, now Douglas. They were harking back to their childhoods, the years before they had a record deal, before they met Robert Stigwood, before they had anything much materially. In July 1999, Barry had written a letter for the Redcliffe Museum in Australia, the town that was effectively the birthplace of the Bee Gees as a group with its talent shows and its speedway track, but one that was also somewhere the Gibbs had lived for no more than eighteen months. The letter was probably way more poetic than anything the museum had expected. Robin and Mo had always been hand on heart, barely flinching from putting their personalities out there for the public to scrutinise. But Barry was different, and this was a rare glimpse into his mind:

> If you ask me about Redcliffe I could tell you a hundred stories about my life here in this wonderful place. As a twelve-year-old emigrant, I was a stranger in a strange land . . . it was a wonderful tropical existence that I re-live over and over in my heart and mind. Playing between the fishing boats when the tide was out at night . . . eating fruit from the trees . . . the 4KQ talent show we never won, the Saturday night dance which always ended with a pie floating in peas . . . I have changed, but the child inside me has not. I'm still here on Redcliffe beach . . . It is held in time deep inside my soul.

---

[30] The poem was set to music at some point in the late nineteenth century by the otherwise unknown 'J. Townsend' and published in the book *Manx National Songs* in 1896.

Redcliffe, Chorlton, Ellan Vannin. 'I feel very much a sort of a gypsy,' explained Barry about his torn devotions. 'I feel very patriotic to all these countries. I'm not a gypsy, but I feel that way.' When they called their next album *This Is Where I Came In*, that feeling of going home intensified.

Released in April 2001, it was their twenty-second album and took more of a White Album approach than any since *Odessa*, with individual songs from each of the three brothers. Canadian writer Gary Pig Gold said that it 'put those Gibbs right back upon a plateau every note the equal of their mid-'70s and even mid-'60s glory daze. Near complete credit for this sobering turn of fortunes [was due to] Maurice's greatly increased role.'

Thoroughly dried out, Maurice was revelling in his new lease of life. 'I used to look in the mirror and just see darkness. Now I look and see little cherubs with flowers flying around my head. Well, it's not quite like that . . .' His shrugging, self-analysing 'Man in the Middle' came over like a rainy TV theme, with Mo as a private detective, the Isle of Man's answer to *Public Eye*'s Frank Marker, trying and failing to crack a betting racket at the TT Races. Around the time they recorded the album, he became consumed by his new-found love for paintball combat, and it was no half-assed hobby – he had been introduced to the sport by friends at Alcoholics Anonymous, and his team, the Royal Rat Rangers, impressively reached the semi-finals of paintball's World Campaign Cup at Crystal Palace. Mo was on a roll. His other contribution to the album, 'Walking on Air', had an undertow of powerpop in its Euro melancholy; if they had recorded it in 1973 instead of 'Wouldn't I Be Someone' it could have been a huge hit . . . and possibly derailed their Arif Mardin moment. 'Loose Talk Costs Lives' looked back to the rich layers and sly touches of *Guilty* or *Mr Natural*. 'We're basically the same,' sang Barry, and he was right. *This Is Where I Came In* somehow reminded you of almost every period of their career.

The brothers sang many of the harmonies around one microphone, again something they hadn't done in many years. The album also featured more live instruments and fewer synths than anything since the mid-'70s. Possibly influenced by famous fan Noel Gallagher, they also looked back to the Beatles for inspiration. 'She Keeps on Coming' had strong *Rubber Soul* vibes on its chorus, specifically reminiscent of 'Drive My Car'; and Robin's 'Déjà Vu' borrowed George Harrison's arpeggio moves, along with John Lennon's 'telephone voice' from 'Tomorrow Never Knows'. Robin described the album as 'getting back to that original feeling, that human feeling that we had on the *Bee Gees' 1st* album in 1967. The only real difference is now you have videos and things like that.'

'Sacred Trust' – which had already been recorded by the Backstreet Boys – was on more solid R&B ground, 'Embrace' was another Europop Robin moment, while 'Wedding Day' had the feel of an old doo wop song, only with added turn-of-the-21st-century Miami gloss. 'Wedding Day'! Why hadn't it been done before? It was rather like writing a song called 'Happy Birthday'; Barry's commercial instincts were still functioning – I mean, it wasn't like Billy Idol was likely to get played for most couples walking down the aisle. The unexpected thirties throwback 'Technicolor Dreams' found Barry cutting into Peter Skellern's tea-dance market: 'I'll give you Panavision pictures / 'Cause you give me Technicolor dreams.' Could it have been looking back to Hugh's early days in Australia, working in door-to-door sales? *This Is Where I Came In* was the album where they afforded themselves more than just a quick backward glance, finally happy to dip into their past without caution, and it worked beautifully.

Ending with the thoroughly atypical 'Voice in the Wilderness' – Status Quo boogie rock, except with the requisite multiple Gibb chord changes – was a typically spanner-in-the-works Bee Gees move.

This Is Where I Came In sounded like no other Bee Gees album. *Rolling Stone* wrote of how the group 'winningly assume the mantle of boy-band elder statesmen. Each Gibb stakes out a portion of the album for his own. As ever, though, Barry is the Bee Gee MVP. The blow-dried love-song bard makes like Noël Coward on "Technicolor Dreams" and sounds like he rediscovered cocaine on the frantic "Voice in the Wilderness". He powers through terrific ballads such as "The Extra Mile" and "Loose Talk Costs Lives" like he's been doing them since Max Martin was in nursery school. Which, of course, he has.'

Released as the first single, the essentially acoustic title track – with thrillingly live vocal harmonies – peaked at number eighteen in Britain, sandwiched between the R&B-flavoured soft pop of Samantha Mumba and the post-mod revival, archive-digging guitar sound of Ocean Colour Scene. It was where they belonged as well as where they came in. 'At long last I'm not a teenager trying to make it,' confessed Barry. 'I'm not that person who was desperately changing everything about himself in order to have a hit record.'

Still, they remained world champions of sniping at each other. Petty disagreements could get acrimonious, even as the brothers turned fifty. Engineer John Merchant reckoned the spats were part of the work process: 'They always knew what the other person was capable of, and so they would not rest until their brother had delivered that. It could be in terms of writing lyrics or melody or song structure or performances or arrangements. In all those things, they would challenge each other consistently.' And, like an unrealistic sitcom, everyone else in the studio knew the situation would be resolved as soon as the kettle went on. 'Sure enough, they would walk in with a cup of tea . . . and that was the indication that they were done and it was time to get back to work.'

So steeped was it in Gibb lore that if *This Is Where I Came In* had been announced as a full stop, nobody would have been surprised. With its joyful variety of styles, it almost had the feel of a posthumous compilation.

In August 2001, Barry's father-in-law George Gray died. Barry was deeply affected, and wrote a poem called 'I Once Knew a Man' which he read out at the funeral. He saw that 51 Keppel Road, Chorlton, was on the market and, perhaps with mortality on his mind, bought it. Fans secretly hoped he had plans to create some kind of Bee Gees museum.

The brothers continued to take their lives at an unusually leisurely pace. They were each awarded the CBE early in 2002, and Barry would become the first Bee Gee grandad, when his son Stephen's wife Gloria gave birth to baby Nina in December that year. Cover versions kept their names on the charts: Steps had a hit with 'Chain Reaction', and Destiny's Child remade Samantha Sang's 'Emotion'.

Still they wrote, recorded, created. In December 2002, *Billboard* reported that Barry had co-written a song in protest at the Bush government's plan to invade Iraq. That summer, Michael Jackson had turned up at Barry's house with the beginnings of a song which they then worked up into 'All in Your Name', a reiteration of the anti-war 'Not in My Name' slogan. It seemed the stuff of rumour, but it would eventually be released in 2011. The recording was clearly a demo, but a highly emotional performance by both men, the impact of which might have been lost if they had spent too long on it. The lyric took a pessimistic view of the governments in Britain and the States, and their desire to acknowledge the will of the people: 'And it looks like we fall / And it burns like a flame / Any ground that I claim,' sang Barry on the first chorus, before a key change and a second chorus, on which Michael Jackson lifted the song with a quavering power, much as Robin had elevated the tearful 'Let There Be Love' on *Idea* back in 1968.

Jackson would be a regular visitor to Barry and Linda's home in the early 2000s, and sometimes he would crash out and stay overnight. 'We would just sit around and write and get drunk,' laughed Barry. 'Michael liked wine – there were a few nights when he just went to sleep on the floor. He'd sit in the kitchen and watch the fans outside his hotel on TV, just giggling – "Hee hee!"' Apparently, they never discussed his child abuse court case. Barry also told the *Daily Mirror* that he never saw Jackson unhappy.

Robin was less content. The slowing pace of the Bee Gees' career made him antsy. 'I'm not happy doing nothing,' he said. And so he set to work on an album which was initially to be called *robin* but would be released in 2002 as *Magnet*: 'I just woke up one morning and thought, well, I'll go into the studio and make a solo album.' He regarded the contemporary pop scene as 'a bit of a beauty contest . . . I really want to get attention to new young songwriters which aren't getting the encouragement and development from record companies as they used to.' He signed to a German label, SPV, and asked writers to submit songs. Deconzo 'Deacon' Smith ended up producing and penning most of the album, along with one Michael Graves and former China Black ('Compliments on Your Kiss') singer Errol Reid. None had much of a track record, and none went on to do much else of note.

Aside from a rather pat update of 'Another Lonely Night in New York' and a cover of the Everly Brothers' 'Love Hurts' (which was, very much, where the Bee Gees had come in), the album was impressively contemporary without sounding awkward. Robin's voice was given a good setting by Smith; 'Special' was a ballad that evoked God; 'Please' was a catchy lead single that made the UK top thirty; the intro to 'Don't Rush' still sits there waiting to be discovered by Frank Ocean. The melodies were uniformly strong, Robin was clearly fully invested in the contemporary R&B scene, and – with outside writers – the songs shunned his usual quirkiness for lyrics about clubs, rocking, freaking, even drinking. It was a superior British R&B album.

There was no reason on earth why *Magnet* shouldn't have sold a ton. Well, there was one. The obvious thing against Robin was his age, and he had entered a world where that counted for a lot; the market for British R&B in 2002 would have been looking at someone like Craig David to put it in the mood rather than a skinny white dude in his early fifties. What's more, Bee Gees fans were confused and maybe rather let down by an album of, for the most part, cover versions; the only song on which Robin claimed a writing credit, 'Insepa- rable', had melodic similarities to the decades-old 'Indian Gin and Whisky Dry' from *Idea*. There was an intriguing analogy to be made with fellow '60s heartthrob Scott Walker, who had moved into ever more esoteric territory since his com- mercial heyday, and was working on an avant garde album called *The Drift* at the time *Magnet* came out. *The Drift* would emerge as a dark and painful listen, setting Walker's beautiful baritone against intentionally ugly sounds with misanthropic lyrics. 'Jesse' used the image of Elvis Presley's stillborn twin to evoke the emptiness left by the disappearance of New York's twin towers: 'Nose holes caked in black cocaine . . . six feet of foetus flung at sparrows in the sky.' It may seem odd, but a fifty-something Scott Walker's obliterating darkness was easier for critics to digest than a fifty-something Robin Gibb singing, 'It's Friday night, and I just got paid / Going out on the town, trying to get my freak on.'

Magnet's monochrome album cover, with Robin pulling off what looked like an advanced yoga position, conspired to make him seem even more skeletal and elastic than he did in real life. One track that stood out was a new recording of 'Wish You Were Here', the Gibbs' tribute to lost boy Andy, now stripped of its '80s production baggage and given an easy acoustic feel that emphasised the lyric. *Mojo* reviewed it enthusiastically – 'a veteran leopard changes his spots' – and you had to admire Robin's spirit, but *Magnet* wasn't a commercial success. A bootleg edition of the album from Russia contained half a dozen bonus tracks – 'Massachusetts', 'Love Me', 'You Should Be Dancing' . . . this, the bootleggers appeared to be saying, is how we want our Bee Gees to sound.

Right through 2002, Maurice just carried on shooting paintball, eating corned beef hash and enjoying sobriety. He joined Barry for the twenty-eighth Love & Hope charity ball in Miami, and they sang the Beatles' 'Get Back' and 'Lady Madonna', the Everly Brothers' 'Bye Bye Love' and 'Love Hurts', and Roy Orbison's 'Shahdaroba', a deep cut and family favourite that had originally been on the B-side of the brothers' copy of 'In Dreams' back in 1963. Mo also appeared on ITV's *An Audience with Lulu* and suggested that they sing 'Islands in the Stream'. Instead, Lulu asked Mo to sing 'First of May', a song they had performed together on TV when they were just married. It was a very touching moment.

As Robin's *Magnet* single 'Please' nudged its way up to number twenty-three in December 2002, the joint winners of reality show *Popstars: The Rivals*, One True Voice, took their cover of *This Is Where I Came In*'s 'Sacred Trust' up to number two. It was only pipped to the Christmas number one spot by the thundering 'Sound of the Underground' sung by their distaff counterparts on the show, Girls Aloud. Robin appeared on the surreal BBC quiz show *Shooting Stars*, looking uncomfortable next to Vic Reeves and Bob Mortimer, and was interviewed on a bunch of regional radio and TV shows, including *Scotland Today*. 'I'm still a Bee Gee,' he told them. 'I still love being a Bee Gee.'

On 8 January 2003, Maurice began complaining to Yvonne about stomach pains. He collapsed at their Miami Beach home and was rushed to Mount Sinai medical centre. Surgeons discovered he had a congenital intestinal blockage but, before they could operate, Maurice had a heart attack. He died on 12 January. Robin was block-booked on British TV to promote *Magnet* but, instead, found himself having to talk about the death of his twin brother, 'the most sweetest, generous of people you could ever meet'. It was shockingly sudden. Mo had only just turned fifty-four. It was no age at all.

After Mo's death, Barry hid himself away; workaholic Robin kept going, the best way he found to get through his grief. He talked to *GMTV*'s Lorraine Kelly on 22 January and announced what many had been expecting to hear. 'I think the important thing is we go forward for Maurice,' he explained. 'Anything we do, we will do together, but it'll be as brothers and not under the name of the Bee Gees. That will be preserved in history as the three of us.'

EPILOGUE

'I don't understand people who say, "I've done enough, I'm gonna sit back and relax." It's beyond my comprehension. The three of us are driven – I don't think we'll stop until we drop.'

– Robin Gibb, 2001

'Like the breath of a child from the moment he's born
To the very last day when the curtains are drawn.'

– 'Children of the World'

The end of the Bee Gees had been horribly abrupt. Without any warning, overnight, the group ceased to exist. Mo's contribution had never been as obvious as Barry's or Robin's. It wasn't just his third harmony, or his bass lines, or that compressed piano, or his gags, or his smile; the centre of the family was lost with him. Barry and Robin would now pursue almost entirely separate careers, and continue to live in different countries. What's more, the ever-brightening public perception of the group that had been building steadily through the '90s and into the new century – the good-time party group, '70s pop totems, the Manx ABBA with a Beatle back story – was now changed to one of sadness. Like so much of their music, the death of Maurice in 2003, following that of Andy in 1988, coloured their story in shade and shadows.

Given the Gibbs' tragedies, it had been easy, if understandable, for the public to forget the other Bee Gees who had come and gone but contributed so much over a career that stretched back to 1958. Of the Australian lads who fled to London at the same time as the Gibbs, Colin Petersen had returned to Sydney in 1974 after Humpy Bong broke up, and took up work as a painter. In 2023 he was fronting a band called the Best of the Bee Gees with Colin Petersen and playing shows around Australia. Vince Melouney was also playing shows in 2023, with impressive names like drummer Clem Burke from Blondie and former Stingrays bassist Alec Palao in his band. They knocked out a terrific version of 'Come Some Christmas Eve or Halloween', a Robin obscurity from 1968 which had finally been issued in 2006 on a boxset called *The Studio Albums 1967–68*. An exemplary piece of archive work put together by Bee Gees fan Andrew Sandoval, this boxset contained umpteen other fine outtakes like 'Ring My Bell', 'Gena's Theme' and 'Chocolate Symphony', which had previously only circulated among fans as low-grade bootlegs. After a similarly excellent and thorough *Odessa* set in 2009, the deluxe editions stopped dead. Endless hits compilations aside, the Bee Gees catalogue has remained largely dormant since; even classics like *Main Course* are currently out of print.

Neither Karl Richardson nor Albhy Galuten would produce any more groundbreaking music after splitting from the Bee Gees. Albhy realised he was more 'interested in technology related to music – future delivery systems, electronic distribution, new formats, and so forth' and was last seen working for the world's largest record company, Universal. Karl produced albums for Latin singer Ana Rodríguez and southern rock band China Sky in 1988 before going to work in Broadway productions like Leslie Bricusse's *Jekyll & Hyde* (1990) and producing multiple albums for stage star Linda Eder.

Of the other official and semi-official Bee Gees, Geoff Bridgford went back to Australia and became a singer-songwriter, recording the 1978 album *My Heart Has Turned My Head Around*, which never got further than the test pressing stage; Dennis Bryon wrote his memoir *You Should Be Dancing: My Life with the Bee Gees* in 2015, and toured with Vince and Blue Weaver as 'The Italian Bee Gees'. Blue – who had a much richer CV for his pre-Bee Gee years than the other affiliated members (replacing Rick Wakeman as keyboardist in the Strawbs, touring the US with Mott the Hoople) – has kept busiest. In 2019, he played with the Strawbs at their fiftieth anniversary concert in New Jersey, along with a thirty-piece orchestra and a forty-piece choir. He has also played in *Massachusetts – The Bee Gees Musical*, which toured Europe: 'I'm re-creating the sounds I used on all the Bee Gees records,' Blue told mixonline.com. 'The show that we do is the life story of the Bee Gees from the early days up until the last song they recorded together.'

After Mo's death, Robin, as he had many times before, used work as a prop. His eagerness to engage with any TV shows or charity work that could benefit from his experience was commendable. He didn't need a doctor to confirm that whatever had been twin brother Maurice's genetic bad luck could just as easily be his. Like the pop stars he grew up with who had known they were living on borrowed time – Bobby Darin, Billy Fury – he aimed to get as much variety into his life as possible. First, he became a judge and a mentor on the BBC's *Fame Academy*, set in Witanhurst, a semi-derelict mansion in Highgate, north London, and a building with a rather shocking history (Robin must have loved that).[31]

Unlike most reality TV talent show hosts, Robin clearly devoted much time and effort into mentoring his three 'students'. Having duetted with Robin on the *Still Waters* track 'My Lover's Prayer', Alistair Griffin made it through to the final where he was beaten by Alex Parks. Singing outside the front door of Witanhurst, with a full TV crew and sound system, Robin's voice could be heard drifting over Hampstead Heath once a week in the autumn of 2003. His duet with Alistair Griffin would be released in January 2004 and reach number five in the UK chart. Arguments, possibly staged to raise viewing figures, had regularly broken out on the show – Robin's role appeared to be that of a neutral observer, a voice of calm, a man in the middle; he would have picked up plenty of tips from Mo over the years. A full-length album of Bee Gees songs performed by the contestants was also released by Polydor. Robin would become a regular BBC presence, appearing on *Later with Jools Holland* in 2004, at the 2008 Electric Proms, and as the subject of family tree show *Who Do You Think You Are?* in 2011.

He also continued to play charity shows, including a concert for the Diabetes Research Institute in February 2006, where he shared a stage with Barry for the first time since Maurice's death. There were occasional new songs: in 2006

---

[31] It was built for soap magnate Arthur Crosfield, who, egged on by his wife, wanted to live in the biggest house in London. Crosfield later fell to his death from a train having lost his entire fortune. The house is now reputedly owned by an acquaintance of Vladimir Putin.

came 'Mother of Love' and 'Wing and a Prayer', the latter incorporating verses from the then-still-unreleased title song from *Sing Slowly Sisters*. A couple of years later he made the *50 St Catherine's Drive* album, named after the Gibbs' childhood semi in Douglas; it was similar in style to *This Is Where I Came In* and notably more acoustic than anything he had recorded solo since 1970. (It would remain unreleased until 2014. Dwina tweaked the posthumous album to include the nostalgic 'Sydney', the last song Robin wrote.) Then, for a couple of years, Robin and his youngest son Robin-John worked on the epic *Titanic Requiem* to commemorate the 100th anniversary of the disaster. It premiered on 10 April 2012 at Westminster Central Hall, but by then Robin had terminal cancer, and was too frail to attend – the performance climaxed with a pre-recorded version of the standout 'Don't Cry Alone', with Robin's voice already sounding like a ghost. Most of the people in the room were holding back tears. He died on 20 May, aged sixty-two.

When Robin died in 2012, it tilted the Bee Gees narrative completely into shadow. Books have since emerged with tell-tale titles like *Stayin' Alive* and *Tragedy*. Barry has been incredibly open about the deep sadness in his life, having lost all of his younger brothers, just like Brian Wilson before him. He has even confessed to dimming the bathroom lights so that when he looks in the mirror he can squint and see a fuller mane of hair, a younger man, Barry Gibb in his pomp as if it was still 1978. The last Gibb standing has become a lonely figure, and the pop world has been thoroughly sympathetic.

Barry had thought about retiring after Robin's death, but realised that, as the last surviving Bee Gee, he was the only one who could keep their music alive: 'I care that the music lives, and I do everything in my power to enhance that. That's my mission.'

What's more, Barbara, the Gibb matriarch, was still alive at ninety-three, and what kind of signal would his retirement have sent out to her? Unsurprisingly, she was finding the losses hard to deal with. 'She can't understand losing three of her kids: she thinks it's her fault,' said Barry in 2012. 'So I spend a lot of time trying to convince her that there's no blame. She thinks it's genetic, or she says things like, "What did I do to deserve this?" and I think, *That's a mother*. I say, "Come on, Mum, we had a fantastic time. This is life – death is life." I try to be spiritual with her, try to comprehend what's really happened here. We'll never understand it, but we'll celebrate them. Don't be wringing your hands all the time, because there's no time left.'

The 'legend' spot at Glastonbury – the UK equivalent of France's Chevalier des Arts – was offered to Barry in 2016 but he had to pull out for family reasons. Still, he appeared on stage that year with Coldplay, the biggest group in the world, singing 'To Love Somebody' and 'Stayin' Alive'. The following year he was well enough to take up his 'legend' solo spot. 2016 also saw the release of *In the Now*, his only album of new compositions since 2001's *This Is Where I Came In* – it was co-written with sons Stephen and Ashley and co-produced by John Merchant.

Barry would call the sessions for his 2020 duets album *Greenfields* 'the thrill of a lifetime', and he probably wasn't exaggerating. But it took his boy Stephen to convince him that the likes of Dolly Parton and Alison Krauss would be interested in working with him. All these decades later, the violent backlash the Bee Gees suffered in the wake of *Saturday Night Fever* was still there in his mind, the notion that anyone who enjoyed 'Stayin' Alive' must be doing it for some youthful, ironic reason he didn't get. But disco is now regarded as a '70s pop cultural phenomenon with at least as much heft as punk, its critical fall at the turn of the '80s now widely seen as being fuelled by homophobia and racism. You get the feeling Barry Gibb has heard this many, many times, not least from his kids, but somehow he still can't quite believe it. He'll start hearing it from his grandchildren soon enough.

Still, Barry can sit back and enjoy what he's done. He can leave his Miami home and be feted as a legend somewhere in the world on a weekly basis if he wants. As for working on reissues and deluxe editions of the Bee Gees catalogue, or revisiting *The Kid's No Good* or other half-forgotten daydreams, maintaining the Bee Gees legacy is a full-time job – and who needs a full-time job in their mid-seventies? Besides, he's got seven grand-children. He's also aware that neither Mo or Robin really had the opportunity to relax and reflect on what they had achieved. 'They were just too restless. I spend a lot of hours just being happy about what happened, because it may never have happened, any of those hits. We could have still been in clubs in Queensland. So I've always managed to feel, somehow, that we ought to appreciate what happened: the dream came true. And it's okay. It's okay.'

ACKNOWLEDGEMENTS

There are a few people I would like to thank for their help, without whom I'd probably still be writing this book now.

Pete Selby, for commissioning *Bee Gees: Children of the World* and placing his trust in me; Mark Sinker for reading through it and gently making umpteen improvements; and Melissa Bond for editing it with sensitivity and patience.

Nik Cohn for kindly allowing me to borrow sections of his *New York Magazine* article 'Tribal Rites of the New Saturday Night'. If that piece didn't exist, whole chunks of this story may never have happened.

Andrew Môn Hughes and Grant Walters, Bee Gees historians who replied to rather a lot of email queries. They truly know more about the Bee Gees than anyone I've ever met. Thanks so much for your generosity, and good luck with the ongoing *Decades* project.

Sheila Burgel, Matthew Lees, Pete Paphides, Alexis Petridis and Harvey Williams – friends and fellow travellers, who were happy to discuss the Gibbs and lend their insights over a bottle or two of wine.

I would also like to say a special thanks to Andrew Sandoval for his years of research, friendship and Bee Gee-related anecdotes; Geoffrey Weiss for the stash of Australian 45s, including the mighty 'Raining Teardrops', that he has helped me to amass (Geoffrey is also the only person I know with an original copy of the first Bee Gees album); Andy Zax for the beautiful *Trafalgar* trade poster; Kenny Clayton and Chris Hutchins for enlightening me on Robin's solo '60s records; and Joe Brennan for his astonishingly in-depth blog, gibbsongs, which always made me think two, three, four times about songs I thought I knew inside out.

Lastly, much love to Tessa Norton and Leonard Shukman, my smashing family, who never once complained when I played 'I Just Want to Be Your Everything' every day for eighteen months. I love you very much.

BIBLIOGRAPHY

Arnold, P. P., *Soul Survivor: The Autobiography* (Nine Eight Books, 2022)

Beck, Christopher, *On Air: 25 Years of TV in Queensland* (One Tree Hill, 1984)

Berman, Connie and Daly, Marsha, *Andy Gibb* (Xerox Education Publications, 1979)

Brown, Peter and Gaines, Steven, *The Love You Make: An Insider's Story of the Beatles* (McGraw Hill, 1983)

Bryon, Dennis, *You Should Be Dancing: My Life with the Bee Gees* (ECW Press, 2015)

Bullock, Darryl W., *The Velvet Mafia: The Gay Men Who Ran the Swinging Sixties* (Omnibus, 2021)

Cohn, Nik, *Pop from the Beginning* (Weidenfeld & Nicolson, 1969)

Coleman, Ray, *Brian Epstein* (Penguin, 1990)

Considine, Shaun, *Barbra Streisand: The Woman, the Myth, the Music* (Delacorte, 1985)

Cook, Hector, Môn Hughes, Andrew and Bilyeu, Melinda, *The Bee Gees: Tales of the Brothers Gibb* (Omnibus, 2001)

English, David, *Bee Gees: The Legend* (Quartet, 1983)

Ertegun, Ahmet, *What'd I Say: The Atlantic Story* (Welcome Rain, 2001)

Haden-Guest, Anthony, *The Last Party: The Life and Times of Studio 54* (William Morrow, 1998)

Hild, Matthew, *Arrow Through the Heart: The Biography of Andy Gibb* (Bear Manor, 2022)

Leaf, David, *Bee Gees: The Authorised Biography* (Octopus, 1979)

Lulu, *Her Autobiography* (Granada, 1985)

Marsh, Dave, *The Heart of Rock and Soul* (Penguin, 1989)

Martin, George, *All You Need Is Ears* (St Martin's Press, 1979)

Môn Hughes, Andrew, Walters, Grant and Crohan, Mark, *Decades: The Bee Gees in the 1960s* (Sonicbond, 2021)

Preedy, Bob, *Live Like a Lord: James Corrigan and Batley Variety Club* (Amadeus Press, 2002)

Pryce, Larry, *The Bee Gees* (Granada, 1979)

Pye, Michael, *Moguls: The Business of Show Business* (Temple Smith, 1980)

Sandoval, Andrew, *Bee Gees: The Day by Day Story 1945–1972* (Retro Future, 2012)

Spence, Simon, *Staying Alive: The Disco Inferno of the Bee Gees* (Jawbone, 2017)

Spencer, Chris, *Who's Who of Australian Rock* (Five Mill Press, 1997)

Stevens, Kim, *The Bee Gees* (Quick Fox, 1978)

Tatham, Dick, *The Incredible Bee Gees* (Futura, 1979)

Wexler, Jerry and Ritz, David, *Rhythm and the Blues* (Alfred A. Knopf, 1993)

Windsor, Barbara, *The Laughter and Tears of a Cockney Sparrow* (Arrow, 1991)

DISCOGRAPHY

NOTE: All releases are on vinyl, unless (CD) is stated. For the sake of space, I have stuck to these two formats and not included cassettes, eight-track cartridges, minidiscs or digital-only releases.

BEE GEES STUDIO ALBUMS

1965 ***Barry Gibb & the Bee Gee's Sing and Play 14 Barry Gibb Songs*** Aus: Leedon LL-31 801 mono
I Was a Lover, a Leader of Men / I Don't Think It's Funny / How Love Was True / To Be or Not to Be / Timber! / Claustrophobia / Could It Be / And the Children Laughing / Wine and Women / Don't Say Goodbye / Peace of Mind / Take Hold of That Star / You Wouldn't Know / Follow the Wind

1966 ***Spicks and Specks*** (1) Aus: Spin EL 32031 mono
Monday's Rain / How Many Birds / Playdown / Second Hand People / I Don't Know Why I Bother with Myself / Big Chance / Spicks and Specks / Jingle Jangle / Tint of Blue / Where Are You / Born a Man / Glass House

1967 ***Bee Gees' 1st*** UK: Polydor 583 012 stereo, 582 012 mono; US: ATCO 33-223 stereo and mono
Turn of the Century / Holiday / Red Chair Fade Away / One Minute Woman / In My Own Time / Every Christian Lion Hearted Man Will Show You / Craise Finton Kirk Royal Academy of Arts / New York Mining Disaster 1941 / Cucumber Castle / To Love Somebody / I Close My Eyes / I Can't See Nobody / Please Read Me / Close Another Door

1968 ***Horizontal*** UK: Polydor 583 020 stereo, 582 020 mono; US: ATCO SD 33-233 stereo and mono
World / And the Sun Will Shine / Lemons Never Forget / Really and Sincerely / Birdie Told Me / With the Sun in My Eyes / Massachusetts / Harry Braff / Day Time Girl / The Earnest of Being George / The Change Is Made / Horizontal

1968 ***Idea*** UK: Polydor 583 036 stereo, 582 036 mono; US: ATCO SD 33-253 stereo and (promo-only) mono
Let There Be Love / Kitty Can / In the Summer of His Years / Indian Gin and Whisky Dry / Down to Earth / Such a Shame / Idea / When the Swallows Fly / I've Decided to Join the Air Force / I Started a Joke / Kilburn Towers / Swan Song

1969 ***Odessa*** (2) UK: Polydor 583 049–50 stereo, 582 049–50 mono; US: ATCO TL-ST-142 stereo
Odessa (City on the Black Sea) / You'll Never See My Face Again / Black Diamond / Marley Purt Drive / Edison / Melody Fair / Suddenly / Whisper Whisper / Lamplight / Sound of Love / Give Your Best / Seven Seas Symphony / With All Nations (International Anthem) / I Laugh in Your Face / Never Say Never Again / First of May / The British Opera

1970 ***Cucumber Castle*** (3) UK: Polydor 2383 010; US: ATCO 33-327

If I Only Had My Mind on Something Else / I.O.I.O. / Then You Left Me / The Lord / I Was the Child / I Lay Down and Die / Sweetheart / Bury Me down the River / My Thing / The Chance of Love / Turning Tide / Don't Forget to Remember

1970 ***2 Years On*** (4) UK: Polydor 2310 069; US: ATCO SD 33-353

2 Years On / Portrait of Louise / Man for All Seasons / Sincere Relation / Back Home / The First Mistake I Made / Lonely Days / Alone Again / Tell Me Why / Lay It on Me / Every Second Every Minute / I'm Weeping

1971 ***Trafalgar*** UK: Polydor 2383 052; US: ATCO SD 7003

How Can You Mend a Broken Heart / Israel / The Greatest Man in the World / It's Just the Way / Remembering / Somebody Stop the Music / Trafalgar / Don't Wanna Live Inside Myself / When Do I / Dearest / Lion in Winter / Walking Back to Waterloo

1972 ***To Whom It May Concern*** UK: Polydor 2383 139; US: ATCO SD 7012

Run to Me / We Lost the Road / Never Been Alone / Paper Maché, Cabbages and Kings / I Can Bring Love / I Held a Party / Please Don't Turn Out the Lights / Sea of Smiling Faces / Bad Bad Dreams / You Know It's for You / Alive / Road to Alaska / Sweet Song of Summer

1973 ***Life in a Tin Can*** UK: RSO 2394 102; US: RSO SO 870

Saw a New Morning / I Don't Wanna Be the One / South Dakota Morning / Living in Chicago / While I Play / My Life Has Been a Song / Come Back Johnny Bridie / Method to My Madness

1973 ***A Kick in the Head Is Worth Eight in the Pants*** unreleased
Elisa / Wouldn't I Be Someone / A Lonely Violin / Losers and Lovers / Home Again Rivers / Harry's Gate / Rocky L.A. / Castles in the Air / Where Is Your Sister / It Doesn't Matter Much to Me / King and Country / Jesus in Heaven / Dear Mr Kissinger

1974 ***Mr Natural*** UK: RSO 2394 132; US: RSO SO 4800
Charade / Throw a Penny / Down the Road / Voices / Give a Hand, Take a Hand / Dogs / Mr Natural / Lost in Your Love / I Can't Let You Go / Heavy Breathing / Had a Lot of Love Last Night

1975 ***Main Course*** UK: RSO 2394 150; US: RSO SO 4807
Nights on Broadway / Jive Talkin' / Wind of Change / Songbird / Fanny (Be Tender with My Love) / All This Making Love / Country Lanes / Come On Over / Edge of the Universe / Baby As You Turn Away

1976 ***Children of the World*** UK: RSO 2394 169; US: RSO RS-1-3003
You Should Be Dancing / You Stepped into My Life / Love So Right / Lovers / You Can't Keep a Good Man Down / Boogie Child / Love Me / Subway / The Way It Was / Children of the World

1979 ***Spirits Having Flown*** UK: RSO RSBG 001; US: RSO RS-1-3041

Tragedy / Too Much Heaven / Love You Inside Out / Reaching Out / Spirits (Having Flown) / Search, Find / Stop (Think Again) / Living Together / I'm Satisfied / Until

1981 ***Living Eyes*** UK: RSO RSBG 002; US: RSO RX-1-3098

Living Eyes / He's a Liar / Paradise / Don't Fall in Love with Me / Soldiers / I Still Love You / Wildflower / Nothing Could Be Good / Cryin' Every Day / Be Who You Are

1987 ***E.S.P.*** UK: Warner Bros 925 541-2; US: Warner Bros 1-25541

E.S.P. / You Win Again / Live or Die (Hold Me like a Child) / Giving Up the Ghost / The Longest Night / This Is Your Life / Angela / Overnight / Crazy for Your Love / Backtafunk / E.S.P. (vocal reprise)

1989 ***One*** UK: Warner Bros 925 887-1; US: Warner Bros 25887-1

Ordinary Lives / One / Bodyguard / It's My Neighbourhood / Tears / Tokyo Nights / Flesh and Blood / Wish You Were Here / House of Shame / Will You Ever Let Me

1991 ***High Civilization*** UK: Warner Bros WX417; US: Warner Bros 9 26530-2 (CD)

High Civilization / Secret Love / When He's Gone / Happy Ever After / Party with No Name / Ghost Train / Dimensions / The Only Love / Human Sacrifice / True Confessions / Evolution

1993 _Size Isn't Everything_ UK: Warner Bros 519945-1; US: Warner Bros 314 521 055-2 (CD)

Paying the Price of Love / Kiss of Life / Paying the Price of Love Part 1 / Omega Man / Haunted House / Heart Like Mine / Anything for You / Blue Island / Above and Beyond / For Whom the Bell Tolls / Fallen Angel / Decadance

1997 _Still Waters_ (5) UK: Polydor 36 546 0 (CD); US: A&M 31453 7302 2 (CD)

Alone / I Surrender / I Could Not Love You More / Still Waters (Run Deep) / My Lover's Prayer / With My Eyes Closed / Irresistible Force / Closer than Close / I Will / Obsessions / Miracles Happen / Smoke and Mirrors

2001 _This Is Where I Came In_ (5) UK: Polydor 549 625-2 (CD); US: Universal 549 626-2 (CD)

This Is Where I Came In / She Keeps on Coming / Sacred Trust / Wedding Day / Man in the Middle / Déjà Vu / Technicolor Dreams / Walking on Air / Loose Talk Costs Lives / Embrace / The Extra Mile / Voice in the Wilderness

(1) Reissued as _Rare Precious and Beautiful_ in 1968 (UK: Polydor 236 221; US: ATCO SD 33-264). UK and US editions both in 'reprocessed' stereo.

(2) Also issued in the UK as two separate LPs, _Marley Purt Drive_ and _Sound of Love_, on Polydor's budget 99 label. In South America the album was released two separate discs, Part 1 and Part 2. The US had a partially mixed, single LP, in-store promo version, same cat number. This was the last Bee Gees album to be issued in mono as well as stereo.

(3)   Released in Germany with different artwork as *Songs of Cucumber Castle*.

(4)   'Club edition' released in Germany and Switzerland as *Lonely Days*. Also issued as *Lonely Days* in South America.

(5)   Not issued anywhere on vinyl.

BEE GEES LIVE ALBUMS

1977 ***Here at Last – Live*** UK: RSO 2658 120; US: RSO RS-2-3901
I've Gotta Get a Message to You / Love So Right / Edge of the Universe / Come On Over / Can't Keep a Good Man Down / New York Mining Disaster 1941 / Run To Me–World / Holiday–I Can't See Nobody–I Started a Joke–Massachusetts / How Can You Mend a Broken Heart / To Love Somebody / Boogie Child / Down the Road / Words / Wind of Change / Nights on Broadway / Jive Talkin' / Lonely Days

1998 ***One Night Only*** (1) UK: Polydor 559 220-2 (CD); US: A&M 31455 220 2 (CD)
Intro–You Should Be Dancing–Alone / Massachusetts / To Love Somebody / Words / Closer than Close / Islands in the Stream / Our Love (Don't Throw It All Away) / Night Fever–More than a Woman / Lonely Days / New York Mining Disaster 1941 / I Can't See Nobody / And the Sun Will Shine / Nights on Broadway / How Can You Mend a Broken Heart / Heartbreaker / Guilty / Immortality / Tragedy / I Started a Joke / Grease / Jive Talkin' / How Deep Is Your Love / Stayin' Alive / You Should Be Dancing

(1)   The CD is edited down from the VHS release, omitting some songs. The 1999 reissue included a bonus CD with the missing songs.

BEE GEES COMPILATIONS

There are literally dozens of budget-priced Bee Gees compilations, including a peculiar 1992 one from Australia which they share with the Archies. I have only listed official ones, most of which include previously unavailable material. I haven't mentioned the numerous official ones that recycle hits over and over (e.g. *Very Best of the Bee Gees*, *Ultimate Bee Gees*) or the numerous bootlegs either, though YouTube is probably the best place to look if you are curious about the rarer Gibb recordings.

1968 ***Rare Precious and Beautiful Vol. 2*** UK: Polydor 236 513; US: ATCO SD 33-321
I Was a Lover, A Leader of Men / Follow the Wind / Claustrophobia / Theme from Jaimie McPheeters / Everyday I Have to Cry / Take Hold of That Star / Could It Be / To Be or Not to Be / The Three Kisses of Love / Cherry Red / All of My Life / Don't Say Goodbye

1969 ***Rare Precious and Beautiful Vol. 3*** UK: Polydor 236 556
Wine and Women / I Don't Think It's Funny / Turn Around, Look at Me / I Am the World / The Battle of the Blue and Grey / How Love Was True / And the Children Laughing / You Wouldn't Know / I Want Home / Timber! / I Was a Lover, a Leader of Men / Peace of Mind

1969 ***Best of Bee Gees*** UK: Polydor 583 063; US: ATCO SD 33-292
Holiday / I've Gotta Get a Message to You / I Can't see Nobody / Words / I Started a Joke / Spicks and Specks / First of May / World / Massachusetts / To Love Somebody / Every Christian Lion Hearted Man Will Show You / New York Mining Disaster 1941

1970 ***Inception / Nostalgia*** Ger: Karussell 2674 002
See *Brilliant from Birth*

1973 ***Best of Bee Gees Vol. 2*** (1) UK: RSO 2394 106; US: RSO SO 875
How Can You Mend a Broken Heart / I.O.I.O. / Don't Wanna Live Inside Myself / Melody Fair / My World / Let There Be Love / Saved by the Bell / Lonely Days / Morning of My Life (In the Morning) / Don't Forget to Remember / And the Sun Will Shine / Run to Me / Man for All Seasons / Alive

1974 ***Gotta Get a Message to You*** UK: Contour 2870 404
Budget compilation notable for including two otherwise unavailable recordings: 'It Doesn't Matter Much to Me', from *A Kick in the Head Is Worth Eight in the Pants*, and a version of Robin's 1969 single 'One Million Years' with an alternative vocal.

1979 ***Bee Gees Greatest*** (2) UK: RSO RSDX 001; US: RSO RS 2-4200
Jive Talkin' / Night Fever / Tragedy / You Should Be Dancing / Staying Alive / How Deep Is Your Love / Love So Right / Too Much Heaven / (Our Love) Don't Throw It All Away / Fanny (Be Tender with My Love) / If I Can't Have You / You Stepped

into My Life / Love Me / More than a Woman / Rest Your Love on Me / Nights on Broadway / Spirits (Having Flown) / Love You Inside Out / Wind of Change / Children of the World

1990 ***Tales from the Brothers Gibb: A History in Song 1967–1990*** UK: Polydor 843 911-1; US: Polydor 843 911-2 (CD)
A four-CD – or six-LP – box set that is still the best career overview, even though, being thirty-plus years old, it misses their last four albums and later solo work.

1998 ***Brilliant from Birth*** Aus: Spin D 46066 (CD)
The Battle of the Blue and Grey / The Three Kisses of Love / Timber! / Take Hold of That Star / Peace of Mind / Don't Say Goodbye / Claustrophobia / Could It Be / Turn Around, Look at Me / Theme from Jaimie McPheeters / Everyday I Have to Cry / You Wouldn't Know / Wine and Women / Follow the Wind / I Was a Lover, a Leader of Men / And the Children Laughing / I Don't Think It's Funny / How Love Was True / To Be or Not to Be / Cherry Red / I Want Home / The End / Hallelujah I Love Her So / I Love You Because / Somewhere / The Twelfth of Never / You're the Reason / You're Nobody till Somebody Loves You So / All by Myself / Butterfly / Can't You See That She's Mine / From Me to You / Monday's Rain / All of My Life / Where Are You / Playdown / Big Chance / Glass House / How Many Birds / Second Hand People / I Don't Know Why I Bother with Myself / Jingle Jangle / Tint of Blue / Born a Man / Spicks and Specks / I Am the World / Daydream / Forever / Coalman / Exit Stage Right / Paperback Writer / I'll Know What to Do / In the Morning / Like Nobody Else / Lonely Winter / Lum-Dee-Loo / Storm / Terrible Way to Treat

Your Baby / Yesterday's Gone / You Won't See Me / Top Hat / Just One Look / Ticket to Ride

Sixty-three recordings squeezed onto two CDs, every known Australian Bee Gee recording including the run-throughs of 'Ticket to Ride' and 'Paperback Writer'. This collection superseded the *Rare Precious and Beautiful* trio, *Inception / Nostalgia* (1970), which had been in awful reprocessed stereo, and *The Birth of Brilliance* (1978).

2001 ***Their Greatest Hits – The Record*** UK: Polydor 589 446-2 (CD); US: Universal 314 589 400-2 (CD)

Includes 1994 recordings of 'Emotion' and 'Heartbreaker', originally intended for the unreleased *Love Songs* album; 'Islands in the Stream' was recorded for this album; 'Immortality' is the 1997 demo for Celine Dion. The UK version added 'Jumbo' and 'My World', while the initial pressing accidentally used an otherwise unreleased 1971 recording of 'How Can You Mend a Broken Heart', with a lead vocal by Barry.

2006 ***The Studio Albums 1967–1968*** US: Reprise RHI1 74872 (LP), R2 74117 (CD); UK/Europe: Reprise 8122 74117-2 (CD)

Turn of the Century (early version) / One Minute Woman (early version) / Gilbert Green / New York Mining Disaster 1941 (version 1) / House of Lords / Cucumber Castle (early version) / Harry Braff (early alternative version) / I Close My Eyes (early version) / I've Got to Learn / I Can't See Nobody (alternative take) / All Around My Clock / Mr Waller's Wailing Wall / Craise Finton Kirk Royal Academy of Arts (alternative take) / New York Mining Disaster 1941 (version 2) / Out of Line / Ring My Bell / Barker of the UFO / Words / Sir Geoffrey Saved the World / Sinking Ships / Really and Sincerely (alternative version) / Swan

Song (alternative version) / Mrs Gillespie's Refrigerator / Deeply Deeply Me / All My Christmases / Thank You for Christmas / Silent Night–Hark! The Herald Angels Sing / Chocolate Symphony / I've Gotta Get a Message to You (mono single) / Jumbo / The Singer Sang His Song / Bridges Crossing Rivers / Idea (alternative version) / Completely Unoriginal / Kitty Can (alternative version) / Come Some Christmas Eve or Halloween / Let There Be Love (alternative version) / Gena's Theme / Another Cold and Windy Day (Coke Spot no. 1) / Sitting in the Meadow (Coke Spot no. 2)

As well as the original albums in mono and stereo (on the CD version), this set contains these unreleased tracks and demo versions, all beautifully remastered – an entire bonus disc for each of *Bee Gees' 1st*, *Horizontal* and *Idea*. Essential for fans of their '60s work, as is the three-CD reissue of *Odessa*, released in 2009. A model example of how to treat back catalogue.

2010 ***Mythology: The 50th Anniversary Collection*** UK/ Europe/US: Reprise 8122-79859-9 (CD)

A compilation that accepts that Andy is 25 per cent of the story, with one disc given to each brother. There's a lot of unnecessary replication of *Tales from the Brothers Gibb*, and nothing unreleased from the 1970 split recordings, so it feels like a missed opportunity. Andy and Maurice are the real beneficiaries here: Barry's disc is almost all from *Main Course* and later, with nothing unreleased; Robin's focuses more on the '60s; Andy's unreleased 'Arrow Through the Heart' finally sees the light of day; and Maurice's rare single side 'Hold Her In Your Hand' appears on CD for the first time.

(1)   The US edition adds 'Wouldn't I Be Someone'. A com-
        pilation called *Best of Bee Gees Vol. 2* was issued in Europe
        as early as 1971 – the track listing seems to be different in
        almost every territory.

(2)   The 2007 CD reissue would include the otherwise unissued
        1977 recording of 'Warm Ride' as a bonus track.

ORIGINAL FILM SOUNDTRACKS, WITH VARIOUS ARTISTS

1971 ***Melody*** (1) UK: Polydor 2383043; US: ATCO SD 33-363
In the Morning / In the Morning (Reprise) [Richard Hewson
Orchestra] / Melody Fair / Melody Fair (Reprise) [Richard Hew-
son Orchestra] / Spicks and Specks [Richard Hewson Orches-
tra with Children from Corona School] / Romance Theme in F
[Richard Hewson Orchestra] / Give Your Best / To Love Some-
body / Working on It Day and Night [Richard Hewson Orches-
tra w/ Barry Howard] / First of May / First of May (Reprise)
[Richard Hewson Orchestra] / Seaside Banjo [Richard Hewson
Orchestra] / Teachers Chase [Richard Hewson Orchestra] /
Teach Your Children [Crosby Stills Nash & Young]

1976 ***All This and World War II*** UK: Riva RVLP2; US: 20th
Century 2T-522
Magical Mystery Tour [Ambrosia] / Lucy in the Sky with Dia-
monds [Elton John] / Golden Slumbers/Carry That Weight /
I Am the Walrus [Leo Sayer] / She's Leaving Home [Bryan Ferry] /
Lovely Rita [Roy Wood] / When I'm Sixty Four [Keith Moon] /
Get Back [Rod Stewart] / Let It Be [Leo Sayer] / Yesterday [David
Essex] / With a Little Help from My Friends/Nowhere Man [Jeff
Lynne] / Because [Lynsey de Paul] / She Came in Through the

Bathroom Window / Michelle [Richard Cocciante] / We Can Work It Out [Four Seasons] / The Fool on the Hill [Helen Reddy] / Maxwell's Silver Hammer [Frankie Laine] / Hey Jude [Brothers Johnson] / Polythene Pam [Roy Wood] / Sun King/Getting Better [Status Quo] / The Long and Winding Road [Leo Sayer] / Help [Henry Gross] / Strawberry Fields Forever [Peter Gabriel] / A Day in the Life [Frankie Valli] / Come Together [Tina Turner] / You Never Give Me Your Money [Wil Malone & Lou Reizner] / The End [London Symphony Orchestra]

1977 ***Saturday Night Fever*** UK: RSO 3517 014; US: RSO RS-2-4001
Stayin' Alive / How Deep Is Your Love / Night Fever / More Than a Woman / If I Can't Have You [Yvonne Elliman] / A Fifth of Beethoven [Walter Murphy] / More Than a Woman [Tavares] / Manhattan Skyline [David Shire] / Calypso Breakdown [Ralph McDonald] / Night on Disco Mountain [David Shire] / Open Sesame [Kool & the Gang] / Jive Talkin' / You Should Be Dancing / Boogie Shoes [KC and the Sunshine Band] / Salsation [David Shire] / K-Jee [MFSB] / Disco Inferno [The Trammps]

1978 ***Sgt Pepper's Lonely Hearts Club Band*** (2) UK A&M AMLZ 66600. US RSO RS-2-4100
Sgt Pepper's Lonely Hearts Club Band (w/ Paul Nicholas) / With a Little Help from My Friends (w/ Peter Frampton) / Here Comes the Sun [Sandy Farina] / Getting Better (w/ Peter Frampton) / Lucy in the Sky with Diamonds [Dianne Steinberg, Stargard] / I Want You (She's So Heavy) (w/ Dianne Steinberg, Paul Nicholas, Donald Pleasence, Stargard) / Good Morning Good Morning (w/ Peter Frampton, Paul Nicholas) / She's Leaving Home

(w/ Jay MacIntosh, John Wheeler) / You Never Give Me Your Money [Paul Nicholas, Dianne Steinberg] / Oh! Darling (Robin Gibb) / Maxwell's Silver Hammer [Steve Martin] / Polythene Pam / She Came in Through the Bathroom Window (w/ Peter Frampton) / Nowhere Man / Sgt Pepper's Lonely Hearts Club Band (Reprise) (w/ Peter Frampton) / Got to Get You into My Life [Earth, Wind & Fire] / Strawberry Fields Forever [Sandy Farina] / When I'm Sixty-Four [Frankie Howerd, Sandy Farina] / Mean Mr Mustard [Frankie Howerd] / Fixing a Hole [George Burns] / Because (w/ Alice Cooper) / Golden Slumbers [Peter Frampton] / Carry That Weight / Come Together [Aerosmith] / Being for the Benefit of Mr Kite (w/ Peter Frampton, George Burns) / The Long and Winding Road [Peter Frampton] / A Day in the Life / Get Back [Billy Preston] / Sgt Pepper's Lonely Hearts Club Band [the cast]

1983 ***Staying Alive*** UK: RSO RS BG3; US: RSO 813 269-2
The Woman in You / I Love You Too Much / Breakout / Someone Belonging to Someone / Life Goes On / Stayin' Alive / Far from Over [Frank Stallone] / Look Out for Number One [Tommy Faragher] / Finding Out the Hard Way [Cynthia Rhodes] / Moody Girl [Frank Stallone] / (We Dance) So Close to the Fire [Tommy Faragher] / I'm Never Gonna Give You Up [Frank Stallone, Cynthia Rhodes]

(1) 'In the Morning' is a re-recording of the Australian-era song.
(2) This movie – Beatles songs, covered by the biggest names of 1976, coupled with footage of the Second World War – has been all but buried by time, even more deeply than *Cucumber Castle* and *Sgt Pepper*. As a snapshot of who's who in pop in 1976, it's intriguing – the Bee Gees are as big as Leo Sayer.

ROBIN GIBB SOLO ALBUMS

1970 ***Robin's Reign*** (1) UK: Polydor 583 085; US: ATCO SD 33-323
August October / Gone Gone Gone / The Worst Girl in This Town / Give Me a Smile / Down Came the Sun / Mother and Jack / Saved by the Bell / Weekend / Farmer Ferdinand Hudson / Lord Bless All / Most of My Life

1970 ***Sing Slowly Sisters*** (2) unreleased
Sing Slowly Sisters / Life / C'est la Vie, Au Revoir / Everything Is How You See Me / I've Been Hurt / Sky West and Crooked / Irons in the Fire / Cold Be My Days / Avalanche / Engines, Aeroplanes / The Flag I Flew / Return to Austria / It's Only Make Believe / All's Well That Ends Well / A Very Special Day / Great Caesar's Ghost / Anywhere I Hang My Hat / Loud and Clear

1983 ***How Old Are You*** UK: Polydor POLD 5099; US: Polydor 422-810 896-1
Juliet / How Old Are You / In and Out of Love / Kathy's Gone / Don't Stop the Night / Another Lonely Night in New York / Danger / He Can't Love You / Hearts on Fire / I Believe in Miracles

1984 ***Secret Agent*** UK: Polydor POLD 5142; US: Mirage 90170-1
Boys Do Fall in Love / In Your Diary / Robot / Rebecca / Secret Agent / Livin' in Another World / X-Ray Eyes / King of Fools / Diamonds

1985 ***Walls Have Eyes*** UK: Polydor 827 592-1; US: EMI America SJ-17176

You Don't Say Us Anymore / Like a Fool / Heartbeat in Exile / Remedy / Toys / Someone to Believe In / Gone with the Wind / These Walls Have Eyes / Possession / Do You Love Her

2003 *Magnet* UK/Europe SP Recordings SPV 085-71472 CD (CD)
Please / Don't Wanna Wait Forever / Wish You Were Here / No Doubt / Special / Inseparable / Don't Rush / Watching You / Earth Angel / Another Lonely Night in New York / Love Hurts

2005 *Live* (with the Neue Philharmonie Frankfurt Orchestra) (3) US: Eagle ER20073-2
Night Fever / I've Gotta Get a Message to You / How Deep Is Your Love / Nights on Broadway / Love Hurts / Massachusetts / My Lover's Prayer / New York Mining Disaster 1941 / Please / Saved by the Bell / To Love Somebody / Words / You Win Again / Juliet / Tragedy / Stayin' Alive

2006 *My Favourite Carols* US: Koch KOC-CD-4203
In the Bleak Midwinter / O Come All Ye Faithfull / Silent Night / God Rest Ye Merry Gentlemen / Good King Wenceslas / Away in a Manger / Once in Royal David's City / Three Ships / Hark the Herald Angels Sing / Noel

2012 *The Titanic Requiem* (4) (with RJ Gibb, performed by the Royal Philharmonic Orchestra) UK: Rhino 2564661065
Triumph (Shipbuilding) / Farewell (The Immigrant Song) / Maiden Voyage / New York Suite in C major / Sub Astris (Under the Stars) / Kyrie / SOS (Tract) / Distress (Confutatis) / Salvation (Gradual) / Reflections / Daybreak / Christmas Day / Libera Me / Don't Cry Alone / In Paradisum (Awakening)

2014 *50 St Catherine's Drive* (5) US: Reprise R2-544945
Days of Wine and Roses / Instant Love / Alan Freeman Days /
Wherever You Go / I Am the World (new version) / Mother of
Love / Anniversary / Sorry / Cherish / Don't Cry Alone / Ava-
lanche / One Way Love / Broken Wings / Sanctuary / Solid /
All We Have Is Now / Sydney (demo)

(1) The Japanese issue has a cover shot of Robin in profile,
    leaning moodily against a wall.
(2) No finalised running order exists, but all of these songs were
    potentially recorded for the album and would be released
    on the second disc of the essential *Saved By the Bell* three-disc
    set in 2015.
(3) No UK release, but the album was released in most of
    Europe.
(4) Recorded between 2010 and 2011, except 'Don't Cry
    Alone', recorded 2008.
(5) Originally due for release in 2008, then in 2009 (with
    added tracks). Remixed and issued posthumously. The Isle
    of Man Post Office edition came with a DVD, a booklet
    containing Robin Gibb stamps, and an insert signed by
    Dwina Gibb.

ROBIN GIBB COMPILATIONS

2015 *Saved by the Bell: The Collected Works of Robin
Gibb 1968–1970* UK/Europe: Reprise 081227954574; US:
Reprise R2 549315

BARRY GIBB SOLO ALBUMS

1970 *The Kid's No Good* unreleased

Born / One Bad Thing / The Day Your Eyes Meet Mine / Happiness / Peace in My Mind / Clyde O'Reilly / It's Over / I'll Kiss Your Memory / The Victim / This Time / What's It All About / Mando Bay

1984 ***Now Voyager*** UK: Polydor POLH 14; US: MCA 5506
I Am Your Driver / Fine Line / Face to Face / Shatterproof / Shine Shine / Lesson in Love / One Night (For Lovers) / Stay Alone / Temptation / She Says / The Hunter

1988 ***Music from the Original Soundtrack 'Hawks'*** UK/ Europe: Polydor 837 264-1
System of Love / Childhood Days / My Eternal Love / Moonlight Madness / Where Tomorrow Is / Célébration de la Vie (instrumental) / Chain Reaction [Diana Ross] / Cover You / Not in Love at All / Letting Go

2016 ***In the Now*** UK: Columbia 88985328341; US: Columbia 88985 32835 2 (CD)
In the Now / Grand Illusion / Star Crossed Lovers / Blowin' a Fuse / Home Truth Song / Meaning of the Word / Cross to Bear / Shadows / Amy in Colour / The Long Goodbye / Diamonds / End of the Rainbow

2021 ***Greenfields: The Gibb Brothers' Songbook Vol. 1***
UK: Capitol 0060243138855; US: Capitol B003319901
I've Gotta Get a Message to You (w/ Keith Urban) / Words of a Fool (w/ Jason Isbell) / Run to Me (w/ Brandi Carlile) / Too Much Heaven (w/ Alison Krauss) / Words (w/ Dolly Parton) / Jive Talkin' (w/ Miranda Lambert and Jay Buchanan) / How Deep Is Your Love (w/ Little Big Town and Tommy

Emmanuel) / How Can You Mend a Broken Heart (w/ Sheryl Crow) / To Love Somebody (w/ Jay Buchanan) / Rest Your Love on Me (w/ Olivia Newton-John) / Butterfly (w/ Gillian Welch and David Rawlings)

NOTE: In 2006, the demos for *Guilty, Heartbreaker, Eyes That See in the Dark* and *Eaten Alive* were all made available on iTunes, but not physically.

MAURICE GIBB SOLO ALBUMS

1970 ***The Loner*** unreleased
Journey to the Misty Mountains / The Loner / Please Lock Me Away / I've Come Back / Soldier Johnny / She's the One You Love / Railroad / Laughing Child / Something's Blowing / Silly Little Girl / Insight

ANDY GIBB SOLO ALBUMS

1977 ***Flowing Rivers*** UK: RSO 2394 183; US: RSO RS-1 3019
I Just Want to Be Your Everything / Words and Music / Dance to the Light of the Morning / Too Many Looks in Your Eyes / Starlight / (Love Is) Thicker than Water / Flowing Rivers / Come Home for the Winter / Let It Be Me / In the End

1978 ***Shadow Dancing*** UK: RSO RSS 0001; US: RSO RS-1-3034
Shadow Dancing / Why / Fool for a Night / An Everlasting Love / (Our Love) Don't Throw It All Away / One More Look at the Night / Melody / I Go for You / Good Feeling / Waiting for You

1980 ***After Dark*** UK: RSO 2394 247; US: RSO RS-1-3069
After Dark / Desire / Wherever You Are / Warm Ride / Rest
Your Love on Me / I Can't Help It / One Love / Someone I
Ain't / Falling in Love with You / Dreamin' On

ANDY GIBB COMPILATIONS

1991 ***Andy Gibb*** UK: Polydor 511 585-2 (CD); US: Polydor
P2-11585 (CD)

BEE GEES SINGLES

Mar 63 The Battle of the Blue and Grey / The Three Kisses of
Love (1)
Jul 63 Timber! / Take Hold of That Star (1)
Feb 64 Peace of Mind / Don't Say Goodbye (1)
Aug 64 Claustrophobia / Could It Be (1)
Oct 64 Turn Around, Look at Me / Theme from Jaimie
McPheeters (1, A)
Apr 65 Every Day I Have to Cry / You Wouldn't Know
(1, A)
Jul 65 Wine and Women / Follow the Wind (1, A)
Nov 65 I Was a Lover, a Leader of Men / And the Children
Laughing (1, A)
Mar 66 I Want Home / Cherry Red (1)
Jun 66 Monday's Rain / All of My Life (1)
Sep 66 Spicks and Specks / I Am the World
Jan 67 Born a Man / Big Chance
Apr 67 New York Mining Disaster 1941 / I Can't See Nobody
Jul 67 To Love Somebody / Close Another Door
Sep 67 Holiday / Every Christian Lion Hearted Man Will Show
You (2)

Sep 67 Massachusetts / Barker of the UFO

Nov 67 World / Sir Geoffrey Saved the World

Jan 68 Words / Sinking Ships

Feb 68 And the Sun Will Shine / Really and Sincerely (3)

Mar 68 Jumbo / The Singer Sang His Song

Jul 68 I've Gotta Get a Message to You / Kitty Can

Oct 68 I Started a Joke / Kilburn Towers (4)

Mar 69 First of May / Lamplight

May 69 Tomorrow Tomorrow / Sun in My Morning

Jul 69 Marley Purt Drive / In the Morning (5)

Aug 69 Don't Forget to Remember / The Lord

Sep 69 Don't Forget to Remember / I Lay Down and Die (6)

Feb 70 Let There Be Love / Really and Sincerely (7)

Mar 70 I.O.I.O. / Sweetheart

Mar 70 If I Only Had My Mind on Something Else / Sweetheart (8)

Nov 70 Lonely Days / Man for All Seasons

Apr 71 Melody Fair / First of May (9)

Jun 71 How Can You Mend a Broken Heart / Country Woman

Aug 71 When the Swallows Fly / Give Your Best (10)

Aug 71 Melody Fair / In the Morning (11)

Oct 71 Don't Wanna Live Inside of Myself / Walking Back to Waterloo

Oct 71 In the Morning / To Love Somebody (9)

Jan 72 My World / On Time

Apr 72 Israel / Dearest (7)

Jun 72 Run to Me / Road to Alaska

Aug 72 Sea of Smiling Faces / Please Don't Turn Out the Lights (9)

Nov 72 Alive / Paper Maché, Cabbages and Kings

Mar 73 Saw a New Morning / My Life Has Been a Song

Jun 73 Wouldn't I Be Someone / Elisa

Feb 74 Mr Natural / It Doesn't Matter Much to Me

Jul 74 Throw a Penny / I Can't Let You Go

Sep 74 Charade / Heavy Breathing

May 75 Jive Talkin' / Wind of Change

Sep 75 Nights on Broadway / Edge of the Universe

Dec 75 Fanny (Be Tender with My Love) / Country Lanes

Jun 76 You Should Be Dancing / Subway

Sep 76 Love So Right / You Stepped into My Life

Jan 77 Boogie Child / Lovers

Feb 77 Children of the World / Boogie Child (12)

Jul 77 Edge of the Universe (live) / Words (live)

Sep 77 How Deep Is Your Love / Can't Keep a Good Man Down

Dec 77 Stayin' Alive / If I Can't Have You

Jan 78 Night Fever / Down the Road

Jun 78 More than a Woman / Children of the World (13)

Jul 78 A Day in the Life / Sgt. Pepper's Lonely Hearts Club Band (14)

Nov 78 Too Much Heaven / Rest Your Love on Me

Feb 79 Tragedy / Until

Apr 79 Love You Inside Out / I'm Satisfied

Oct 79 (Our Love) Don't Throw It All Away / Spirits (Having Flown) (15)

Dec 79 Spirits (Having Flown) / Wind of Change

Sep 81 He's a Liar / He's a Liar (instrumental)

Oct 81 Living Eyes / I Still Love You

Jan 82 Paradise / Nothing Could Be Good (16)

May 83 The Woman in You / Stayin' Alive

Aug 83 Someone Belonging to Someone / I Love You Too Much (instrumental)

Jan 84 Life Goes On / Breakout (9)

Sep 87 You Win Again / Backtafunk

Dec 87 E.S.P. / Overnight

Dec 87 Live or Die (Hold Me like a Child) / Giving Up the Ghost (5)

Feb 88 Crazy for Your Love / You Win Again (remix) (17)

Feb 88 Angela / You Win Again (remix) (18)

Mar 89 Ordinary Lives / Wing and a Prayer

Jun 89 One / Flesh and Blood

Nov 89 Tokyo Nights / Will You Ever Let Me (19)

Jan 90 Bodyguard / Will You Ever Let Me (20)

Feb 91 Secret Love / True Confessions

May 91 When He's Gone / Massachusetts (live) (21)

Jun 91 The Only Love / You Win Again (live)

Aug 93 Paying the Price of Love / My Destiny

Nov 93 For Whom the Bell Tolls / Decadence

Jan 94 Kiss of Life / 885 7019 (CD, 12″) (22)

Apr 94 How to Fall in Love Part 1 / 855 7019

Feb 97 Alone / Closer Than Close / Rings Around the Moon (promo 7″, CD, cassette)

Jun 97 I Could Not Love You More / Love Never Dies (CD, cassette)

Nov 97 Still Waters (Run Deep) / Obsessions / Stayin' Alive (live)

Apr 01 This Is Where I Came In / Just in Case / I Will Be There (CD, cassette)

(1)   Australia only.

(2)   Canada, US only. Released in mainland Europe with 'Red Chair Fadeaway' on the B-side.

(3)   France only.

(4)   Released in almost every territory except UK. 'Swan Song' was the B-side in France; 'When the Swallows Fly' in Rhodesia and South Africa.

(5)   Canada only, with a unique mix of the B-side.

(6)   Belgium, Netherlands only.

(7)   Australia, Canada, New Zealand, US only. 'Then You Left Me' was the B-side in New Zealand.

(8)   Japan only.

(9)   Netherlands only.

(10) Guatemala, Hong Kong, Portugal, Singapore, Venezuela only.

(11) Germany, New Zealand, Spain, UK, Yugoslavia only.

(12) Australia, Italy, Portugal only.

(13) France, Italy only.

(14) New Zealand only.

(15) Japan, Netherlands only.

(16) UK only.

(17) Australia, mainland Europe, New Zealand only.

(18) Australia, France, Germany only.

(19) Australia, US only.

(20) Germany only.

(21) France, Germany only.

(A) credited to Barry Gibb and the Bee Gees

SINGLES CREDITED TO THE BEE GEES AND OTHER ARTISTS

Jan 65 House Without Windows / And I'll Be Happy (Trevor Gordon and the Bee Gees)

Jul 98 Immortality / Immortality (version) (Celine Dion with the Bee Gees)

ROBIN GIBB SINGLES

Jun 69 Saved by the Bell / Alexandria Good Time (UK, withdrawn)

Jun 69 Saved by the Bell / Mother and Jack

Nov 69 One Million Years / Weekend

Jan 70 August October / Give Me a Smile

Jul 78 Sesame Street Fever (w/ The Count, Grover, Ernie and Cookie Monster) / Trash

Jul 78 Oh Darling / She's Leaving Home (The Bee Gees, Jay MacIntosh and John Wheeler)

Oct 80 Help Me (w / Marcy Levy) / Help Me (instrumental)

Apr 83 Juliet / Hearts on Fire

Oct 83 How Old Are You / I Believe in Miracles

Jan 84 Another Lonely Night in New York / I Believe in Miracles

Jun 84 Boys Do Fall in Love / Diamonds

Sep 84 Secret Agent / Robot

Jan 85 In Your Diary / Robot

Sep 85 Like a Fool / Possession

Jan 86 Toys / Do You Love Her

Feb 03 Please / Watching You / Don't Rush (CD)

Mar 03 Wait Forever (edit) / Wait Forever (Shanghai Surprise remix) (CD)

Jan 04 My Lover's Prayer (w/ Alistair Griffin) / Bring It On (Alistair Griffin) (CD)

Nov 11 I've Gotta Get a Message to You (The Soldiers with Robin Gibb) (CD)

Robin also guested on G4's cover of 'First of May' (2004) and US5's recording of 'Too Much Heaven' (2007).

BARRY GIBB SINGLES

Jun 70 I'll Kiss Your Memory / This Time

Sep 70 One Bad Thing / The Day Your Eyes Meet Mine (Canada, withdrawn)

Nov 71 King Kathy / Summer Ends / I Can Bring Love (UK fan club release)

Oct 80 Guilty / Life Story (w/ Barbra Streisand)

Jan 81 What Kind of Fool / The Love Inside (w/ Barbra Streisand)

Aug 84 Shine Shine / She Says

Nov 84 Fine Line / Stay Alone

Dec 84 Face to Face (w/ Olivia Newton-John) (Europe, promo only, same both sides)

Aug 88 Childhood Days / Moonlight Madness

NOTE: Barry featured on Jamie Jo's 'U Turn Me On' (2008). There were also CD promo singles for his duet with Barbra Streisand 'Above the Law' (2005), and two *In the Now* tracks – one for the title song and one for 'Star Crossed Lovers' (both 2016).

MAURICE GIBB SINGLES

1970 Railroad / I've Come Back

1984 Hold Her in Your Hand / Hold Her in Your Hand (instrumental)

ANDY GIBB SINGLES

Aug 75 Words and Music / Westfield Mansions (Australia only)

Sep 76 Can't Stop Dancin' / In the End (Australia only)

Apr 77 I Just Want to Be Your Everything / In the End

Oct 77 (Love Is) Thicker than Water / Words and Music

Apr 78 Shadow Dancing / Let It Be Me

Jul 78 An Everlasting Love / Flowing Rivers

Oct 78 Why / One More Look at the Night (UK only)

Oct 78 (Our Love) Don't Throw It All Away / One More Look at the Night

Sep 79 Rest Your Love on Me (w/ Olivia Newton-John) (short version) / Rest Your Love on Me (long version) (US promo)

Jan 80 Desire / Waiting for You

Mar 80 I Can't Help It (w/ Olivia Newton-John) / Someone I Ain't

Nov 80 Time Is Time / I Go for You

Feb 81 Me (Without You) / Melody

Aug 81 All I Have to Do Is Dream (w/ Victoria Principal) / Good Feeling

INDEX

INDEX

INDEX